MW01026098

International Relations Theory

A Primer

ELIZABETH G. MATTHEWS

CALIFORNIA STATE UNIVERSITY SAN MARCOS

RHONDA L. CALLAWAY

SAM HOUSTON STATE UNIVERSITY

New York   Oxford

OXFORD UNIVERSITY PRESS

Oxford University Press is a department of the University of Oxford. It furthers
the University's objective of excellence in research, scholarship, and education
by publishing worldwide. Oxford is a registered trade mark of Oxford University
Press in the UK and certain other countries.

Published in the United States of America by Oxford University Press
198 Madison Avenue, New York, NY 10016, United States of America.

© 2017 by Oxford University Press

For titles covered by Section 112 of the US Higher Education
Opportunity Act, please visit www.oup.com/us/he for the
latest information about pricing and alternate formats.

All rights reserved. No part of this publication may be reproduced, stored
in a retrieval system, or transmitted, in any form or by any means, without
the prior permission in writing of Oxford University Press, or as expressly
permitted by law, by license, or under terms agreed with the appropriate
reproduction rights organization. Inquiries concerning reproduction outside
the scope of the above should be sent to the Rights Department, Oxford
University Press, at the address above.

You must not circulate this work in any other form
and you must impose this same condition on any acquirer.

Library of Congress Cataloging-in-Publication Data
Names: Matthews, Elizabeth G., author. | Callaway, Rhonda L., 1965-
author.
Title: International relations theory : a primer / Elizabeth G. Matthews,
    California State University San Marcos ; Rhonda L. Callaway, Sam Houston
    State University.
Description: New York, NY : Oxford University Press, 2016. | Includes
    bibliographical references.
Identifiers: LCCN 2016014868 | ISBN 9780190268671 (pbk. : acid-free paper)
Subjects: LCSH: International relations. | International
    relations—Philosophy.
Classification: LCC JZ1305 .M346 2016 | DDC 327.101—dc23 LC record
    available at https://lccn.loc.gov/2016014868

Printing number: 9 8 7 6 5 4 3 2 1

Printed in the United States of America
on acid-free paper

To our parents
and
for our students

BRIEF CONTENTS

TABLE OF CONTENTS

....

LIST OF TABLES/FIGURES

Tables

Figures

ACKNOWLEDGEMENTS
....

We have many people to thank for their assistance and encouragement as we made our way through this process. The idea for this book came from years of teaching our students about theories of international relations and witnessing the difficulties they encountered in the learning process. Much of the material in this book came from our experiments in delivering theoretical explanations in a way the students could not just understand, but be excited by. Thus, we thank all of our students over the years for their interest in theoretical approaches to understanding the world and in their willingness to embrace even the most difficult of theoretical concepts. We would like to thank California State University San Marcos and Sam Houston State University for their support of our professional development, in particular our professional leaves in Fall 2013 that allowed us to develop this project. We are indebted to Rhonda's colleague at SHSU, Ken Hendrickson, for his expertise and editorial eye. We would like to thank Rhonda's research assistant, Mariia Domina, for her work editing the bibliography, and Elizabeth's colleague at CSUSM, Ashley Fogle, for her assistance with the design of the figure in Chapter 7. We would also like to thank Jennifer Carpenter, our Acquisitions Editor, for her faith in this project and in us. We also appreciate the guidance and assistance provided to us by Matt Rohal, Assistant Editor. We extend our thanks to our copy editor, Emmeline A. Parker, and our indexer, Mary J. Harper. We would also like to thank SPi Global for their assistance in the production of this book. Lastly, we would like to thank our families, friends, and colleagues for their endless support and encouragement through this process. Without your shoulders to cry on and ears to bend, we might not have made it to this point.

CHAPTER 1

Introduction

"[T]he study of international affairs is best understood as a protracted competition between the realist, liberal and radical traditions . . . The boundaries between traditions are somewhat fuzzy and a number of important works do not fit neatly into any of them, but debates within and among them have largely defined the discipline."
—Stephan M. Walt, "International Relations: One World, Many Theories." (1998, 29)

S tudents of international relations face a daunting task. In order to understand the complex world of international relations, we must devise explanations for the myriad of activities and behaviors we see on a daily basis. We are faced with an ever-growing number of state and non-state international actors, a complex and growing set of issues, and shifts in attitudes, response choices, government structures, weapons, technology, and environmental factors. As such, means of organizing this vast amount of information is vital to understanding it; further, creating analytical tools allows for a deeper appreciation and comprehension of the events that take place in world politics. One of the ways in which we seek this clarity is through the use of theory. **Theory** refers to frameworks of thought or knowledge that we use to engage and give meaning to the world around us. A theory contains a set of statements that explains particular events and acts as a conceptual framework to understand phenomena in world politics. Practitioners of international relations utilize theories to analyze and inform policies and practices. Some theories aim to explain, categorize, and establish causal relationships regarding state behavior, ultimately leading to predictive capabilities on the part of analysts and policymakers alike. For example, if state A went to war under a certain set of conditions, and those conditions are repeated, state A should theoretically go to war again. Other theories opt to focus less on universal claims and explanation and more on understanding and interpreting the meaning and context of state and non-state behavior. Thus, extending our war example, critical theorists might ask whether a particular war is a just war, thus, taking a normative approach to conflict studies. As will be seen throughout this book, predictive power of some theories is often lacking while the normative approach is often viewed as naïve and incomplete, but that does not stop theorists from all perspectives from trying to simplify reality and better understand international relations.

This book presents a comprehensive overview of the five main theories or approaches in international relations. There are a number of other theoretical approaches in international relations, but realism, liberalism, economic structuralism, constructivism, and feminism have been, and continue to be, the five predominant theories of international relations (Maliniak et al., 2012). Before proceeding, we offer an explanation for the inclusion of these specific approaches. In your study of international relations, you will see these five described by a number of terms: images, paradigms, approaches, worldviews, and perspectives. What explains the use of these different terms? The answer lies in the fact that they do different things and serve different purposes. Realism and liberalism are the dominant theoretical frameworks utilized in international relations and scholars, in general, agree that these are indeed "theories." In addition, these are most often held and articulated by the practitioners of foreign and national security policy even if they do not self-identify as a realist or a liberal. This use of the term "theory" is consistent with the definition of a theory found in discussions regarding the philosophy of science. That is, a theory consists of a set of statements that help to explain events, in this case, the behavior of states and non-state actors in the international system. It is a simplified view of reality. Furthermore, a set of hypotheses can be derived from such theories and empirically tested.

It becomes more complicated when we move to the critical approaches of economic structuralism, constructivism, and feminism, perhaps more correctly referred to as **worldviews** rather than theories. A worldview (*Weltanschauung* in German) is simply how one looks at the world and a belief about how the world works. It denotes a broader perspective than a theory. In the early stages of international relations theory, the focus was primarily war; although this remains an important area of study, we are inundated with an increasing number of issues and interactions we seek to explain, such as human rights, the environment, globalization, and poverty. This has helped create a growing number of perspectives seeking to explain the causes of global phenomena and how those phenomena are created. Constructivists, feminists and economic structuralists ask different questions than those asked by realists and liberals; they look at the world differently and provide different answers and interpretations of phenomena. To fully appreciate the range of explanations available in international relations, exposure to all five approaches is essential, regardless of what they are named.

What follows in this chapter is foundational information you need to have to begin your study of international relations theory. Before you can dive into the paradigms presented in the subsequent chapters, you need to be introduced to the evolution of international relations theory. Where did these ideas come from? How are they tied to the historical narrative of world politics? The following sections will also provide you with an explanation of the research process in international relations and an introduction to one of the central organizing features of study in this field, the levels of analysis. We will also provide you with foundational material to help you understand the case studies that will be analyzed throughout the chapters, the issues of proliferation and trade (specifically, the role of the **World Trade Organization—WTO**). The first represents a classic security concern, with the latter focusing on issues associated with economic cooperation as well as conflict. As you will see, there are many facets to both cases, and we will apply each theory to an aspect of proliferation and trade to illustrate how theory helps to describe, explain, predict, or at least better understand phenomena in world politics. Finally, we will explain how this book is organized and present you with a series of questions you should consider as you make your way through the following chapters. You should pay close attention to these questions, as well as the bolded terms in the text, as they will come up throughout the chapters.

Evolution of International Relations Theories

Although the discipline of political science is relatively young, the subfield of international relations traces its origins to Thucydides'

The History of the Peloponnesian War and, more specifically, a section describing a conversation between Athenian and Melian generals called "The Melian Dialogue" (see Chapter 2). With the writings of Niccolo Machiavelli, Hugo Grotius, Thomas Hobbes, Immanuel Kant, and many others, international relations theorists have delved into the past to help explain current, as well as to predict future, state behavior. Thus, the evolution of theories within international relations is intrinsically tied to history; in fact, much of theoretical development is in response to international conditions and events (see Figure 1.1). One prevailing paradigm guiding policymakers and analysts in decision-making is replaced when the assumptions underlying that paradigm fail to adequately explain reality. Ultimately, decision-makers want the ability to understand and predict systemic conditions as well as state behavior. When the theory fails to help in these two areas, decision-makers and theorists search for alternative explanations. Over the past couple of centuries, the primary event leading to the demise of a particular paradigm and the emergence of another has been international war.

After World War I, for example, policy-makers and philosophers sought to replace the realist-based **balance-of-power** system with a different understanding of state relations based on a utopian or **idealist** perspective. The ultimate goal of policymakers as well as the burgeoning field of international relations was to find ways to avoid war. The balance-of-power model served European decision-makers well during the **Concert of Europe** where peace among the great powers existed for almost a century in the years between the end of the Napoleonic wars in 1815 to the start of World War I in 1914; however, changes in domestic conditions within the European states altered the rules and subsequently the assumptions of the balance-of-power paradigm culminating in the Great War. One of these domestic changes occurred in czarist Russia when revolutionaries ushered in an alternative worldview based on Marxist ideology as interpreted by the leadership of Vladimir Lenin in October 1917.

The failure of the League of Nations and **collective security** to deter aggression in the interwar period (1919–1939) followed by World War II led policymakers and international relations theorists to deem the utopian view as too naïve and realism returned as the predominant theory to explain interstate relations. Realism posits that states, as unitary and rational actors, are the most important actors in the

FIGURE 1.1 Theories of International Relations Timeline.

Concert of Europe 1820
- Balance of Power System
- Multipolar System

WWI 1914–1919
- Russian Revolution 1917
- Marxist/Leninist Theory

Interwar Period 1919–1939
- Utopianism
- Idealism & Collective Security
- Woodrow Wilson

Cold War Begins 1945
- Realism
  - Morgenthau
- Liberalism
- Bipolar System

1960–1970s
- Vietnam War
- Neorealism & Neoliberalism
- Waltz 1979
- Marxist Influenced Theories
  - Dependency Theory
  - World Systems Theory

End of Cold War 1989
- Constructivism & Feminism emerge
- Unipolar System?

September 11, 2001 and Beyond
- Wars in Iraq & Afghanistan
- Multipolar System?

international system. These states exist in a self-help system where national security and survival are paramount issues for the state. For a realist, states seek to maximize their relative power in an **anarchic** and **zero-sum** environment where conflict is inevitable. Realism will be fully explained in Chapter 2.

While conflict between the superpowers dominated the forty years after World War II, realism failed to explain many of the cooperative actions on the part of state actors in areas such as trade and international finance, leading to a resurgence of idealism in the form of liberalism. Liberals contend that while states are important, non-state actors such as **intergovernmental (IGOs)** and **nongovernmental (NGOs) organizations** play an important and mitigating role in the international system. States seek absolute gains in a **positive-sum** environment where shared interests tend to mute the potential for conflict. Liberals argue that these non-state actors serve as arenas for states to meet and compromise on disagreements alleviating some, if not all, of the conflict between states that previously would have led to war. Moreover, liberals consider individuals, terrorist organizations, and multinational or transnational organizations such as Apple, IBM, and Coca-Cola, to be additional actors that operate within the system, as well. Thus, there are multiple channels by which states interact with one another. For liberals, states learn to cooperate leading to win-win situations (positive-sum game), thus overcoming the self-help and conflictual nature of the anarchic international system. Liberalism is the focus of Chapter 3.

During the Cold War, Marxist-influenced theories also emerged as explanations for the disparate levels of economic development found in the international system. Often referred to as economic structuralism today, this family of theories focuses on economic class as the key element in the international system rather than power for realists or shared interests for liberals. Economic structuralists argue that economic class, that is, the general level of economic development, determines a state's position in the international system in a hierarchical fashion. They reject the liberal notion that all states benefit from capitalism, rather capitalism is exploitative in nature and has subsequently created a structure that consists of poor and rich states, the haves and have-nots, with the latter in a perpetual state of underdevelopment. Marxist-based theories help explain this subservient position as smaller states view **multinational corporations (MNCs)** as tools of both larger states and the elites within their own countries. Attempts at breaking these dependent relationships focused on domestic economic policies and a strategy of non-alignment during the Cold War. The family of theories that fall under the umbrella of economic structuralism, Marxist and non-Marxist alike, will be fully explored in Chapter 4.

The inability of realism to provide an explanation for the end of the Cold War and the collapse of the **bipolar** system without an actual war is perhaps its greatest weakness and led to the suggestion that we had reached the "end of history" with liberalism as the final victor in the battle of worldviews (Fukuyama, 1989). Liberal theories continued to gain favor in the post-Cold War period as they explained greater and greater levels of cooperation (for example, regional trade agreements and supra-national organizations, such as the WTO and the European Parliament). However, the conflicts that emerged during this time (including Somalia and the Balkans) provided realist theorists additional cases to rest their assumptions upon and with the terrorist attacks on September 11, 2011, realism seemed to return to its place of dominance.

The end of the Cold War also witnessed the emergence of constructivism and feminism as major paradigms within international relations. If realism is based on power, liberalism on shared interests, and economic structuralism on class, constructivism is based on ideas and identity. Often described as an approach rather than a theory, constructivism suggests that the structure of the international system, as well as relations between states, is an artifact of the ideas, norms, values, and identity of the participants in the system. Conflict is a product of people and their shared experiences rather than a product of the structure of the system. Thus, the idea that what occurs within the state has relevance to the international system has gained traction amongst international relations scholars. Constructivism is fully discussed in Chapter 5.

Feminism is an interdisciplinary approach focusing on gender and how it is a socially constructed concept rather than simply a biological one (although some feminists focus on biological differences). International relations feminists examine the experiences of individuals based specifically on gender and the influence this has on state behavior and relations between states. As in constructivism, feminist theorists look inside the state to see how gender influences domestic decision-making not only in high politics issues of national security and war, but also in the so-called low politics issues of health, education, and poverty. Feminists reject the claim that a fixed reality and structure based solely on anarchy and inter-state relations exists in the international system and instead address how the concept of gender influences the way the world works and questions why there is a lack of women in positions of power in domestic and international politics as well as a lack of female international relations scholars. Feminism is explored in Chapter 6.

The Study of International Relations

While the theories of international relations have evolved over time, so has the approach to the study of international relations. Theories are a tool for academics (and decision-makers) in that they help guide the research process. However, within the field of international relations there are several debates regarding this process. These debates focus on the **ontological**, **epistemological**, and **methodological** aspects of theory. Succinctly stated, "to make sense of the world one needs an ontology (a general, theoretically charged account of what there is and how it works), a methodology (for revealing, and explaining or understanding, that picture of the world), and an epistemology (which shows how we can know (or reasonably believe) that the methodology gives us the picture)" (Hollis and Smith 1996, 112).

Ontology is the theory or study of being and refers to the nature of existence, that is, what kinds of things actually exist and operate in the universe. For our purposes, it might be easier to think about ontology as "the world as political scientists assume it to be" (Stanley 2012, 95). On the surface, this is quite an abstract concept. As applied to international relations, we might question whether there is any structure to the international system or whether different actors in the international system exist. Furthermore, ontology addresses the question of whether there is a fixed reality or whether there is no single reality in the universe. In other words, ontology "concerns the implicit and simplifying assumptions about political 'reality' that *underpin* explanations of political phenomena" (Stanley 2012, 95). Each theory of international relations presents a different belief or assumption about what exists in the international system. For example, when it comes to anarchy, realists assume that anarchy is a fixed reality and, as such, it creates a self-help environment that states must navigate. On the other hand, liberals accept anarchy as a fixed reality but assume that its negative consequences can be overcome through cooperative efforts. Economic structuralists' ontological perspective is more complicated. Marxist-based theorists generally assume that there is a known world or fixed reality, one apart from our own existence, whether people are aware of it and experience it or not, while non-Marxist economic structuralists are more likely to question whether there is a fixed reality. Finally, constructivists and feminists not only question the existence of anarchy as fixed, they take a relativist position arguing that there is no such thing as a real world apart from our construction of one, thus, it is impossible to exist apart from our interpretations of what we observe. Ultimately, they assume that the world and concepts such as gender are socially constructed, generally through language and discourse, and anarchy is simply what states make of it (Wendt 1992).

The study of knowledge and how humans acquire knowledge is known as **epistemology**. We need an ontological perspective in order to pursue an epistemological one. So, how do we come to know the things we know (epistemology) about the things we believe exist (ontology) in the universe? How do we discover knowledge about the world? Among political scientists, epistemological positions generally can be divided into **positivists** and **post-positivists** camps; however, keep in mind that these are not mutually exclusive categories. Positivists are theorists that approach the study of international relations from an ontological position that there is a known reality apart from our own existence, and this knowledge is acquired in an empirical (but not necessarily a quantitative) fashion. Of the five theories discussed in this book, realist and liberal theorists tend to be positivists. Conversely, post-positivists contend that there is no single reality (ontology) and contend that the acquisition of knowledge (epistemology) is multifaceted. At the heart of the post-positivists position is the argument that it is impossible to apply the standards utilized by the hard sciences, such as biology or chemistry, to the study of human behavior. Most constructivists, feminists, and many economic structural theorists adhere to a post-positivist perspective. Beyond the acquisition of knowledge, epistemological issues focus on whether certain knowledge should be accepted or rejected. For example, at some point in time, philosophers and explorers decided to reject the knowledge claim that the world was flat. Likewise, we accept that the claim that placing your hand on a hot burner will be painful without having to actually experience the pain. Thus, the acquisition of knowledge can occur through experience, empiricism, and objective observation or through reasoning, that is, through subjective and even reflective analysis of the ideas and beliefs underlying the observed phenomena.

Last, the theories of international relations differ in their methodological approaches, that is, how data is acquired and ultimately analyzed. The **methodology** employed in international relations can take many forms; however, we highlight the three main methodological approaches in the field—case studies or qualitative analysis, quantitative analysis, and formal modeling. For example, if a researcher questions whether states are more or less likely to go to war with trading partners, a case study approach or qualitative analysis would entail the selection of a sample of cases including both instances when the parties went to war and when they did not, with a detailed analysis of primary and secondary sources, interviews, or fieldwork to reach conclusions concerning the decision-making process to engage in conflict or not. A quantitative analysis would likely include a large-N study where data is gathered across time (years) and space (countries in the international system) resulting in a large number of observations. The power of the analysis would rest on the statistical significance of the variables chosen to explain the decision to go to war. Last, there are numerous types of formal modeling, but in this case a game theoretical approach might be adopted. Game theory is the rigorous consideration of the possible outcomes of a situation in which state A impacts state B that in turn impacts state A; thus it is about interaction. As such, states in our example would be in an iterated (repeated) game and decisions would be made based on rational calculations of self-interested benefits. In the most famous game, the Prisoner's Dilemma (discussed in Chapter 3), both sides would choose either to cooperate or defect leading to the avoidance or outbreak of war. The methodology chosen generally rests upon the research question put forth by scholars in international relations. Ultimately, these concepts "are like a skin not a sweater: they cannot be put on and taken off whenever the researcher sees fit." To move forward with an in-depth understanding of the application of international relations theories, "all students of political science should recognize and acknowledge their own ontological and epistemological positions and be able to defend these positions against critiques from other positions" (Marsh and Furlong 2002, 17).

There have been four distinct waves or debates regarding the issues of ontology, epistemology, and methodology as applied to the research process in international relations with each of the five theories we present playing major roles. As you will see, the core concerns are repeated with new actors entering the theoretical landscape in each debate asking, what and how should scholars pursue the study of international relations? The first debate between realists and liberals (idealists) occurred during the years before and after World War II, when the discipline was still in its infancy. At this time, both realists and liberals relied on case studies to describe and explain political phenomena such as diplomatic relations and the characteristics and functions of institutions. These case studies tended to be historical and legalistic in nature with a focus on governments and their power. As previously discussed, idealists were driven by a desire to avoid war and motivated to establish a world order that embraced a collective response to the problems states faced in the international system. Scholars such as E.E. Carr before World War II and Hans Morgenthau after World War II (both of whom will be discussed in later chapters) chastised the idealist perspective's subjective view of how the world ought to be rather than focusing on the objective view of how the world really works.

The second debate centered on the behavioral revolution that swept through academic circles in the decades following World War II calling for a more rigorous research agenda, particularly in the social sciences. This marks the emergence of the positivist movement in international relations. The field of political science, in general, was criticized for its inability to predict political behavior and thus turned to the scientific method and statistical analysis to bolster their theoretical claims. On one hand, many scholars embraced the systematic and empirical approach of the scientific method as well as statistical analyses in addressing their research questions. However, it should be noted that empirical and quantitative analysis are not synonymous. While quantitative analysis is by definition empirical, not all empirical studies include quantitative analysis. There are plenty of empirical studies that employ qualitative methodologies. In the international relations discipline, the levels of analysis (see below) were introduced to provide a more systematic approach to understanding political behavior (Waltz 1959; Singer 1961). On the other hand, traditionalists argued for a program that maintained the notion that research should be conducted as if individuals mattered without the obsession of collecting and analyzing data. In fact, traditionalists suggested that the study of international relations was predicated on human behavior that required subjective judgment rather than the scientific method. This debate would be replayed between the positivists and post-positivists in what is referred to as the Third Debate (see below).

What is known as the interparadigmatic debate pitted realists, liberals, and Marxist-based theorists against one another regarding questions of how the international system is structured, how states and non-state actors behave in such a system, and perhaps most importantly, how change occurs in the international system. At the same time, the adoption of the methods that moved the field along a more rigorous scientific research path also led some in the discipline to argue that researchers lost sight of the substantive issues in favor of methodological squabbles. In the 1970s and 1980s, researchers once again turned to institutions as a focal area, this time, they combined institutions with the study of human behavior, particularly the preferences, norms, and ideas of actors. Nonetheless the rigorous methodologies endured as many turned to economics and other disciplines for methodological guidance. In addition, leading scholars sought to formalize the theories of realism and liberalism, with special attention paid to systemic analysis (Waltz 1979; Keohane and Nye 1977) thus introducing the second generation of the mainstream theories: neorealism and neoliberalism.

Finally, the current debate, known as the Third Debate, began toward the end of the Cold War when the post-positivists (elements of economic structuralism, constructivism, and feminism) emerged and gained momentum to challenge the dominance of positivists in international relations.[1] Post-positivists argue that the researcher inherently influences the search for true knowledge. Thus, the ideas, norms, values, beliefs, identity and discourse of individuals influence the events and issues in international relations making the study of world politics far more subjective than positivists allow. Leading scholars such as Alexander Wendt and J. Ann Tickner (both of whom will be discussed in later chapters) brought constructivism and feminism into the mainstream of discussion within international relations circles emphasizing the influence of norms, values, gender, and identity on the structure of the international system as well as on the relations between states, societies, and individuals.

Looking at the four debates over time, we see the ebb and flow of interests and concerns as well as some symmetry. As one generational debate focuses on substantive issues, the next debate tends to focus on issues related to the philosophy of science. For example, the first and interparadigmatic debates emphasized *what* to study (i.e., institutions, identities, norms), while the second and current debates focus(ed) more on the *how* or the approaches to the study of international relations (i.e., scientific method and rationale analysis versus post-positivist, and subjective analysis). Each of the theoretical chapters will touch on how these issues affected and influenced the evolution of the theory.

Levels of Analysis

Theories of international relations are often intertwined with another analytical tool—the levels of analysis. As mentioned earlier, world politics is a complicated, complex, and evolving environment. The levels of analysis are used (especially by positivists) to simplify and divide the phenomena we see in world politics by parsing out manageable pieces used to explain behavior, outcomes, and events. Although there is some debate concerning the number and names of the levels, typically there are three: individual, state (domestic), and international system. The use of the levels of analysis helps us determine where to focus our study by choosing certain variables to analyze. As the different theories are explained in the following chapters of this book, the levels of analysis will periodically assist in situating the theoretical principles on the international stage. Each level will be briefly described to provide a foundation for their application.

We will begin with the largest unit of analysis—the international system. From this perspective, it is the characteristics of the system that guide behavior and the interactions between actors. Systems analysts believe that actors will behave in somewhat predictable patterns given the structure of the system. States are viewed as unitary actors; there is no concern about, or attention paid to, actors within the states. Domestic-level actors, such as legislatures, judiciaries, the public, and interest groups are irrelevant, as are the individual decision-makers within state. The interactions of states are driven by the structure of the system, thus the constraints are external, not provided by the groups or people within the states. The number of poles (powerful actors) in the system has a profound effect on, and can often constrain, state behavior. For example, during the Cold War the international system was bipolar in nature, that is, there were only two superpowers. In that system, the United States and Soviet Union behaved in certain ways because the power dynamics of the system guided their choices. There were only two states battling for supremacy, creating a situation in which they were locked in a zero-sum game (meaning that a loss for one was necessarily viewed as a victory for the other). Thus, at every possible opportunity the superpowers were trying to undermine each other's power while increasing their own power relative to their opponent. It was this structure that determined relations and interactions, and when the structure changed at the end of the Cold War, so did the interactions.

The state or domestic level of analysis looks inside the state, that is, at the internal processes, to determine how each makes and implements foreign policy. The unit of analysis includes factors or variables within each state, such as bureaucracies, standard operating procedures, political culture, ideology, regime type, executive-legislative relations, public opinion, interest groups, and the strength of civil society. The key at this level of analysis is how these internal forces compel the state to adopt one foreign policy or another. These variables differ between states, across issue areas (some issues are more impactful on domestic audiences than others), and types of decisions. For example, decision-making in a crisis is very different than in a non-crisis situation. In non-crises, many more domestic variables will come into play because there is not a time-constraint on the decision-making process. If we return to our Cold War example, the roughly forty years of hostility between the United States and Soviet Union can be explained as a battle of ideologies and regime types. The Soviet Union was a closed totalitarian communist state while the United States was an open capitalist democracy. These were viewed as incompatible as each saw the other as a threat, and the Cold War became a battle of ideological expansion. The United States attempted to spread democracy; the Soviet Union was trying to spread communism. The Cold War ended when communism failed in the Soviet Union closing the ideological divide between the two states.

The individual level of analysis focuses on the people who make the decisions on the world stage. Decision-making is a complex process, and this level delves into the individual characteristics that make each one of us tick. Analyzing decisions from this level requires that we understand how people make choices and to accomplish this goal we must look at human qualities and idiosyncrasies. It must first be accepted that individuals do not always behave rationally; people do not conduct a cost-benefit analysis of every decision they make guaranteeing arrival at the rational, best choice. Given our cognitive limitations, deficiency in information, and biases, rationality simply cannot be guaranteed. As such, this level of analysis requires investigation into cognitive functioning, as well as emotional and psychological factors. For example, humans are seekers of **cognitive consistency**—that is, we are uncomfortable with ideas that contradict what we believe to be true. As a consequence, we create cognitive consistency by making available information fit our pre-existing beliefs. We also must consider heuristic devises such as schemas and analogies that people use as shortcuts in decision-making. If we can convince ourselves that a new event is just like a previous one, choosing a response is much easier than gathering all the necessary information to make a "new" decision. When we add emotions to our cognitive limitations, rationality is even harder to obtain. Among other responses, human beings get angry, sad, happy, frustrated, afraid, surprised, and disgusted, and these emotions can dramatically impact how we respond to situations. Policymakers are simply people, and while we might be comforted in thinking they can suppress their basic emotions, in reality that is unrealistic. Looking at the Cold War from this level of analysis, we can highlight specific individuals who made decisions that either started or ended the hostility, or instigated specific crises or tension reduction. For example, an individual level analyst might explain the end of the Cold War using the "great man theory." From this perspective, Mikhail Gorbachev can be credited with ending the conflict by seeking an improvement in relations with the United States through concessions in major issue areas. He took numerous steps to demonstrate his goodwill; he withdrew the Soviet military from Afghanistan, released dissidents, opened churches, stopped jamming foreign radio broadcasts, and agreed to the Intermediate Nuclear Forces (INF) Treaty. These were all actions the United States had been pressing for, but previous Soviet leaders refused to take them. The argument contends that without Gorbachev, these tension-reducing polices would not have been adopted.

As you can see, the levels of analysis are a useful methodological framework that aids in analyzing political phenomena and human behavior. Political scientists, regardless of the theoretical approach, inherently utilize one of the levels in their analysis. As you read the case studies below, keep in mind the different levels of analysis to ascertain whether the issue can best be explained from the individual, domestic, or system level of analysis. In each of the following chapters, we revisit these two issues and illustrate how each theoretical approach takes a different perspective.

Case Study I: Proliferation

In each theoretical chapter, different elements of the same issues—proliferation and trade—will be examined through the particular theoretical lens. This will allow for a more thorough understanding of the application of each theory. This section provides foundational information on proliferation to help provide a framework for applying each theory. **Proliferation** is a multi-faceted and highly contentious issue in world politics. In international relations, when we talk of proliferation, we mean one of two things. Horizontal proliferation is an increase in the number of actors possessing certain weapons. Vertical proliferation is the expansion of already existing arsenals. Our focus in the case studies in this book will concern the former. These weapons can be conventional (for example, warplanes, missiles, helicopters, and missile defense components), but more often than not, when proliferation is a hot issue on the international stage, it is about the spread of **weapons of mass destruction (WMD)**, and in particular the spread of nuclear weapons or the material with which to make them. Sanctions, diplomatic wrangling, and even war can be the outcome of states trying to prevent WMD proliferation. Conventional weapons tend to be a different story. States with significant and prosperous military industrial complexes are eager to sell conventional weaponry to allies (and sometimes non-allies). In 2011, global arms sales reached $85.3 billion, more than three quarters ($66.3 billion) sold by the United States (Shanker 2012). As such, our proliferation discussion will focus on WMDs, the attempts to prevent their spread, and the theoretical arguments underpinning those attempts.

The prevailing sentiment is that any horizontal proliferation of nuclear weapons is dangerous, meaning it threatens the stability of the international system, and from the perspective of many nations, including the United States, it threatens national interests and security. This is not a universally accepted idea, however. There are scholars and policymakers who disagree about the impact of proliferation. The scholarly differences are best demonstrated by the debate between prominent international relations theorists Scott Sagan and Kenneth Waltz. Sagan represents the pessimistic view of proliferation arguing that states cannot, and do not, always act in a manner that serves their best interests. As such, even though the use of nuclear weapons entails potentially exceedingly high costs (up to annihilation), bureaucratic and organizational obstacles within states can cause irrational and incoherent policy choices (note that this is a domestic-level argument). For example, military organizations, given their biases, routines, and interests, are unlikely to fulfill the requirements for nuclear **deterrence** to work (Sagan 1994). This is critical, in that, deterrence is the key to undermining concerns about the dangers of proliferation. Waltz, an optimist about nuclear proliferation, argues that the fear of retaliation to a nuclear attack is enough to deter any use of the weapons. He goes as far as to argue that with this deterrent in place, the probability of a major war between nuclear powers "approaches zero" (Waltz 1988, 627).

Sagan's bureaucratic argument is not the only problem with the issue of nuclear deterrence. No state since 1945, when the United States used them against Japan to end World War II, has ever launched a nuclear attack. As such, many view the threat of their use as hollow, that is, lacking credibility. There is a general consensus in international relations that no state wants to be the next to use such weapons thus welcoming the condemnation of the global community. Other scholars note that the destructive capability of a state's nuclear arsenal plays into deterrence calculations. During the Cold War, the United States and Soviet Union never engaged in direct military confrontation and stability existed as they eventually created a condition known as **Mutually Assured Destruction (MAD)**. The condition of MAD guarantees that if one side launched a nuclear strike, the other side could retaliate, inflicting unacceptable losses. As a consequence, neither launched a nuclear strike. In today's world, MAD does not exist between all states possessing nuclear weapons. India and Pakistan, for example, both possess nuclear weapons, but neither controls a stockpile capable of completely destroying the other. If conditions remain the same, however, Pakistan could become the world's fifth largest nuclear weapon state by 2025 (Kristensen and Norris 2015).[2] Currently, their relationship is unstable, in that one side might try to destroy the existing weapons of the other through a preemptive strike, thus instigating a nuclear conflict. The scholarly debate concerning this issue will be further explored in Chapter 2 with a more in-depth look at prominent realists and the view that proliferation does not necessarily create the doomsday scenario promoted in the conventional wisdom. In addition, as will be explained in Chapter 6, feminism provides an alternative view of weapons and proliferation focusing on the gendered nature of the study of proliferation and the impact of conflict in general.

When we look at policymakers and the view of proliferation, it is often a case of "where you stand depends on where you sit." Nations possessing nuclear weapons are usually (if not always) opposed to any additional states developing these weapons. For example, in 2012, French President Francois Hollande, told the United Nations General Assembly, there is "an urgent need to combat the greatest threat to global stability: I mean the proliferation of nuclear weapons" (Hollande 2012). France, of course, is a recognized nuclear state and one of the five permanent members of the UN Security Council. States already possessing WMDs have taken a range of measures to prevent their spread to both state and non-state actors (although our focus here is on state actors). The United States, for example, has imposed economic sanctions, sought actions by the UN Security Council, and even gone to war to halt or prevent the acquisition of WMDs by other states. It is easy for one state that possesses such weapons with no intent to give them up to argue others should not have access to the same. It is also a significant bone of contention between the "haves" of nuclear weapons and the "have-nots." The "have-nots" fall into three basic categories: 1) those who want to acquire them; 2) those who exist under the umbrella of an established nuclear state with no need to build their own (for example, states under the US nuclear umbrella in NATO); and 3) those who do not want to acquire them and often call for those who possess them to relinquish them. The latter category opens the door for compelling rhetoric and heated debate on the international stage. For example, in 2012, a South African diplomat said that there is a rejection of "any justification for the continued retention" of nuclear weapons (Minty, 2012). Further, in an interesting combination of the first and third categories, in September 2013, Iranian President Rouhani called for all states (in particular, Israel) to eliminate their nuclear weapons: "No nation should possess nuclear weapons . . . As long as nuclear weapons exist, the risk of their use, threat of use and proliferation persist.

The only absolute guarantee is their total elimination" (Rouhani, 2013). This statement is interesting on several fronts, most notably because Israel does not acknowledge its possession of nuclear weapons and Iran is under heavy scrutiny for its alleged nuclear weapons program (see below). The debate between the "haves" and the "have-nots" will be further explored through the economic structuralist lens in Chapter 4.

In addition to nuclear weapons, WMDs also include chemical and biological weapons. While there is a general acceptance that the use of these weapons is a human rights violation and a war crime, there are still states who possess them (with no intent to destroy them) and even those who use them. Many states have acknowledged chemical and biological weapons programs in the past and ended those programs. These states include Canada, France, Germany, Iraq, Japan, Libya, South Africa, South Korea, the Soviet Union, the United Kingdom, and the United States. Although some of these states continue to work to destroy their stockpiles of weapons, this is not the hot-button issue in international relations concerning these types of weapons. The controversy comes with those states that possess and/or continue research on such weapons, and, of course, those who use them. It is difficult to confirm the existence of these programs as they are conducted clandestinely, but it is generally believed that programs exist for chemical and/or biological weapons in Algeria, China, Cuba, Egypt, Ethiopia, Iran, Israel, Myanmar, North Korea, Pakistan, Russia, Sudan, Syria, and Taiwan.[3] The controversy reaches a zenith when a state uses them, as was the case with Syria in summer 2013. The United Nations confirmed that the nerve agent sarin was used around Damascus on August 21, but did not confirm who used the agent. Western powers, including the United States, have insisted it was the Syrian government that used the weapons against civilians in an ongoing civil war in the state. The Syrian regime insists it was the rebels seeking to overthrow the rule of President Bashar Assad. In response, there was outcry from numerous states, human rights organizations, and publics around the globe.

In an effort to control the proliferation of WMDs, the international community has negotiated multilateral treaties, held conferences, and pressured governments through the use of both carrots and sticks. The most comprehensive effort to contain the spread of nuclear weapons has been the Non-Proliferation Treaty (NPT). The treaty was originally opened for signature in 1968 and was extended indefinitely in 1995 (there is a treaty review every five years). There are 191 parties to the treaty (only North Korea, India, Israel, Pakistan, and South Sudan are nonmembers) and its main provisions are two-fold. One, states possessing nuclear weapons are prohibited from helping non-nuclear states acquire them. Second, non-nuclear states agree not to develop or otherwise acquire nuclear weapons. The goals of the treaty include controlling the spread of nuclear weapons, facilitating the peaceful use of nuclear energy, and furthering efforts towards nuclear and complete disarmament. Chemical and biological weapons also have multilateral treaties aimed at their control. The 1993 Chemical Weapons Convention (CWC) bans countries from possessing, acquiring, stockpiling, transferring, and using chemical weapons. There are 192 members of the treaty (with Myanmar becoming the latest in August 2015). The Biological Weapons Convention (BWC) was opened for signature in 1972 and went into effect in 1975. The BWC was the first multilateral treaty that banned the development, production, and stockpiling of an entire class of WMD. There are 174 states-parties to the treaty. Both the CWC and the BWC advanced the tenets of the 1925 Geneva Protocol that prohibited the use, but not the possession or development, of chemical and biological weapons. The establishment and functioning of these treaties will be discussed in the subsequent theoretical chapters with a specific focus on the liberal view in Chapter 3.

Currently, there are two major international disputes over the proliferation of nuclear weapons: North Korea and Iran. North Korea's nuclear program became an issue of contention in 1994 and again in 2002 through today. In 1994, Pyongyang refused to allow international inspectors access to its plutonium processing plant. An agreement was reached in which North Korea agreed to halt suspicious activity in exchange for assistance with its civilian nuclear energy program. This agreement proved to be short lived, as in 2002 North Korea admitted that it had been carrying on a secret program to enrich uranium. In January 2003, North Korea withdrew from the NPT and by the end of the year it had processed enough nuclear material to make as many as six nuclear weapons. In 2006, the country conducted its first nuclear test. Although an agreement was reached through six-party talks (with China, Japan, North Korea, Russia, South Korea, and the United States) in 2007 that called for North Korea to close its main reactor in exchange for fuel, the agreement fell apart and North Korea withdrew from the six-party talks in 2009. North Korea conducted its second nuclear test that same year, and a third followed in 2013. There have been numerous attempts to restart the six-party talks, but no breakthrough is in sight as tensions continue to be high between North Korea and South Korea and Pyongyang continues its pursuit of more powerful weapons output and increased delivery capability. North Korea's nuclear program will be discussed in greater detail in Chapter 2 as we will look at a realist explanation for why North Korea endeavors to build these weapons and why the international community seeks to stop them.

Iran also presents the international community with a conundrum over nuclear proliferation. Although Iran remains a member of the NPT, it is widely believed that Tehran is producing weapons-grade material for nuclear weapons. It is also believed that Iran manufactures chemical agents, including sarin and mustard gas. An agreement was reached in 2004, but was soon, and repeatedly, violated by Iran. The UN Security Council imposed sanctions on Iran, although Tehran continues to assert its nuclear program is for peaceful, civilian purposes (a goal supported by the NPT). China and Russia, two veto-wielding members of the UN Security Council, do not view Iran's nuclear ambitions with the same level of concern as the United States and its closest allies. This has produced considerable diplomatic wrangling between the great powers in the international system. Since 2012, there have been high-level discussions between Iran and the P5+1 (the US, Russia, China, Britain, France, and Germany), and in July 2015 an agreement was reached (the Joint Comprehensive Plan of Action) that will lift decades of sanctions imposed against Iran in return for limitations on its nuclear program. The agreement places strict limits on Iran's ability to produce weapons-grade material, but allows the regime to enrich uranium to levels suitable for civilian (energy) use. The deal is controversial, due particularly to the fact that Iran can continue to enrich uranium, thus not ending its nuclear program, and questions and concerns over the inspection regime put into place to ensure Iran complies with the deal. Iran's nuclear program will be explored further in Chapter 5 as we highlight the constructivist view of Iran's pursuit of these weapons.

Case Study II: Trade and the World Trade Organization (WTO)

International trade is an essential element of the global economy. Trade is the movement of goods and services from one nation to another in exchange for money or different goods and services.

Since the inception of the modern state system with the Treaty of Westphalia in 1648, the level, pace, and growth of international trade can be divided into four distinct phases. Before 1800, the sum of exports plus imports as a percentage of global GDP never rose above 10%. A second phase occurred in the 19th century as the industrial revolution spread resulting in a 3% annual increase in global trade until 1913. The two world wars stifled global trade as nations opted for protectionist and nationalist policies. The process of globalization and the corresponding interdependence between nations after World War II increased the demand for goods and services that could not be produced locally. This coupled with the allure of the money to be made by selling products internationally resulted in the growth of the international trading system during this fourth phase (Nagdy and Roser, 2015). For example, in 2014, exports amounted to $19.06 trillion (in current US dollars) and imports equaled $19.01 trillion (in current US dollars) (World Bank, 2015). This equates to more than 50% of global production (Nagdy and Roser, 2015).

Trade is a perfect example of the competing impulses in international relations. On the one hand, it brings people together while fostering political, economic, and social interactions and other international norms consistent with the liberal approach. Consumers in the United States, for example, buy products imported from all over the globe. Americans purchase and enjoy imported cars, pharmaceuticals, electronic equipment, alcoholic beverages, and rely on the country's largest import, oil. In addition, the United States imports large quantities of resource materials, such as rubber, tin, copper, iron, steel, and chemicals. On the other hand, trade is often the source of disagreement and conflict. States are compelled to protect their domestic producers and manufacturers and this often results in the imposition of all types of trade barriers including **tariffs**, **quotas**, **subsidies**, and **nontariff barriers**. This type of state behavior is best explained by the realist approach, where economics are a means to an end, specifically, power in the international system. In an effort to promote growth in trade, the international community created the General Agreement on Tariffs and Trade (1947), which evolved into the WTO in 1995. This case study will focus on the theoretical perspectives and their view of trade liberalization and specifically the role of the WTO in regulating the global trading system. The remainder of this section provides foundational information on the WTO to help provide a framework for applying each theory.

Prior to the World Wars and the economic collapse in the interwar period, **protectionism** was common and trade was regulated by the larger powers in the system for their own benefit. For example, the US Congress passed the Smoot-Hawley Tariff Act in 1930 effectively raising tariffs to historical levels on over 20,000 products. In Europe, the sum of exports and imports as a percentage of GDP fell precipitously during this period; for example the ratio in the United Kingdom fell from 58% in 1920 to 14% in 1932 while the Netherlands saw their percentage cut in half from a high of 81% in 1920 to 44% in 1932 (Nagdy and Roser, 2015).[4] Many attributed this type of protectionism and the subsequent retaliation from US trading partners as a factor that prolonged the Great Depression. Economic collapse during the Great Depression and the catastrophe of World War II prompted the creation of several international economic institutions, including the International Trade Organization (ITO) and the General Agreement on Tariffs and Trade (signed in 1947 in Geneva, Switzerland). The ITO sought to liberalize all trade and prescribe standards for open markets and full domestic employment. The United States was not prepared to liberalize agriculture or accept intrusive policies from an international organization, and hence the US Congress refused to ratify the ITO in 1950. As a consequence, GATT, which was an agreement not an organization, was left as the default structure to regulate international trade. GATT was limited, however, in that its sole focus was liberalizing trade in industrial and manufactured goods.

GATT is based on the principle of reciprocity and nondiscrimination, in that all member nations agree to lower trade barriers as a group. The allure of increased access to foreign markets works to discourage nations from enacting trade barriers to protect their domestic industries. **Most Favored Nation (MFN)** status constitutes a policy of nondiscrimination in the organization by ensuring that an importing country will not discriminate against another country in favor of a third. For example, if the United States allows the importation of bananas from India with a $2 duty, all countries with MFN status can import bananas to the United States with a $2 duty. If the United States negotiates a duty of $1 on bananas with Ecuador, all countries with MFN status, including India, will be granted the new, lower duty.

The United States could not require any state with MFN status to pay a higher duty than the lowest it grants.

Reciprocity and nondiscrimination form the basis for the agreements made under the auspices of the WTO. Beginning in 1947, GATT supervised nine rounds of multilateral talks designed to promote the reduction of protectionist policies as well as freer access to each other's markets. In 1947, as part of the first round, 56 member states met in Havana Cuba and succeeded in reducing bilateral tariffs on approximately 45,000 products accounting for 20% of world trade, effectively reversing much of the protectionist policies enacted during the interwar period. The third round of talks in Torquay, England in 1950 resulted in states cutting the 1948 tariff levels by 25%. The Dillon Round that lasted from 1960–1962 focused on not only cutting tariffs but included discussions on the emerging economic agreement among Western European States that would eventually become the European Union. In the Dillon Round, states began negotiating the European Economic Community (ECC). The Kennedy Round (1964–1967) addressed the issue of anti-dumping and saw membership increase to 62 countries (Love and Lattimore, 2009).

The most famous of these is the eighth round—the Uruguay round—which ran from 1986 to 1993. This round succeeded in bringing some protectionist policies under control (including decreases in agricultural export subsidies and the elimination of quotas), and as a result there was an increase in trade and foreign direct investment. The Uruguay round also created the WTO, currently comprised of 162 members[5] and headquartered in Geneva, Switzerland. The WTO oversees trade negotiations, monitors the implementation of members' trade policies, engages in dispute settlement through the Dispute Settlement Body (DSB), assists developing countries in building trade capacity, and seeks to enhance cooperation and awareness through outreach activities to the public, media, other international organizations, and nongovernmental organizations. Economic liberals promote an open market and international organizations like the WTO, the International Monetary Fund (IMF), and the World Bank. The liberal economic perspective will be discussed further in Chapter 3. Through the constructivist lens, Chapter 5 will discuss the creation of the norm of free trade as well as China's identity as a developing country in the WTO and developing countries evolving ideas and views regarding the free trade regime.

There are significant issues of controversy with the WTO, often resulting in dramatic public protests, but for the sake of our discussion, we will focus on two. First, membership in GATT and later the WTO has been controversial. Technically, membership is open to any country, but politics has played a significant role with some states refusing to join and other states being kept out. For example, prior to the 1980s, communist countries refused to join GATT as it was seen as a tool of Western capitalist imperialists. The liberalization of the Soviet Union and subsequent collapse of communism abridged these concerns. Further, countries can use trade, and WTO membership in particular, as a foreign policy tool to compel another state to comply with demands. For example, after the massacre in Tiananmen Square in 1989 in which the Chinese government violently suppressed pro-democracy protesters, the United States attempted to tie an improvement in human rights in China to the granting of MFN status. This proved to be a hollow threat as the United States continually granted and renewed China's MFN status despite disturbing reports on China's human rights. The United States proved unwilling to pursue a political policy (promote human rights) that acted as a detriment to economic policy (decreased trade). Although China's human rights record continued to be a subject of debate, the communist nation joined the WTO in 2003. The use of the WTO as a political tool will be further explored through a realist lens in Chapter 2.

Second, "implementation" or the problem developing countries have in implementing WTO agreements is a second source of major controversy. A majority of members of the WTO are developing countries, and they are categorized in two groups: "developing countries" and "least developed countries." The WTO does not define the terms "developed" and "developing" and countries self-identify as to which category they belong (although that assessment can be challenged by other WTO members). "Least developed countries" are identified by the United Nations.[6] One of the main goals of the WTO is to enhance the trade capacity of developing nations to assist them in benefitting from the international trading system. This has been the focus of what is known at the Doha Round (ninth round), or the Development Round, that began in 2001 and is technically still underway. There are significant benefits that come with a designation of "developing" country, including technical assistance to aid officials in better understanding WTO rules, allowing developed countries to treat them with more favorable terms than other WTO members, and extra time to fulfill their commitments.[7] These benefits, however, have not overcome a major obstacle for developing countries. There is much debate concerning whether WTO rules and procedures are suited to developing countries mired in debt (Stiglitz, 2007). The disparity of power, the exploitation of developing countries, and the trouble with the Doha Round will be further explored in Chapter 4. Furthermore, chapter 6 will address the impact of WTO policies on women in the workforce and discuss the role, or lack thereof, of women decision-makers in the WTO as many of the issues concerning developing countries are magnified when it comes to issues of gender.

Organization of the Book

In this chapter we provided an introduction to the concept of international relations theory and its importance and well as an historical overview of the discipline. We also provided the background on the two cases that we will applied throughout the textbook. Each subsequent chapter will cover one of the five main theories providing the history, main theorists, central assumptions, variants, and criticisms, and then the theory will be applied to an aspect of both case studies, proliferation and trade. Each chapter will also contain the family of theories that exists under the umbrella of the main paradigm. The final chapter will tie the theories together by demonstrating the explanatory power derived from a holistic approach to theoretical study.

Throughout the text, you are encouraged to consider a series of questions to help illuminate the meaning of each theory. This will help you think systematically about the purpose, direction, application, and weaknesses of each theory. The questions to be considered are:

- Who are the actors/agents?
- What are the explicit and perhaps implicit assumptions of each theory?
- What are the sources and key contributors to each theory?
- How does each theory view:
  - The individual
  - The state
  - The system
- According to each theory, how does change occur in the international system?

- What are the sub-theories, if any?
- How does the theory describe, explain, or predict state behavior in both high and low issue areas?
- What are the weaknesses of the theory in explaining behavior?

Once you have completed this textbook, you will have the tools necessary to develop your own worldview and theoretical orientation. The book is designed for cumulative learning; allowing you to see the similarities and differences among theories and judge the power of the theoretical application to a real-world example. Each chapter ends with a list of readings to guide the interested student to some of the classics of each theory as well as to works that elaborate on the theoretical application.

Key Terms

Anarchic (anarchy)
Balance-of-power
Bipolar
Cognitive consistency
Collective security
Concert of Europe
Deterrence
Epistemological (Epistemology)
Idealist
Intergovernmental Organizations (IGOs)
Methodological (Methodology)
Most Favored Nation (MFN)
Multinational Corporations (MNCs)
Mutually Assured Destruction (MAD)
Nongovernmental Organizations (NGOs)
Non-tariff barriers
Ontological (Ontology)
Positivists
Positive-sum
Post-positivists
Proliferation

Protectionism

Quotas

Subsidies

Tariffs

Theory

Weapons of Mass Destruction (WMDs)

World Trade Organization (WTO)

Worldviews

Zero-sum

For Further Reading

Sagan, Scott and Kenneth Waltz. 2012. *The Spread of Nuclear Weapons: An Enduring Debate*, 3rd Edition. New York: W.W. Norton and Company.

Singer, David J. 1961. "The Level-of-Analysis Problem in International Relations," *World Politics*, 14, (1961), pp. 77–92.

Waltz, Kenneth N. 1993. "The Emerging Structure of International Politics," *International Security*, Vol. 18, No. 2 (Fall 1993), pp. 51–55.

———— 1959. *Man, the State, and War*. New York: Columbia University Press.

Wight, Colin, Lene Hansen, and Tim Dunne. 2013. "The End of International Relations Theory," *European Journal of International Relations*, Vol.19(3), pp. 405–425.

Zeng, Ka. 2013. "US-China Disputes under the World Trade Organization (WTO)," *Asian Journal of Social Science*, Vol. 41, Issue 3/4, pp. 352–380.

Endnotes

[1] A majority of the discipline refers to the positivists/post-positivists debate as the Third Debate as they do not view the inter-paradigmatic debate between realists, liberals, and economic structuralists as one of the major debates in international relations.

[2] According to estimates by the Bulletin of the Atomic Scientists, India has 110 nuclear warheads, while Pakistan has 110–130. All of these warheads are stockpiled, however, not deployed.

³ For a full list and explanation of states believed to possess chemical and/or biological weapons, see "Chemical and Biological Weapons Resource Page," James Martin Center for Nonproliferation Studies, Monterey Institute of International Studies, http://cns.miis.edu/cbw/possess.htm. Accessed October 14, 2013.

⁴ Nagby and Roser use data from International Historical Statistics available at Available at: http://www.palgraveconnect.com/pc/doifinder/10.1057/9781137305688.0001

⁵ For the current list of members, see http://www.wto.org/english/thewto_e/whatis_e/tif_e/org6_e.htm.

⁶ For a list of "least developed countries," see http://www.wto.org/english/thewto_e/whatis_e/tif_e/org7_e.htm.

⁷ For more on how the WTO treats developing countries, see http://www.wto.org/english/thewto_e/whatis_e/tif_e/utw_chap6_e.pdf.

CHAPTER 2

....

Realism

". . . [T]he standard of justice depends on the equality of power to compel and that in fact the strong do what they have the power to do and the weak accept what they have to accept."

—Thucydides, *The Melian Dialogue*

In January 2013, North Korea's National Defense Commission announced a new round of nuclear and long-range rocket tests. In doing so, they declared this was part of an "upcoming all-out action" against the United States, "the sworn enemy of the Korean people" (Kwon and Mullen, 2013). This was another salvo in the long-running, and continuing, controversy surrounding North Korea's nuclear program (see Chapter 1). To the casual observer, North Korea would appear to be biting off more than it can chew. The regime is believed to possess between four and eight nuclear weapons with tested short- and medium-range missiles (and no long-range missile capability). The United States, on the other hand, has 1,585 strategic nuclear warheads deployed through its nuclear triad: ICMBs, SLBMs, and long-range bombers.[1] As such, the United States possesses the capability to destroy North Korea with nuclear weapons without a single American leaving US soil. It is currently debatable whether North Korea possesses the capability to strike the United States with their weapons in any capacity.

So, why does North Korea make such threats at a larger and clearly more powerful opponent? For a realist, the answer is clear: power politics. North Korea pursues its nuclear and missile programs for several reasons. The publically stated reason is to deter the United States from a direct attack and continued hostile policies, such as sanctions and joint military exercises with South Korea. The larger objectives, however, include the survival of the regime (as North Korea believes the

United States desires regime change) and the power and prestige that comes with being a recognized nuclear power. Nuclear weapons convey a sense of legitimacy and power on the international scale that no other weapon, policy, or action can match. That being the case, North Korea is pursuing power politics in its relations with South Korea, the United States, and Japan (amongst others). This is a pure realist approach to international relations. The following sections will highlight the theory of realism and at the end of this chapter, we will return to our discussion of North Korea's nuclear program to further illustrate the goals and strategies of the regime, as well as the attempts of other states to stop and reverse its programs.

Roots and Evolution of Realism

Realism remains the most venerable paradigm in international relations. Although it is certainly not without its detractors, realism occupies a central position in the study of international relations. The realist tradition traces back more than 2,000 years to the Chinese strategist Sun Tzu, who wrote his classic study, *The Art of War*, describing the Period of Warring in China during the fourth and third centuries BCE. As much about avoiding war as fighting one, Sun Tzu demonstrated the importance of power in seeking interests and survival (Tzu, 1963). The focus of Sun Tzu's work brings us to the meaning of realism. Realism is often referred to as **realpolitik** or power politics, and its focus is the ability of states to acquire, exercise, and maintain power. Realist direct their focus to issues of security, including war and other forms of violent conflict, and the exercise of power in these arenas. Although we talk about power as if there is consensus on what that means, there is actually great debate on its definition and measurability. Generally, power is the ability to make another do what it otherwise would not do, or prevent it from doing what it wants to do. When discussing power, however, we must be careful not to engage in circular logic: power explains the behavior change and thus the behavior change is a measurement of power. Since international relations operate in an environment of incomplete information, we cannot know the true motives or decision-making process of the second state in the wake of the first state's power.

Measuring power can be difficult, but it is widely discussed in two categories. The first is hard power. This is most likely what one thinks of when considering the power of a state. Hard power includes tangible military capabilities: troops, tanks, aircraft, missiles, nuclear weapons, and advanced military technology. These types of capabilities are relatively easy to measure, but determining their impact is something quite different. As mentioned in Chapter 1, although many states now possess nuclear weapons, no state since the United States in 1945 has used them. Yet, their possession still confers legitimacy and power. If no one intends to use them, how much power can they create? The second category of power, which is widely dismissed by realists, is **soft power**. Developed by Joseph Nye Jr. of Harvard University, this concept describes the exercise of power through a state's own values, ideas, wealth, and culture. Hard power focuses on the ability to coerce others to do what you want, whereas soft power is about the ability to attract and influence others because they respond positively to your values and beliefs (Nye 2005). Despite debates over measuring power, all realist focus on power as the central feature of state-to-state relations.

Central Assumptions

While there are several types of realists (explained below), most realists share certain central assumptions.

- States are the principal actors in international relations and each enjoys **sovereignty**.
- States exist in a self-help system of anarchy, in which survival is the top priority.
- States are disposed toward conflict rather than cooperation.
- States are unitary rational actors.

Since 1648 and the Treaty of Westphalia (which ended the Thirty Years' War), states have been the primary political unit in international relations. The treaty created the principal of sovereignty and territorial integrity upon which the nation-state system was founded. The Thirty Years' War was the revolt against the rule of the Holy Roman Empire, and the establishment of sovereignty was a blow to the rule of the Church. Monarchs could now decide domestic policy for themselves, including the recognition of an official religion within their borders. Sovereignty paved the way for the recognition of constitutional governments as the seat of legal authority rather than authority derived from a religious institution, namely the Catholic Church.

All realists accept that we live in a condition of anarchy, meaning there is no recognized legitimate hierarchical structure (such as a world government) to control the behavior of states. As such, all states must fend for themselves, providing for their own security and survival. If they fail to do so, they risk succumbing to another state. As a consequence, states must prioritize security through the acquisition of power usually through military might. Realists view this as the most important function of the state. This focus on a state's own survival through the acquisition and maintenance of power leads to a more conflictual environment as states are compelled to arm themselves for self-defense. This leads to a condition known as the **security dilemma**. As one state arms itself for self-defense, other states become fearful of this build-up of weaponry and view it as aggressive rather than defensive. The result is a spiral of arms build-ups as each state seeks to increase its own safeguards from attack. The environment is inherently conflictual as states view each other with suspicion and fear decreasing the likelihood of cooperation.

This condition highlights a prominent disagreement within the realist school. **Defensive realists** (including Kenneth Waltz, Barry Posen, Jack Snyder, and Stephen Van Evera) believe that states seek power as a means of security to balance and defend themselves against other states. They argue that there is an offense-defense balance that weighs in the defender's favor—in other words, offense does not pay. Aggressive states seeking additional power and territorial gains will end up fighting a string of losing wars or expending significant resources holding conquered territories that in the end will be detrimental to their own power. **Offensive realists** (including John Mearsheimer) work from the assumption that more power is always better in securing the survival of the state, thus states seek maximum or dominant power. Advocates of this type of realism argue that offense does indeed pay, and the historical record supports their claim showing that the side that takes the offensive wins more often than not. Moreover, conquered territories can indeed be successfully held and resources extracted without debilitating costs to the conqueror. Thus, great powers will constantly be seeking dominance over one another with the ultimate prize being hegemony (Mearsheimer, 2013). Later in this chapter, we discuss the balance versus imbalance of power debate rooted in the arguments of defensive and offensive realists.

Although realists recognize that there are multiple entities within states—individuals, interest groups, bureaucracy, and others—to simplify the complex environment in which decision are made, most realists deemphasize the role of these actors and focus on the state as a single, that is, unitary actor. We presume that the state acts rationally in conducting a cost-benefit analysis and making the decisions that best suit its interests. The state identifies goals, interests, preferences, and the means to achieve them and acts accordingly. Realists also tend to be skeptical that there is a set of universal moral principles by which actions are judged in pursuit of these goals and preferences. The determinants of ethical conduct can vary and leaders should not undermine the interests of their state by trying to achieve them. Further, many realists declare the existence of a dual moral standard, one by which leaders live and one that applies to everyone else. The morality of leaders is based on what is in the best interest of their state, even if that means lying, cheating, torturing, killing, or engaging in other acts of cruelty. For individuals we would find these characteristics morally reprehensible, but in a leader, realists accept they may be necessary to ensure the survival of the state.

While these are the central assumptions of realism, there are many variations of realist thought. Within these variations, there are also a series of sub-theories that explain a specific phenomenon. Figure 2.1 demonstrates the variants and sub-theories of realist thought we explore in the sections below, including the evolution of realism focusing on some of the great thinkers of this tradition. In doing so, we highlight two important elements. First, what are the different variations of realist thinking? Second, where did these ideas come from?

Classical Realism

Classical realists have a pessimistic view of human nature and focus on the inherent dark side of human beings. We are amoral, selfish, and aggressive and given that humans create states, we must assume states possess similar features. This inevitably leads to a conflictual international environment resembling Darwin's survival of the fittest. In this dog-eat-dog world, states must arm themselves to ensure their own survival or natural selection will weed out the weak. Although classical realism begins with the individual-level assumption that people matter (see Chapter 1 for the levels of analysis), the state is still the primary unit of analysis. The state takes on the characteristics of human beings, namely the fearful and conflictual nature of humankind, leading to the condition in which survival is the top priority of the state.

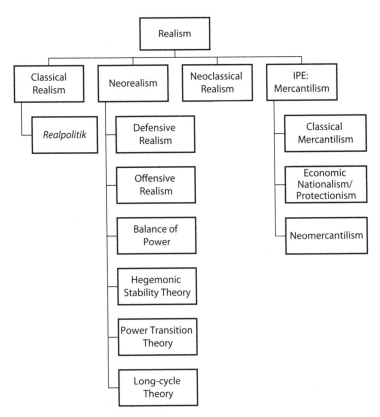

FIGURE 2.1 Realism Family Tree.

Like all variations of realism, power politics is the central feature of international relations, but the key for classical realists is why states want power. It is based on human nature; our inherent need to dominate others and in return the need to protect ourselves from others.

To protect a state's vital interests, material capabilities and alliances with other states are central. Although alliances are seen as a means to increase one's power, some famous classical realists (see below) viewed them with skepticism. The world remains a self-help system—if a state does not protect itself, no other state in the system will. Thus, alliances take a backseat to a state's own military preparation. There is no absolute guarantee that an alliance partner will be there when push comes to shove, but if a state has prepared itself for battle, it can be confident in its own capabilities. The build-up of military capabilities and the creation of alliances come with their own set of problems however. As mentioned above, the security dilemma can result when a state is trying to create a favorable balance of power in relation to other states. A build-up of capabilities can be seen as threat, and thus precipitate conflict. These ideas developed roughly 2,500 years ago with writers and works that have become classics in the field. The following section will discuss these origins.

Pioneers in the Field

The Greek historian Thucydides (460–395 BCE) is often credited with being the first to write in the realist tradition and his account of the Peloponnesian War (431–404 BCE) is a classic statement on the nature of war.[2] In what became arguably the most influential segment of his book, "The Melian Dialogue," Thucydides clearly lays out the role of power in international relations: it is the final authority in disputes. The quote that began this chapter epitomizes this argument. In the discussions between the Melians and Athenians, the Athenians make it clear that Melos must accept that the powerful do what they want and the weak must accept it. This argument is made when the Athenians arrive on Melos and demand they surrender or be destroyed. The Melians attempt to convince the Athenians that there is another way, namely allowing Melos to remain neutral in Athens' war with Sparta, but the Athenians conclude that such an action would make them look weak and decrease their power.

In addition to the enunciation of the crude use of power, Thucydides points out the "folly" of relying on alliances for one's own security. With Sparta as an ally, the Melians tell the Athenians that it would be in their best interest to leave Melos be, as Sparta will come to their aid if attacked. The Athenians scoff at this idea, arguing that the Spartans would serve their own self-interest and as a consequence not assist Melos in defending against an attack. In the end, Melos refused to surrender and the Athenians were correct. Sparta did not come to their aid and the Melians were defeated, resulting in the slaughter of the adult males and the enslavement of the women and children. What is the lesson here? That international relations is a self-help system, meaning one's own survival is only guaranteed through the development and maintenance of one's own military power. This is one of the central assumptions of realism; this is a self-help system in which survival is a state's top priority.

Another pioneer of realist thought, Niccolo Machiavelli (1469–1527) is most famous for his ruthless advice in *The Prince*, which resulted in the term "Machiavellian." The purpose of this work was to provide sound advice to the prince on how to accumulate and use his power in the attainment of not only political goals; ultimately, however, the advice was for survival. A different moral standard exists for the prince than for others. He must be willing to be ruthless and cruel to ensure survival, and a reputation for cruelty is beneficial in keeping his subjects in line. Machiavelli contends that the only way to maintain a conquered land accustomed to liberty is to destroy it, and while a prince should be good when possible, he should never do so at the expense of his power. He should avoid needless cruelty because being hated may prove to be counterproductive. Do what one must to maintain power, but do not unnecessarily harm others or risk the potential undermining of one's rule. Machiavelli asks the famous question, "Is it better to be loved or feared?" He tells the prince it is best to be both loved and feared, but if only one is possible, fear will maintain his power, love will not. Love is fleeting, but fear is powerful and lasting, resulting in more cautious behavior by one's subjects. Machiavelli is also suspicious of the utility of alliances, and ultimately advises the prince to avoid them. There is no guarantee that alliance partners will fulfill their commitments as they have different interests and goals. Likewise, the prince should never be bound by any other interests than his own. Ultimately, in this self-help system, building military capabilities is crucial and the pursuit of power is the only way to ensure survival. Much like Thucydides, these arguments helped lay the foundation for the central assumptions of realism.

Carl von Clausewitz (1780–1831) was a Prussian general who fought in the Napoleonic Wars. His most famous work, *On War*, highlights the role of military power in the attainment of political ends. The true aim of war is to render one's enemy powerless, a goal achieved through disarmament. To achieve this result, military power is essential, but it must always be subordinate to political goals. War is the means of achieving a political goal, but not an end in and of itself. Clausewitz warns that this can never be forgotten or the consequences can be painful. War is a serious and dangerous business that should not be entered into lightly and leaders should know the last move before taking the first. These are arguments one can hear in present-day analysis concerning decisions to enter conflicts and they tie Clausewitz directly to modern realist thinkers. In addition, the importance he places on military might in the attainment of goals is a clear enunciation of realist thought. This is the approach of the "Powell Doctrine," named after former Chairman of the Joint Chiefs and Secretary of State, Colin Powell. Made famous in the early 1990s, the doctrine promoted war as a last resort, with the use of overwhelming force to minimize US casualties. War should have public support and include a quick exit-strategy with the enemy capitulating.

Hans J. Morgenthau (1904–1980) is arguably the most influential post-war realist and his ideas about international politics are advanced in his book, *Politics Among Nations* (1948). He was born in Germany, but fled when the Nazi regime came to power, a fact that helps to explain his arguments concerning human nature. Morgenthau tells us that there are laws that govern politics and they are rooted in human nature. From his perspective, human beings are flawed, domination is a part of human nature, and power-seeking behavior is a biological drive of human beings. In these conclusions, it is easy to see Morgenthau's classical realist leanings. Beyond the quest for power, he was also concerned with the conditions that would create international peace. He expounded the idea that international conflict can arise if a state pursues interests that are not essential to national survival. As a 20th-century theorist, he was interested in the consequences of the Soviet Union and the United States choosing to spread communism or democracy, respectively. These lofty goals that were not vital to survival led both superpowers during the Cold War to engage in risky and ultimately costly behavior. For example, Morgenthau believed the US venture in Vietnam was unnecessary as it was in a region not vital to US interests. On the other hand, he supported US confrontations over Cuba due to its geographic proximity to the United States. Further, Morgenthau believed two factors in international relations preserved the peace: the balance of power (discussed below) and the use of diplomacy.

There are many other influential thinkers of classical realism, but this brief overview highlights some of the major contributions to the development of the central assumptions of realism. It should already be clear that there is a preoccupation with war and armed conflict, and this focus should help explain why many policymakers hold this world-view. Decisions about conflict are among the most profound and costly made by world leaders, and unfortunately they are forced to make them frequently. Hence, realism tends to speak to their actual experiences. (See Spotlight on Policymakers, below, for the example of George

Kennan.) But, classical realism is only the beginning of the evolution of this school of thought. The world wars brought significant changes in the ways in which international relations theorists viewed the world.

SPOTLIGHT ON POLICYMAKERS: GEORGE KENNAN

George F. Kennan (1904–2005) was an American diplomat and historian best known as the "father of containment." He was a Foreign Service officer and served in numerous locations, including Geneva, Hamburg, Berlin, Estonia, Latvia, Moscow, Vienna, Prague, and London. Beyond his role in the creation of containment, he was the State Department's first policy planning chief, and in that role was an architect of the Marshall Plan, which sent billions of dollars in aid to war-raged Western Europe after World War II. He served as US Ambassador to the USSR in 1952 and Yugoslavia from 1961 to 1963. He authored 17 books, two of which won the Pulitzer Prize, and countless articles, and remained one of the leading thinkers on international affairs until his death in 2005.

Kennan had extensive experience with the Soviet Union and in 1946 he was Charge d'Affaires in Moscow. However, his stint in Moscow was a disaster: he was distrusted by Soviet intelligence, blocked from contact with Soviet citizens, and declared *persona non grata* by the Soviet government. In his capacity as Charge d'Affaires, he sent an 8,000-word telegram—known as the "long telegram"—to the State Department detailing the aggressive nature of Soviet foreign policy under Joseph Stalin. The main elements of the telegram were published as "The Sources of Soviet Conduct" under the pseudonym "Mr. X" in *Foreign Affairs* in 1947. It was there he made public his idea of the US policy of containment, urging that the US should stop the spread of communism by confronting the "Russians with unalterable counterforce at every point where they show signs of encroaching upon the interests of a peaceful and stable world" ("X", 1947, 581). Successive presidential administrations interpreted these words as meaning all necessary measures, but Kennan was promoting the use of diplomacy and covert action, not war. In fact, in a 1948 memorandum, he argued for the use of political warfare against the USSR, and ultimately his ideas became the covert arm of the CIA. In 1975, however, Kennan lamented his role in creating this initiative as "the biggest mistake I ever made" (Weiner and Crossette 2005). He spent much of his post-government career distancing himself from containment and deploring the fact that it was applied incorrectly.

Kennan is a bit of a conundrum in a theoretical sense. On the one hand, he is heralded as a foundational thinker of 20th-century realism.

continued

He believed in the inherent weakness of human beings and hence promoted a foreign policy based on power principles and the inevitability of conflict. He argued for a balance-of-power system and a foreign policy based on the pursuit of national interests. Kennan condemned the liberal internationalist tradition (see Chapter 3), and declared the "legalistic-moralistic approach" as "the most serious fault of our past policy formulation" (Kennan, 1951, 95). He argued that the liberal tradition that guided foreign policy between the two world wars (see Chapter 1) and its reliance on "some system of legal rules and restraints" would actually serve to make the world a more violent and terrible place (Kennan, 1951, 95). Moreover, Kennan rejected international organizations, including the UN, and international law and agreements as impediments to US interests. All of these assertions are consistent with realist tenets.

On the other hand, Kennan's theoretical focus becomes less clear when we look at his position on the Soviet Union. Like Morgenthau, he believed in diplomacy, but the purpose of this diplomacy was to maintain the balance of power, one in which the United States dominated a defeated Soviet Union (Hixson, 1989). Mixing realism and idealism, this dominance would come from more than military might, it would stem from the United States as a "nation among nations" ("X", 1947). He often de-emphasized moral considerations and the importance of ideology (like any good realist), but he countered this theoretical position as a staunch anti-communist. This approach undermined his realist principles by linking pursuits in foreign policy to ideology. Instead of making a rational, calculated decision about what was best for US national interests, he often promoted positions and polices that were simply in opposition to communism. In addition, he became deeply dismayed over the use of containment to justify conventional and WMD buildup, ultimately becoming a hero of the anti-nuclear movement. He questioned the application of power politics in the nuclear age based on morality—the antithesis of realist thinking. Attempts to determine his overriding theoretical perspective are complicated by his own writings, at times espousing ardent realist principles while at others appearing quite idealist in nature. As Henry Kissinger wrote of Kennan, "The debate in America between idealism and realism, which continues to this day, played itself out inside Kennan's soul" (Kissinger, 2011). Regardless of his lack of consistency, Kennan continues to be an influential pioneer of the realist school of thought primarily due to the execution of his ideas by the United States in its foreign policy.

Neorealism (Structural Realism)

In contrast to classical realists who focus on human nature, structural realists or neorealists focus on the lack of overarching authority (anarchy), the structure of the international system, and the relative power distribution among states. In fact, structural realists argue that the relative distribution of power is the central variable in analyzing international interactions. Since one state's standing relative to others is important, states will seek to increase capabilities, both military and economic. Hence, states will pursue power because the structure of the international system forces them to need it. As mentioned above, however, this increase in capabilities leads others to be threatened, creating a security dilemma. This condition also creates the pressures of a zero-sum game; if one state gains another state necessarily losses. In addition to the assumptions of realists (see above), structural realism is based on three additional assumptions.

- The main actors in international relations are the great powers.
- Every state possesses some offensive military capability.
- The intentions of other states are uncertain.

Note that structural realism corresponds most closely with the systemic level of analysis de-emphasizing actors within states (see Chapter 1).

Pioneers in the Field

Structural realism can be traced to the work of Kenneth Waltz (1924–2013), often referred to as the father of neorealism. His *Theory of International Politics* (1979) is the seminal work in the field. John Mearsheimer (2013, 82) argues that this work is "probably the most influential book written in international relations over the past fifty years." Waltz formulated the idea that the interaction between states (their behavior) is based on the system structure and the distribution of power. He ventures away from classical realism in that he ignores human nature and ethics in statecraft, instead creating a scientific explanation (identifying him as a positivist as discussed in Chapter 1) for state behavior focusing on the structure of the system, the interaction of the units in the system, and changes of the system. In doing so, the behavior of states should be predictable. The theory builds from three basic premises. First, all states are basically the same in terms of the functions they must perform: conduct foreign policy, provide for national defense, collect taxes, and so forth. Second, where states differ is in capabilities. They perform similar tasks, but some are better at it than others due to a difference in capabilities. According to Waltz (1979, 97), "The units of an anarchic system are functionally undifferentiated. The units of such an order are then distinguished primarily by their greater or lesser capabilities for performing similar tasks." For example, great power states are better at defense due to their differentiated capabilities, that is, a bigger and stronger military, than a developing state. Third, Waltz argues that a change in the distribution of capabilities across the system's units (states) will lead to a change in the overall structure of the system. Such changes to the structure of the international system will inherently "change expectations about how the units of the system will behave and about the outcomes their interactions will produce" (Waltz, 1979, 97). Changes in system structure are the product of great powers gaining or losing power and the shifting balance of power that accompanies those changes. We see such an example at the end of the Cold War when the capabilities of the Soviet Union changed leading to an adjustment in the international structure from a bipolar to a unipolar (at least temporarily) system.

The core of Waltz's argument is that in a system of anarchy where each state's primary goal is survival, states must compete with each other for power. Hegemony is not the goal (as explained above Waltz is a defensive realist), but states must maintain their power in the system relative to other states. Waltz also explains the logic of balancing and thus controlling the state's lust for power, as well as the arguments for the stability of bipolarity and the system bias against **bandwagoning** (see below). In his theory, state leaders have little room to maneuver as actions to improve their position are countered by the other actors in the system. The system itself is in control. As you read more about neorealism below, you will see how these premises play out in the application of the theory.

John Mearsheimer (1947–) is the leading theorist of offensive realism (discussed above). His book, *The Tragedy of Great Power Politics* (2001), postulates that states are never satisfied with their level of power and will always seek to increase gains relative to other states in the system. Further, states seek hegemony to eliminate threats from other great powers and "[o]nly a misguided state would pass up an opportunity to be the hegemon in the system because it thought it already had sufficient power to survive" (Mearsheimer, 2001, 35). Although both neorealists, this places Mearsheimer at odds with Waltz, who is the leading proponent of defensive realism. As noted above, defensive realists believe that maintaining a balance of power is essential in the system, and if one state becomes too powerful (as in seeking hegemony), balancing will occur among the other great powers to put the system back in alignment. The concept of balancing will discussed in greater detail below.

Before postulating the concept of offensive realism, Mearsheimer was best known for his work on deterrence, both conventional (*Conventional Deterrence*, 1983) and nuclear (*Nuclear Deterrence: Ethics and Strategy*, co-editor, 1985). In recent years, he stirred up controversy with an article (that was turned into a book) that he co-authored with Stephen Walt (another prominent realist) claiming the Israel lobby in the United States is pushing policies that are not in the best interests of the United States or Israel (*The Israel Lobby and US Foreign Policy*, 2007). In his latest book, *Why Leaders Lie: The Truth about Lying in International Politics* (2011), Mearsheimer argues political leaders lie because they believe it is in the best interest of their country and that leaders in democratic regimes lie to their people more often than autocratic leaders. This ties back to the realist idea that there is a different moral code for leaders than average citizens. Throughout these works, Mearsheimer remains a staunch realist and in the following section you will see how many of his ideas play out in a further enunciation of neorealism.

Polarity and Balance Versus Imbalance of Power

Although there are currently 195 independent states, structural realists are primarily concerned only with the **great powers**. The number of great powers determines the structure of the system. The most common way realists define the structure of the system is by the number of poles that exist. A pole is generally one independent state, but could theoretically be an alliance or international organization. Polarity in the international system is usually characterized by unipolarity (one great power or hegemon), bipolarity (two great powers), or multipolarity (at least four great powers). For example, the Cold War was characterized by a struggle between the United States and Soviet Union, creating a bipolar system. Determining the number of poles is not always easy.

In the 1990s, after the shock of the collapse of the Soviet Union had dissipated, there was a debate over whether the system was unipolar (with the United States as the hegemon) or multipolar (including powers such as China, India, and the European Union). Both camps made valid arguments, however, no consensus was reached.

Another debate concerning polarity centers on the question of stability, which means the absence of conflict. This debate is twofold: polarity and balance versus imbalance of power. First, an ongoing debate is which system of polarity is more stable, and this usually centers on bipolarity versus multipolarity. There are three main arguments for the stability of bipolarity, made by such prominent international relations scholars as Kenneth Waltz and John Mearsheimer. First, because the two great powers in the system are comparatively stronger than any other states in the system, the smaller, less powerful states cannot create conflict resulting in fewer points of antagonism. Fewer great powers are involved, thus there are fewer chances for great-power wars. Second, the system is seen as more efficient and deterrence is more effective because there are only two powers. Third, with only two powers dominating the system, chances of misunderstanding and miscalculation are lower. In a bipolar system, there are fewer distractions for the superpowers and they can focus their attention on each other (Waltz, 1979). Bipolarity is a constant struggle between the two great powers ruled by a zero-sum game leading to a balancing game that will prevent conflict. As each great power is jockeying to stay equal to the other in capabilities, they will see the futility of conflict with a roughly equal opponent. For example, during the Cold War, the United States and Soviet Union achieved parity in nuclear weapons—in this case meaning each could destroy the other—thus preventing a nuclear conflict. This created the system of Mutually Assured Destruction (MAD), giving neither side an incentive to begin a war. The Cold War is heralded as the prime example of the stability of a bipolar system. Although there were many smaller conflicts and proxy wars, there was no major war between the two great powers in the system.

On the other hand, there are four main arguments for the stability of a multipolar system, made by such prominent international relations scholars as J. David Singer (1925–2009) and Karl Deutsch (1912–1992). First, because there are a large number of actors, uncertainty leads to caution of the part of states. This caution would prevent states from deviating too far from the normal practices of the past, thus they are less likely to cause tension with the other actors in the system. Second, the larger number of actors also causes a dispersion of attention. When attention has to be paid in several areas, conflict is less likely to occur in any one area (Deutsch and Singer, 1964). Third, a multipolar system is not a zero-sum game. Each state does not have to balance each other state because alliances are a common feature of multipolarity. If one state gets too powerful, the other great powers will ally together to match its strength. This results in a moderation of the security dilemma creating less fear between the powers. Multipolarity requires a fluidity of alliance partners. A state never knows when another will attempt to gain more power. Thus, today's enemy could be tomorrow's ally. Fourth, the great powers are likely to have interests in common leading to an increased number of positive interactions that will moderate any conflictual behavior. If a state shares a common interest, such as trade, with another state, it is less likely to jeopardize that area by becoming hostile in other areas. Instead, they will seek mutually acceptable solutions to protect their area of common interest.

Multipolarity existed between 1648 (**Peace of Westphalia**) and 1914 (World War I). The period saw several wars (War of the Spanish Succession, 1701–1714, War of the Austrian Succession 1740–1745, Seven Years' War 1756–1763, and the Napoleonic Wars 1803–1815), but they were marked by a shifting system of alliances designed to keep the system multipolar. For example, when Napoleon rose to dominate continental Europe by either conquest or alliance, the other powers in the system (Spain, Portugal, Sweden, Russia, Prussia, Austria, and Britain) formed an alliance and defeated him at the Battle of Waterloo. What the great powers (Britain, Russia, Prussia, and Austria) were seeking through the Concert of Europe (see Chapter 1) constructed after the Napoleonic Wars was a return to multipolarity designed to preserve the balance of power. As a consequence of multipolarity (first maintained by the Concert of Europe and then by the **Bismarckian alliance system**), the 99-year period from 1815 to 1914 saw no major European wars and is considered the most peaceful time in human history.

This brings us to the second debate about stability in the system: balance of power versus preponderance of power. Balance of power (or parity) means there is rough equality between the great powers in the system. This is a factor in both bipolarity and multipolarity. The goal is to maintain balance by preventing any single power or combination of powers from dominating the system. Balance of power theorists contend that conflict is less likely in systems of parity largely due to the fact that states will be deterred from entering into conflict with one another because of the fear they could lose in a battle of equal strength or they fear the damage they will incur even if they were to be victorious. Think about a boxing match. If the two fighters are roughly equal in strength, the fight is likely to go all 12 rounds with each of them experiencing serious physical damage along the way. This is analogous to a war between states of roughly equal strength. One may win in the end and the other lose (or it could be called a draw), but the damage they will both incur deters them from entering the ring.

One of the most prominent scholars to explain balance of power is Morton Kaplan (1921–).[3] Kaplan argues that for a balance of power system to function properly, the actors must be states (non-state actors cannot be a pole in this system) and there must be a minimum of five (the number of actors required in a balance of power system differs between scholars) (Kaplan, 1966). He lays out six essential rules of the balance of power system:

> 1) increase capabilities, but negotiate rather than fight; 2) fight rather than fail to increase capabilities; 3) stop fighting rather than eliminate an essential actor; 4) oppose any coalition or single actor that tends to assume a position of predominance within the system; 5) constrain actors who subscribe to supranational organizational principles; and 6) permit defeated or constrained essential national actors to re-enter the system as acceptable role partners, or act to bring some previously inessential actor within the essential actor classification (Kaplan 1966, 297–298).

If an actor violates the rules, the other actors in the system must act in a way that forces the noncompliant actor back into "rule-consonant behavior." The balance of power system is characterized by short-lived, shifting alliances based on advantage not ideology. Any combination of actors is possible within an alliance as long as any alliance does not gain a preponderance of power. States must act to prevent any other actor from gaining preponderance. This is done to protect each state's own national interests. Wars are fought for limited objectives and there are international laws that apply to all actors in the system (for example, rules of war) (Kaplan, 1966).

In a balance of power system, if one state becomes too powerful, the other actors will form a counterbalancing coalition to bring the system back into balance. Recall that this is the argument of defensive realists like Waltz—balance must be maintained in the system and a hegemon must be prevented from rising. This takes us back to our multipolarity example of the Napoleonic Wars. When Napoleon broke the rules of a balance of power system, he was brought back into compliance through the formation of a counterbalancing coalition that ultimately defeated him. Neorealists argue that states will choose this balancing strategy rather than one of bandwagoning. In bandwagoning, states attempt to increase their gains and lessen their losses by jumping on board with the stronger side. For neorealists, this choice is folly. If states strengthen another state through bandwagoning, they court the possibility that the stronger state will eventually turn on them. In fact, in an anarchic system, the likelihood of this happening is very high. By pursuing a balancing strategy, risk is reduced because the more powerful or rising power is opposed by a coalition of the other states. Balancing can be pursued internally, through the reallocation of resources to military/defense, or externally through alliances and other agreements. Beyond bandwagoning, there is an additional dangerous strategy that states pursue to their peril. States can engage in **buckpassing**; allowing other states to do the fighting while they sit on the sidelines. They do not incur the costs of fighting through this strategy, but they run the risk of other states not fighting as well. In this case, the system will come out of balance and states will be subject to the will of the rising power.

Theorists on the other side of the balance of power debate would argue having a preponderant power or a hegemon leads to stability. This is **hegemonic stability theory**. Recall this is the argument of offensive realists like Mearsheimer—hegemony is desired to eliminate threats from other states. Theorists who contend preponderance is more stable argue that the hegemon will have little need to use force to impose its will. The preponderant state is so much more powerful than other states it has no need for feelings of insecurity and can get what it wants without using force. As such, all other states in the system will be deferential to the preponderant power because if they were to pick a fight they would most likely lose. If we return to our boxing analogy, if two boxers were to step in the ring with one being obviously superior in strength, this would most likely be a short fight with a knockout punch by the stronger boxer. As such, the weaker fighter would be wise not to step into the ring. The same goes for weaker states. In a system in which there is a hegemon, weaker states will not start conflicts with the preponderant power out of fear that they will be defeated, losing resources, territory, and perhaps its very existence as an independent entity. In addition, the argument postulates that not just the hegemon benefits from the arrangement, so too do the weaker states. The hegemon creates order and stability and these are conditions from which all states in the system benefit. Without the control of the hegemon, the system unravels into disorder taking with it previously determined international agreements. Agreements falter, collaboration breaks down, disorder prevails, and conflict, costly to many states, ensues.

One of the most prominent theorists of preponderance is A.F.K. Organski, who argues that balance of power theory is false and instead of creating peace, it leads to war. Above, the argument was made that multipolarity and a balance of power within that multipolar system led to the long period of peace following the Napoleonic Wars. Organski argues that this peace was not caused by the balance of power, but that there was a preponderance of power in the hands of England and France that was responsible for the peace of the 19th century. He argues that the balance of power leads to war because "It stands to reason that nations will not fight unless they believe they have a good chance of winning, but this is true for both sides only when they are fairly evenly matched, or at least when they believe they are" (Organski, 1958, 293). On the other hand, a preponderant power does not need to fight to get what it wants and the weaker parties will not start a war because they know they cannot win. So, from this, when do we get war? Organski postulates the **power transition theory**. Conflict is most likely when "a great power in a secondary position challenges the top nation and its allies for control. Thus the usual major conflict is between the top nation (and its allies) and the challenger that is about to catch up with it in power" (Organski, 1958, 325). If we are trying to determine which nations will instigate a conflict, the level of power and the level of satisfaction with the status quo are important. If the preponderant power and its allies are satisfied with the status quo (which they should be because they control the existing international order), they have no need to instigate a conflict. It is the powerful and the dissatisfied that create instability. These challengers desire the creation of a new international order primarily because they do not control the current one and dislike their place in it. They possess enough power to take action to address their dissatisfaction and are risk-acceptant leading them to believe that they can defeat the dominant power and hence become unwilling to continue to assume the position of a subordinate in the system. Thus, according to Organski, war is most likely to occur when the challenger (and its allies) approximates the power of the group that support the status quo (Organski, 1958).

In addition to power transition theory, realists posit other arguments for system change. George Modelski posited **long cycle theory**, identifying regular cycles of world leadership and global war, each of which lasts about 100 years. Since 1494, according to Modelski, there have been four world powers who have guided and maintained the system through five different cycles: Portugal (1494–1580), the Netherlands (1580–1688), Britain (two consecutive cycles from 1688–1792 and 1792–1914), and the United States (1914 to the present). War marks the end of one cycle and the beginning of the next. Portugal became the world power after the Italian/Indian Ocean Wars (1494–1516) and their hegemonic reign ended with the Spanish Dutch Wars (1580–1609) that brought the Netherlands to world power status. Britain assumed the mantle of hegemon after the Wars of Louis XIV (1688–1713) and regained its status after the French Revolution and Napoleonic Wars (1792–1815). The United States assumed the mantle after the two World Wars (1914–1945). While war is the catalyst for change, there is a significant period of decay of the global power and growth of rival powers before a change takes place (and a war results). After the global war and the rise of a world power, there is a period during which the world power sets the rules of, and controls, the system. This is costly and exhausting; hence a period of delegitimation ensues characterized by a decline in relative power of the hegemon. A period of deconcentration follows, during which the hegemon is challenged by emerging rivals and the system becomes multipolar. As such, the system created by the hegemon deteriorates, competition intensifies, and war is the consequence (remember, this is a roughly 100-year cycle). After the completion of the war, the cycle begins again.

Neorealists have sought to create a theory that meets scientific criteria. The outcomes should be predictable of all states in any given situation. The success of this endeavor is hotly debated. Below we will discuss criticisms of realism, and through that lens, you can make your own judgment as to their success. Before embarking on that quest, there is one more, relatively new, branch of realism to discuss—neoclassical realism—and one additional related theoretical perspective—mercantilism.

Neoclassical Realism

Neoclassical realists attempt to take the best elements of classical realism and those of neorealism and bring them together in one framework. An emphasis on foreign policy and leadership are taken from classical realism, while the importance of the structure of the international system and the relative power of states is borrowed from neorealists. Given the previous explanation about classical realism and neorealism, this may seem contradictory. If the structure of the system directs state behavior as believed by neorealists, how does one incorporate leadership in foreign policy, which implies choice, into this paradigm? This is accomplished through a much less rigid view of the control exercised by the structure of the system over world leaders. Neoclassical realists believe that "anarchy gives states considerable latitude in defining their security interests, and the relative distribution of power merely sets parameters for grand strategy" thus leaders' behavior can "inhibit a timely and objectively efficient response or policy adaptation to shifts in the external environment" (Lobell et al., 2009, 7). Neoclassical realists accept that leaders must respond to the external environment, but they must also "extract and mobilize resources from domestic society, work through existing domestic institutions, and maintain the support of key stakeholders" (Lobell et al., 2009, 7).

For neoclassical realists the international system socializes states to respond to the rules and restraints of the system in the aggregate, but system structure cannot explain every individual, short-term policy decision made by states. The pressures of the international system are filtered through individual and domestic factors at the decision-making level. For example, when President Obama was forced to make a decision concerning the Russian encroachment in Ukraine in 2014, there were numerous pressures in play. Obama, along with his senior military and civilian advisors, analyzed US interests in relation to the distribution of power in the international system as well as conducted an assessment of other states' interests, in particular Russia and Ukraine. The pressures on the decision concerning any US response did not exist solely in the White House with an eye to the international system, however. The president had to consider domestic constituencies, such as the public (that at the time was quite war weary), legislators and political parties (concerned about midterm elections and already preparing for the 2016 presidential race), lobbyists and interest groups, and members of the vast US bureaucracy. While the US' position in the world (seen by many as declining hegemony) relative to Russia's (seen by many as a rising power) played a significant role in the US decision to primarily pursue sanctions against Russia in response to its behavior toward Ukraine, many other factors were considered as well. Systemic factors set parameters for state behavior, but domestic processes constrain the ability to respond to systemic pressures. This combination of elements is the heart of neoclassical realism.

Pioneers in the Field

Gideon Rose coined the term neoclassical realism in a 1998 *World Politics* review article. In this article, he identifies this school of thought through reviewing the works of Thomas J. Christensen, Randall L. Schweller, William Curti Wohlforth, and Fareed Zakaria.[4] In his review of these works, Rose expounds that they collectively delineate a new school of thought that "explicitly incorporates both external and internal variables, updating and systematizing certain insights drawn from classical realist thought. Its adherents argue that the scope and ambition of a country's foreign policy is driven, first and foremost, by its place in the international system and specifically by its relative material power capabilities. This is why they are realists" (Rose, 1998, 146). He further explains that in these works the scholars argue, "that the impact of such power capabilities of foreign policy is indirect and complex, because systemic pressures must be translated through intervening variables at the unit level. This is why they are neoclassical" (Rose, 1998, 146). Rose argues that neoclassical realists accept that relative material power establishes a set of parameters within which foreign policy must be made, but "foreign policy choices are made by actual political leaders and elites, and so it is their perceptions of relative power that matter, not simply relative quantities of physical resources or forces in being" (Rose, 1998, 147). Further, systemic elements create broad parameters and illuminate a general direction of foreign policy, but they do not determine with specificity the details of state behavior. Lastly, leaders do not act with complete freedom within their own societies. They must consider these domestic factors because they impact the resources available for foreign policy. As such, countries with similar material power capabilities but different state structures can, and most likely will, act differently (Rose, 1998, 147). Rose determines that these authors have created a distinct school because their quest has a common nature, that is, to develop a generalizable theory of foreign policy by building on the theoretical work of both classical and neorealist scholars "by elaborating the role of domestic-level intervening variables, systematizing the approach, and testing it against contemporary competitors" (Rose, 1998, 153).

Christensen, Schweller, Wohlforth, and Zakaria each identify and explain the creation of the grand strategy of one or more great powers during a specific historical point. Christensen's focus is on the China-US relationship during the Cold War and he builds an explanation for strategy based on several variables. First, he determines that the shifting distributions of power in the international system were the starting point for early Sino-American relations. Second, he identifies the realization of the true extent of the British decline in power in 1947 by the Truman administration as the cause that moved the United States toward containment. Third, he argues that the relative distribution of capabilities was misinterpreted by European leaders propelling them to act counter to the predictions of neorealist theorists. Lastly, the relationship between the United States and China was overly competitive because they both lacked the "national political power" (the ability to mobilize domestic resources for security policy) to do as they pleased, thus they used conflict with each other as ammunition to mobilize against the Soviet Union and pursue their core grand strategies (Christensen, 1996).

Schweller's focus is on Hitler's expansionist grand strategy and he argues that the relative power capabilities between Germany, the Soviet Union, and the United States were critical in the creation of foreign policy in the 1930s and 1940s. He demonstrates that tripolarity had a significant impact on the behavior of numerous states of varying capabilities. Like Christensen, he argues that there was a misinterpretation of the distribution of power, in this case by the Soviet Union believing France and Britain represented a pole in the European system. This misinterpretation led Stalin to ally with Hitler to balance against France and Britain.

Stalin expected a war of attrition in the West, but the quick defeat of France proved him wrong and ultimately paved the way for the German invasion of the Soviet Union. If the Soviets had balanced against Germany, instead of bandwagoning with the Nazi regime, Hitler's strategy of conquest in Europe would have be undermined and perhaps halted. Schweller also argues that Hitler's expansionist grand strategy was aided by the degree that the interests of Germany, the Soviet Union, and the United States were status quo (satisfied with the current distribution of power in the system) or revisionist (dissatisfied with the current situation). Germany was highly revisionist (he terms them "wolves"), the Soviet Union was moderately so (termed "foxes"), but the United States was indifferent (termed "ostriches").[5] These interests were guided by domestic factors and the changes in the international system (Schweller, 1998).

Wohlforth focuses on Soviet grand strategy during the Cold War. Rather than seeing the Cold War as the traditional bipolar struggle, Wohlforth contends that the conflict between the United States and Soviet Union centered on the uncertainty of the relative power between them and the different policymakers' perception of that power. As such, the Cold War was characterized by cycles of tension born from changes in the power relationship and different interpretations of those changes. Finally, Zakaria's argument concerns the United States and its place in the international system in the late 19th century. Although the United States experienced significant growth in economic power in the late 19th century, the federal government did not possess the capacity to propel the United States to great power status. After the Civil War, the United States was a divided, decentralized, and weak state. As such, policymakers could not muster enough state power to ascend to great power status—that is, "that portion of national power the government can extract for its purposes and reflects the ease with which central decision-makers can achieve their ends" (Zakaria, 1998, 9). Policymakers tried to leverage the rising power of the United States into international influence, but were stymied by the lack of ability of the federal government to extract any resources from the states. In the 1880s and 1890s, the United States underwent a structural change brought on by industrialization and policymakers were able to expand US influence abroad. The executive branch gained enough power to avoid or coerce Congress, and the Spanish-American War engrained the perception that the United States was a rising power paving the way for American expansion around the globe (Zakaria, 1998).

As we see from these four works, neoclassical realism combines the structure of the system with unit-level factors (individual and domestic) to construct a theory of foreign-policy decision-making. They seek a fuller explanation as to how states create foreign policy. This approach is particularly useful in cases where neorealism fails to explain state behavior. If a state goes against the rules of the system established by neorealists, neoclassical realists can fill in the gaps. The widespread acceptance of this approach remains to be seen. One of the benefits of neorealism and classical realism is that they are parsimonious. Neoclassical realism undermines this benefit in that an explanation from this approach could include a large number of factors. It crosses the levels of analysis and could result in a laundry list of intervening variables. Keep in mind, all theories have their critics and the criticisms of realism are explored later in this chapter.

Mercantilism

Mercantilism is the oldest theoretical perspective in international political economy (IPE), a subfield of international relations.[6] Mercantilism focuses on creating and sustaining wealth and power to protect a state's national security. This is a view of the role of the state and the market in creating power through wealth. Security is the central concern of states, and mercantilists discuss the importance of military power, which cannot be attained and maintained without economic power. In addition, mercantilists are concerned about non-military threats to states, such as foreign companies and their products. This perspective is often discussed as the economic equivalent of political realism because both seek explanations for the impact of the state and power on the economy. Mercantilists and realists share many of the same tenets—the nation-state is the primary actor in world politics, states compete with each other for limited resources based on national interests, and the competition between states results in a zero-sum game because the resources are limited. The most significant difference between realists and mercantilists is the emphasis realists place on military power. If a realist has to choose between military power and economic power, military power will always win. Realists see military capabilities as the most important factor is protecting a state's most basic interests, independence and survival. Mercantilists do not discount the importance of military capabilities, but argue that states cannot have those capabilities without economic power. In other words, if a state's economy is not strong, it cannot afford to purchase the weapons it requires for defense. It is not that realists fail to understand this principle, but their explanatory focus is on power through military capabilities, while mercantilists' focus is power through wealth.

Mercantilism can refer to a period of history, a philosophical perspective, or policies and behaviors. **Classical mercantilism** as a period of history is the fifteenth through eighteenth centuries, a time when the modern nation-state emerged in Europe. During this period, economies were used to create wealth and power in the name of national security. The philosophical perspective is the way in which wealth promotes security. Power creates wealth and wealth creates power. This is a cycle that leads to a more prosperous, and thus secure, state. While this promotes security for the state acquiring power and wealth, it decreases the wealth and security of other states (a zero-sum game). The set of policies is protectionist and imperialist. Trade restrictions and colonialism were used to promote domestic products and increase resources with raw materials or labor. Mercantilism is thus seen as a driving force of imperialism in the developing world, and as a promoter of trade restrictions (Balaam and Veseth 2005).

In the late eighteenth and nineteenth centuries, **economic nationalism** emerged. To prevent dependency on other nations, economic nationalism promoted strong and independent domestic economies. The interests of the nation superseded the interests of the individual and state action was needed to promote wealth and power. The belief in supporting the domestic economy was widespread and continues to this day. For example, Alexander Hamilton was concerned that the US economy was at risk due to the mercantilist policies of other states (the zero-sum game in play). He argued for an active role for the state in promoting manufacturing and industry, as well as arguing in favor of trade protectionist policies, in particular subsidies and tariffs. In addition to promoting the growth of the US economy, he embraced immigration and encouraged new technologies (Hamilton, 2007). Building a state's domestic economy sounds rational and harmless, but this benign movement spurred the process of imperialism and with it all the negative consequences that continue to plague the developing world. The reasons are two-fold. First, in order to produce manufactured products, the developed countries required resources. They found these, both raw materials and human labor, in the developing world. Second, due to the increase in manufactured goods, the domestic markets simply could not absorb all the products (meaning there were not enough people in the domestic market to purchase all the manufactured goods). States required foreign markets to buy what they produced. As a consequence, they sought foreign sources of resources and markets for their products and this took the form of colonialism.

Following the two world wars, international regimes and organizations began promoting free trade and open markets. The World Trade Organization (WTO) is a prime example of this effort and this is discussed in greater detail later in this chapter. States continue to this day to rhetorically support the idea of free trade and open markets, and neorealists and **neomercantilists** are in complete support of these goals as long as they do not impede national interests. Free trade and open markets promote power, but will never be allowed to adversely impact security interests. Despite the stated benefits, trade is not truly free. Although many trade barriers have fallen, international agreements have been signed, and regional trading blocs created, protectionist policies continue. States continue to be compelled to protect domestic industries from foreign competition even when the state does not have a **comparative advantage** in those goods (comparative advantage is discussed in detail in Chapter 3). Simultaneously, states seek to stimulate economic growth and lower unemployment, but remain concerned about becoming dependent on other states while simultaneously courting the dependency of others.

Even in this period of increased globalization, states continue to pursue protectionist policies and tensions not only remain, they are on the rise given the new or intensified conflicts brought about by globalization. The arguments remain roughly the same as with classical mercantilists, but the means used and promoted by neomercantilists have changed. Tariffs and quotas have fallen out of favor, so neomercantilist policies are more subtle. Nontariff barriers (NTBs) are common and include such limitations as licensing, labeling, and packaging requirements, health and safety standards, customs procedures, additional trade document requirements, import quotas, subsidies, voluntary export restrictions, and lengthy eligibility procedures by the importing country. For example, the US Department of Agriculture subsidizes the sugar industry. Price supports, domestic marketing allotments, and tariff-rate quotas influence the amount of sugar available in the US market as well as keep US sugar prices comparable to worldwide prices

(US Department of Agriculture 2015). The US is not alone is this policy. In 2012, US agricultural subsidies were estimated at $19 billion, while the European Union provided $67 billion, Brazil provided $10 billion, and China provided a whopping $160 billion (Clay, 2013). Thus, neomercantilist policies continue to prevail in many areas and the pursuit of economic power to ensure the survival of the state remains a staple of neomercantilists.

Criticisms of Realism

There are numerous criticisms of the realist approach to explaining international relations. The criticism starts with the name itself, but that is only a symptom of a much larger issue. The term realism indicates that this is the view that is "real" or "realistic." Realists tell us that they view and analyze the world as it actually is, not how they wish it would be, so they most closely approximate "reality." This implies that other approaches are not "real" but instead represent wishful thinking. There are two major problems with this line of argument. First, this assumes that there is a "knowable reality." In Chapter 1, we explained the debates focusing on the ontological, epistemological, and methodological aspects of theory. If realists claim their interpretation of international relations is true, there is an ontological issue in that not all approaches to studying international relations accept the existence all things (see example of anarchy in Chapter 1). Further, the epistemological issue is that realists believe there is a known reality and that we can acquire knowledge of this reality through empirical study, placing them in the positivist camp. Classical realists were seen as "unscientific" (meaning insight without providing evidence), but other realists (structural, defensive, offensive) have sought to develop and test hypotheses (methodologically speaking, this can be qualitative or quantitative), thus claiming their arguments are backed with evidence. If scholars in the social sciences ground their work in the positivist model, they are granted legitimacy above other approaches. In the following chapters, other approaches to studying international relations are explored, and many of them do not take this approach. While liberal theorists tend to be positivists, many economic structuralists, constructivists and feminists are post-positivists arguing there is no single reality and our attainment of knowledge is multifaceted (for example, through experience, observation, reasoning). The question that arises is whether or not there is actually a reality that is waiting to be discovered (so it already exists) or if reality is constructed by actions, behaviors, discourse, and interactions.[7] Realists tell us it is already here and they are the best-suited to explain it. After reading the proceeding chapters, you will make that decision for yourself.

Second, because realists claim to explain the real world, it is somewhat of a self-fulfilling prophecy. Realism is the view of the world held by most policy-makers in that they seek state survival through power, the pursuit of national interests, diplomacy, and force. The "Spotlight on Policymakers" box on George Kennan demonstrates the connection between realism and policy-making. He is but one of many examples of realists as policy practitioners. Critics argue that the influence of realists and the policy prescriptions present in their work serve to perpetuate the violent, untrusting, uncooperative world they analyze. The explanations of the different types of realism presented in this chapter highlight the fact that many realists are concerned with stability (in other words, peace) and hence not consistently promoting war, but their focus on attaining and preserving power adds up to a recipe for conflict. Critics argue there are other ways to secure stability but realists refuse to consider these. As such, policymakers are prone to choose power acquisition and conflict over more creative and less violent solutions. It is important to remember that not all realists are in the business of policy prescription. Some realists attempt to explain how the world works rather than suggest a course of national policy. This of course circles us back to the argument in the previous paragraph about whether or not there is a known reality.

There are several additional criticisms of realism. Critics contend that realists use the structure of the system to over-determine the course of international relations. After reading the sections of this chapter describing structural and neoclassical realism, one should ask, "How powerful is the system in determining behavior and outcomes?" Confusion in coming to a conclusion would be natural. Critics argue that structural realists contend that the system exercises near total control of state behavior leaving no room for human influence or opportunities to change their fate. In this regard, structural realism is seen as fatalistic and deterministic. Following from this, critics argue that realists focus solely on the state and ignore other actors, leading to their inability to explain changes within states. This deficiency was most prominent when the Soviet Union collapsed, much to the surprise of realists. The collapse and ultimate disintegration of the Soviet Union could not adequately be explained without looking inside the country and its debilitating economic situation and dramatic changes in its political structure (perestroika and glasnost). However, there are different approaches to the level of control exercised by the system and the influence of unit level analysis within realism. Structural realists unquestionably focus on the influence of the system, but contend that their approach is not deterministic and does indeed consider units operating at different levels of analysis. While this may be true, the structure of the system is the central explanatory unit of analysis for structural realists and critics see this as overly constraining. Neoclassical realists, on the other hand, clearly argue domestic factors influence decisions made by states (see above). Thus there is variance in the degree to which realists view the impact of the system.

Further, balance of power has been a central feature of realist thought and a lightning rod of criticism. As discussed above, prominent neorealists, such as Kaplan and Waltz, have argued that a balance of power is essential for maintaining stability. Other realists argue that an imbalance of power is best for stability. Hence, realists cannot agree among themselves if the balance of power is the best system structure for peace, and to add to the confusion, realists cannot agree upon a definition of balance of power. In the discussion above, balance of power was defined by its most basic definition—rough equality between great powers in the system. Realists differ, however, on the specifics. How many great powers are required for balance? Is this a policy prescription or an actual state of being? Is this a form of hegemony? Does this lead to peace or war? As a central feature of realism, critics argue it leads to more confusion than answers. Critics also argue that as a guide to policymakers, realism is more likely to lead to war than peace and its most successful function is as a rhetorical tool to argue for increases in defense spending.[8]

Related to stability and peace, the inability of realists to envision a peaceful transformation of international politics is another area of criticism. Realism is viewed as promoting a pessimistic, dismal existence of violence and conflict with no chance of escape (akin to the Hobbesian state of nature). This is partially because realists continually declare state interests as the guiding goal of states, but fail to explain how those interests are determined. A robust investigation of the creation of state interests could lead us down a path of understanding how a peaceful transformation of international politics could occur. Chapter 5 provides a full explanation of the constructivist approach that highlights the notion that interests are constructed through social interaction.

It is important to remember that realists differ in many respects. Some criticisms leveled at realists are actually very specific to certain types of realist interpretations and not the school of thought as a whole. Realists differ as to the influence of unit-level factors, the purpose of military buildup (offensive versus defensive), the best system structure for stability, and how system change is brought about. Thus, in any analysis of realism it is imperative not to condemn the entire approach because of a disagreement with one element. We recommend that students be nuanced and thoughtful in considering the benefits and drawbacks as this will help to become a more advanced student of international relations. To help with this endeavor, the last two sections of this chapter apply realist thought to real-world case studies. Thinking through these cases and how realists of multiple kinds explain these events will help to understand the application of the theory and critique its explanatory capabilities.

Case Study: Proliferation

Returning to the case of North Korea discussed at the beginning of this chapter, why does it matter if North Korea possesses nuclear weapons? Recall the discussion in Chapter 1 concerning the debate over whether the proliferation of nuclear weapons is problematic or not. Kenneth Waltz tells us that the spread of nuclear weapons is not a problem. This conclusion is based on the fact that neorealism is structured on the principle that states are unitary rational actors seeking survival above all else. As such, no rational actor would start a nuclear war because none could rationally believe their state would survive such a conflict. His conclusion also stems from the arguments of a defensive realist. Since states exist in a self-help system, they must maintain their relative power position in relation to other states—that is, maintain a balance of power. Increases in military capabilities are natural in an effort to ensure a state's survival and a system of balance to create stability.

Theoretically, North Korea fits perfectly into Waltz's argument. Despite the fact that popular rhetoric depicts North Korean leaders, first

Kim Jong-Il, then Kim Il-Sung, and now Kim Jong Un, as erratic, unpredictable, and unstable, none took actions that would have resulted in the destruction of their state by an outside power. These leaders have perhaps been erratic, but not suicidal. In addition, the construction of a nuclear arsenal can be viewed as an attempt at balancing against a much larger nuclear power, the United States. Even though North Korea cannot match the might of the world's largest military power, nuclear weapons are international relations' great equalizer. MAD works because each side fears unacceptable damage and most believe that a nuclear strike—even of limited scope—would be unacceptable. Even though it is currently debatable as to whether North Korea can strike the United States with its nuclear weapons, they can undoubtedly strike US allies South Korea or Japan. To the United States, this would be unacceptable. Hence, the North Korean nuclear arsenal deters the United States from using its nuclear weapons against North Korea and the US nuclear arsenal deters North Korea from using its nuclear weapons against its regional neighbors (this is known as **extended deterrence**).

Another relevant point here is what other states would and would not do in response to North Korea's behavior because of their possession of nuclear weapons. This is part of the answer as to why North Korea wants nuclear weapons. For example, in March 2010 the South Korean navy ship Cheonan sank, killing 46 sailors (almost half the crew on board). South Korea claims that North Korea torpedoed the ship, a claim supported by an international investigation. North Korea denies the allegation. South Korea imposed strict economic sanctions, and continues to demand an apology from North Korea before South Korea is willing to lift them. Little else befell North Korea besides rhetorical condemnation from the South's allies. Further, in November 2010 North Korea shelled Yeonpyeong, a South Korean border island, killing four and wounding more than a dozen others in response to a South Korean military exercise. South Korea responded by shelling North Korean gun positions. Again, the communist regime faced little adverse consequences. Is the lack of response to their behavior a consequence of their nuclear arsenal? Does it allow them to behave recklessly with little response or does it create a stability disallowing any major confrontation from occurring? We can consider North Korea's position here from the standpoint of offensive realists. The best way to survive in the anarchic system is to create maximum or dominant power. While North Korea cannot compete with the United States, it can compete and surpass its regional rivals, South Korea and Japan. Thus the creation of a nuclear arsenal places North Korea above its regional foes allowing it to protect itself from them and by extension the United States. In the end, there is an argument from both the defensive and offensive realist perspectives that the North Korean nuclear arsenal appears to create stability.

If Waltz is correct, and nuclear weapons are a stabilizing factor, then why have other states tried to prevent their development by North Korea and when that failed, promoted their dismantling? The Six-Party talks, held intermittently since 2003 (when North Korea possessed enough nuclear material for as many as six nuclear weapons) and suspended since 2009,[9] were aimed at dismantling North Korea's nuclear program. There have also been several stages of UN Security Council sanctions, including an arms embargo in Resolution 1874 on June 12, 2009. On June 13, Pyongyang admitted for the first time that is had a uranium enrichment program. The members of the Six Party talks have varying reasons for pressuring North Korea based on their own political and economic situations, but they all couch their opposition in arguments about stability. Russia's military chief of staff, General Yuri Baluyevsky, stated in 2008 that "it is necessary to do everything possible in order not to allow North Korea to conduct tests; it is necessary to do everything for the resumption of the six-party talks on this problem. It is necessary to do everything in order that the Korean peninsula never becomes an arena of the use of nuclear weapons" (quoted in Toloraya, 2008, 51). Stephen Bosworth, the US Special Representative for North Korean Policy, stated in a press conference in 2010, "[T]he Six-Party process is an essential element in our overall efforts to bring about denuclearization of the Korean Peninsula and stability on the Korean Peninsula" (US Department of State, 2010).

These arguments, coupled with Waltz's position above, highlight the differences between realists. Everyone agrees states want stability, but the question is how they go about achieving it. The states involved in the Six Party talks are adopting the approach of Scott Sagan, rather than Waltz's arguments regarding realism. According to Sagan, states like North Korea lack the organizational mechanisms to adequately control their newly acquired weapons of mass destruction. Thus, the risk is too great to allow proliferation to states that might actually use them. You should be asking yourself at this point, "What kind of realist am I?" Is it more or less stable for North Korea to possess nuclear weapons? Perhaps what you will discover is that you do not gravitate towards realist thinking at all. In the next chapter, we highlight the liberal point of view as to why states try to prevent the spread of nuclear weapons.

TABLE 2.1 **Realism and Proliferation**

Realist Thought	Theoretical Tenet	Proliferation Example
Classical	Humans have an inherent dark side and will seek to dominate others; the main objective of states is survival and military power is the key.	North Korea's possession of nuclear weapons is a threat to other states' survival because their leaders will seek to dominate others. The members of the Six-Party Talks are seeking denuclearization of the Korean Peninsula to ensure their own survival and that of their allies.
Structural (Neorealist)	System structure dictates that great powers must control the rules of the system. The great powers seek stability (peace) by curtailing the strength of rising powers. States seek to increase capabilities because relative power determines survival.	For structural realists who believe the United States is the hegemon, the United States is attempting to bring North Korea into compliance with the US-favored nonproliferation rule. For those who believe the system is multipolar, the United States, Russia, and China are attempting to restrain the power of North Korea to prevent a destabilization of the system. North Korea seeks nuclear weapons to increase its relative power in the region and globally.
Defensive	Rational actors seek survival above all else. Power is the means for states to balance and defend themselves. A balance of power is the best means to achieve stability.	North Korea will not threaten its survival by using nuclear weapons (rational actor). Increases in capabilities are natural as North Korea seeks to balance against the United States. The members of the Six-Party Talks seek to restrain North Korea to maintain a balance of power in the region.
Offensive	States seek to create maximum power and dominate the system.	North Korea's nuclear program is designed to compete with South Korea and Japan, who both fall under the US nuclear umbrella. Although North Korea cannot compete with the United States, they seek regional domination through the acquisition of military power.

continued

Realist Thought	Theoretical Tenet	Proliferation Example
Neoclassical	Creation of foreign policy taking into account the international system and domestic stakeholders.	Concern over North Korea's nuclear program is influenced by the relative power capabilities of the United States and China. China does not want the United States to threaten the survival of its ally and the United States does not want an ally of China's to be a nuclear power. Domestic pressures are influencing behavior. The North Korean regime needs to project an appearance of strength and power to control its domestic society. The United States executive must contend with a legislature and a public that does not want a rogue state to possess nuclear weapons.

Case Study: WTO

Why do states enter into trade agreements or join trade organizations? For a realist, it depends on a state's level of power in the international system. Recall that both neorealists and neomercantilists support free trade and open markets as long as they serve national interests. Active participation in trade is seen as a means to becoming a great power in the system. If, however, participating in the market or engaging in free trade adversely impacts national security, the security interest will always prevail. As such, for great powers, the WTO is at best a useful tool to expand trade and markets, increase wealth and power, and serve the interests of the state. At worst, the WTO is innocuous, in that states with significant economic power and strong influence in the organization can simply ignore WTO rulings that adversely impact their security.

China's long-contested entrance into the WTO, granted in 2001, was preceded by fifteen years of labored negotiations that resulted in China relaxing over 7,000 trade barriers in order to gain the required support. The wait and the concessions appear to have been worth it for China. In the first decade after their accession, China's dollar GDP quadrupled and their exports nearly quintupled (the *Economist*, 2011). Despite these benefits, China has not exactly been a model WTO member. By mid-2015, China was the respondent in 33 cases filed against it in the WTO Dispute Settlement Body (DSB). They are only surpassed in total complaints (meaning all the years they have been members of the WTO) by the European Union with 82 and the United States with 124. Of the 33 cases brought against China, 16 were filed by the United States, and seven by the European Union. In 17 of these cases, the DSB ruled against China in whole or in part with two of those decisions under appeal (WTO, 2015a). The remainder of the cases are either still in consultation or not yet resolved, or were resolved without the need of a ruling from the DSB.

The larger controversy than the fact that China is often out of compliance with WTO rules is the question of whether China abides by the rulings when it loses and consequently alters its behavior. The United States, for one, does not believe it does. In 2014, the United States worked on seven cases against China and, in all instances, the US Trade Representative had serious concerns about China's implementation of changes in response to adverse rulings from the DSB (US Trade Representative, 2014). For example, in March 2014, in a complaint filed by the European Union, the United States, and Japan, the DSB declared that China was in violation of WTO rules for having unjustified export quotas on rare earths. Rare earths are 17 chemically similar elements used in technology, such as mobile phones, electric and hybrid car batteries, DVDs, computer memory, cameras, and fluorescent lighting. China is responsible for 90% of the global production of these minerals. This was an issue of national interest; hence, China appealed to the DSB, but lost that appeal in August 2014. China declared that it would abide by the ruling, but this is in serious question. Rare earths are a vital component of the Chinese economy and the likelihood that China is actually planning to abide by the ruling is unlikely. If they fail to adjust the import quotas, what is the recourse? The complaining states could file another complaint in the WTO, but given China's economic power the lengths states would go to punish them is limited.

In 2013, the Chinese Yuan became the second most used currency in global trade and China became the world's leading trader with imports and exports reaching $4.16 trillion. With nearly 1.4 billion people, which is the equivalent of over 19% of the world's world's population, China is not a country to be trifled with. In October 2014, according to the International Monetary Fund (IMF), China overtook the United States as the world's largest economy based on purchasing power adjusted GDP—China assuming 16.48% of purchasing power compared to the United States at 16.28%. In other economic measures, the United States still tops China, but most economists believe that will change in the next couple of decades. Its economic power affords it great power status (its military is much more questionable despite its nuclear arsenal) and thus the ability of other states, even other great powers, to confront it is limited. So, accession to the WTO provided China increased markets and propelled its economic growth, but its power allows it to skirt some WTO regulations. Although China experienced slowing of its economy in 2014, the benefits of WTO membership will continue. In 2016, China is set to obtain market economy status as a condition of its accession and the limitations on its exports in place for the first 15 years of its membership will expire.

WTO membership for weaker states is a much more mixed bag. While states freely enter into trade agreements, the truth from a realist perspective is that behind these decisions there are stronger states exerting their power. Neorealists stress the relative power between states, so in trade agreements states that are more powerful are coercing weaker states into joining and shaping the institution to meet their needs. In these scenarios, weaker states find themselves in a difficult situation. They can choose to enter an agreement that is less than ideal and perhaps even detrimental to their own interest or they can choose to remain outside the community of nations and experience a situation worse than if they had joined. As mentioned in chapter 1, the Uruguay Round was the eighth multilateral talks sponsored by GATT (the WTO was created in this round) that ran from 1986 to 1993. The negotiations that take place in these rounds are primarily how GATT/WTO rules and regulations are legislated. Rounds end when members have reached a consensus on the results of their negotiations creating binding legal results. Reaching consensus is usually the result of power-based bargaining (Barton et al., 2010).

To end the Uruguay Round and compel an agreement, the United States and the European Community (the precursor to the EU) maximized their bargaining power to cajole developing countries into signing an agreement. This despite the fact that most developing nations had stated from the beginning of the negotiations that they would not sign any agreements involving intellectual property, investment measures, or services. To ensure the inclusion of these issues considered essential to US interests, the United States and European Community used their power to create a Final Draft agreement that released them from their GATT obligation to guarantee MFN status (see Chapter 1) to countries that did not accept the Final Act and join the WTO.

The Uruguay Round resulted in "a set of agreements with highly asymmetrical consequences for the developed and developing countries. Studies have shown high variance in the net trade-weighted tariff concessions given and received" (Barton et al., 2010, 66). The United States received more concessions, while countries like India and South Korea gave more than they received. GDPs in member countries were also impacted, benefitting developed countries and hurting developing countries. Developing countries were forced to accept an agreement that ran counter to their objectives, but they "accepted this outcome because rejection of the WTO agreements would have made them still worse off, eliminating their legal guarantee of access to EC and U.S. markets" (Barton et al., 2010, 66). This example demonstrates the importance of economic power in attaining state interests. The developing countries could not lose access to the huge EC and US markets, hence they had to bow to the will of the more powerful states.

There are times that the WTO goes against the interest of the great powers and they do choose to comply or at least make changes to the trade policy in an attempt to come into compliance. For example, Mexico brought a complaint against the United States concerning its labeling requirements for tuna (a NTB as described above). Tuna caught by US fishers could receive a "dolphin safe" label, but those caught by the Mexican fishers could not because this label was awarded based on the method used to catch the tuna. If the net used would also capture the dolphins along with the tuna (like the method used by Mexican fishers), the tuna was ineligible for the label. The WTO determined this adversely impacted Mexico, but allowed the United States the leeway to prove it was a legitimate regulatory distinction. Instead of easing the conditions, the United States actually strengthened them to demonstrate the policy was not discriminatory towards Mexico, but a legitimate attempt to save dolphins. The new rules require any vessel catching tuna, not just those in the eastern tropical Pacific Ocean, to certify that no dolphins were harmed or killed in their fishing process. This has made it more difficult for vessels around the world to earn the "dolphin safe" label and from the US perspective is sufficient to address WTO regulations. On appeal in April 2015, the WTO disagreed with the United States and declared that the policy still discriminates against Mexico. The United States will likely appeal this decision, but is unlikely to give up attempts to label tuna sold within its borders. One could conclude that this attempt to come into compliance is disingenuous, but it at least demonstrates that great powers do attempt to comply with WTO regulations in cases where national security is not at stake. The United States did not simply ignore the ruling, and while its attempt to comply is questionable, action was at least taken in response.

For neorealists and neomercantilists, these examples highlight the approach states take towards trade and the WTO. Great powers will abide by the rules to experience the benefits of economic growth through trade as long as the rules to not adversely impact their national interests. If a state's national interests are at stake, it will attempt to comply with the rules while continuing to protect that interest, unless it is the state's security that is at stake. If security is at stake, the state will ignore rulings of the WTO as well as other international institutions. Weaker powers need the benefits of engaging in trade and the WTO as well as access to the markets of the great powers to promote their own economic growth. This need, however, makes them vulnerable to compellence by the great powers. Weaker states often have to accept a less than desirable agreement in order to maintain the benefits they so desperately need. Thus we end where we began this chapter. As Thucydides tells us, "the strong do what they have the power to do and the weak accept what they have to accept."

TABLE 2.2 **Realism and the WTO**

Realist Thought	Theoretical Tenet	WTO Example
Classical	Primary focus is military capabilities, but the principle of power is central. "The strong do what they have the power to do and the weak accept what they have to accept."	Weaker states in the WTO can be forced to accept unfavorable agreements. Developing countries were significantly disadvantaged during the Uruguay Round because they could not risk losing the benefits of access to the EC and US markets.
Neorealist	States must seek to increase both military and economic capabilities as both are important in building power relative to other states. States should engage in free trade and open markets as long as security is not threatened. Focus is only on great powers in the system.	The WTO is used by great powers to increase their economic power. China engaged in a protracted campaign to gain WTO membership and its economy has significantly benefited. Many complaints have been filed against China's trade practices, but their compliance with unfavorable WTO rulings is based on their assessment of the national interests.

Realist Thought	Theoretical Tenet	WTO Example
Neoclassical	Power in the international system matters, but so do domestic constituencies.	Trade barriers are erected to protect domestic industries and decrease unemployment. These barriers often conflict with WTO rules and states must determine if they comply with the regulation or side with businesses and employees within their own countries. The domestic pressure can also be ethical. The United States prevents the influx of tuna from states that do not have safeguards for dolphins to both protect the US tuna suppliers, but also because citizens have expressed support for policies that protect dolphins.
Neomercantilism	States create and sustain wealth and power to protect national security interests. States support free trade and open markets as long as they do not impede national interests. Domestic industries should be protected through subtle protectionist policies including NTBs.	The 162 members of the WTO, both great powers and weaker states, join to increase their wealth and prosperity. As with the Uruguay Round, great powers use the WTO to serve their interests even if it is at the expense of weaker states. States use NTBs to promote economic power, but they often run afoul of WTO rules. Great powers may abide by WTO rulings if they do not infringe on national security, or they can alter policies to attempt to come into compliance. The United States attempted to come into compliance on tuna labeling. If a WTO ruling is in conflict with security interests, great powers will refuse to comply.

Conclusion

This chapter provided an overview of the variations of realist thought and the contributions of a sampling of the great thinkers of each. You now have the tools to apply realist thought to events in international relations, as you read with the proliferation debate and the WTO. Keep in mind that as you assess realism, there are numerous realist scholars who approach analyzing international relations in a variety of ways. All realists share some common ground, but each variation, and even each author, provides a different lens through which one can analyze world politics. The easiest events to which realism is applicable are those in which the survival of a state is threatened. As you saw from the case study on the WTO, however, variations of realist thinking are applicable beyond the obvious cases of clear threats to state survival. As stated above, realism is the image of the world adopted by most policymakers and thus, there is an ease with which you might gravitate towards its application. What you will discover in the following chapters is that other approaches to analyzing and explaining events have their own allure and you might find yourself more drawn in those directions if you approach them with an open mind. In the next chapter, the main counter to realism is explored. Liberalism is a philosophical tradition that emerged from the European Enlightenment and focuses on the conditions in which cooperation and collaboration are possible.

Key Terms

Bandwagoning

Bismarckian alliance system

Buckpassing

Classical mercantilism

Comparative advantage

Defensive realists

Economic nationalism

Extended deterrence

Great powers

Hegemonic stability theory

Long cycle theory

Neomercantilists

Offensive realists

Peace of Westphalia

Power transition theory

Realpolitik

Security dilemma

Soft power

Sovereignty

For Further Reading

Buzan, Barry. 1984. "Economic Structure and International Security: The Limits of the Liberal Case." *International Organization* 38, Autumn 1984.

Kaplan, Morton A. 1966. "Some Problems of International Systems Research," in *International Political Communities: An Anthology.* Garden City, N.Y.: Anchor, pp. 469–486.

Kennan, George F. 1951. *American Diplomacy, 1900–1950.* Chicago: University of Chicago Press.

Morgenthau, Hans. 1948. *Politics Among Nations.* New York: Alfred A. Knopf.

Sagan, Scott D. and Kenneth N. Waltz. 2013. *The Spread of Nuclear Weapons: An Enduring Debate*, 3rd edition. New York: W.W. Norton & Company.

Schweller, Randall L. 1998. Deadly Imbalances: *Tripolarity and Hitler's Strategy of World Conquest.* New York: Columbia University Press.

Waltz, Kenneth. 1979. *Theory of International Politics.* New York: McGraw-Hill.

Endnotes

[1] The total US arsenal of nuclear weapons is 4,804, including tactical, strategic, and non-deployed weapons. For more on the numbers of weapons possessed by states, see Arms Control Association, "Nuclear Weapons: Who has What at a Glance." https://www.armscontrol.org /factsheets/Nuclearweaponswhohaswhat. Accessed June 26, 2014.

[2] The book is *History of the Peloponnesian War.*

[3] Kaplan is perhaps most famous for delineating types of international systems and their consequences, of which balance of power was one. He also discussed the loose bipolar system, the tight bipolar system, the universal international system, the hierarchical system, and the unit veto system.

[4] See Gideon Rose, "Neoclassical Realism and Theories of Foreign Policy," *World Politics* 51, no. 1 (October 1998), pp. 144–177. The books reviewed were: Michael E. Brown et al., eds. *The Perils of Anarchy: Contemporary Realism and International Security* (Cambridge: MIT

Press, 1995); Thomas J. Christensen, *Useful Adversaries: Grand Strategy, Domestic Mobilization, and Sino-American Conflict, 1947–1958* (Princeton: Princeton University Press, 1996); Randall L. Schweller, *Deadly Imbalances: Tripolarity and Hitler's Strategy of World Conquest* (New York Columbia University Press, 1998); William Curti Wohlforth, *The Elusive Balance: Power and Perceptions during the Cold War* (Ithaca, NY: Cornell University Press, 1993); and Fareed Zakaria, *From Wealth to Power: The Unusual Origins of America's World Role* (Princeton: Princeton University Press, 1998).

[5] There were also lesser powers who were revisionist like Italy and Japan, termed "jackals" by Schweller.

[6] For a full explanation of issues and approaches in IPE, see David N. Balaam and Bradford Dillman, *Introduction to International Political Economy* (New York: Routledge, 2013).

[7] For a fuller discussion of the ontological and epistemological discussion of realism, see Alexander Wendt, *Social Theory of International Politics* (Cambridge: Cambridge University Press, 1999).

[8] For more on these criticisms and the defense of realism, see Ernst B. Haas, "The Balance of Power: Prescription, Concept or Propaganda?" *World Politics*, 5, no. 2 (July 1953) and Alexander Wendt, *Social Theory of International Politics* (Cambridge: Cambridge University Press, 1999).

[9] Talks were suspended when North Korea withdrew after the UN expanded sanctions against them for test-firing a modified Taepo Dong-2 three-stage rocket.

CHAPTER 3

Liberalism

"For the spirit of commerce sooner or later takes hold of every people, and it cannot exist side by side with war."

—Immanuel Kant, "Perpetual Peace: A Philosophical Sketch"

Beginning in December 2008, the United States has been in a tense trade dispute with Canada and Mexico, its two trading partners in the North American Free Trade Agreement (NAFTA), through the WTO's dispute settlement procedure. Country of Origin Labeling (COOL) requirements imposed by the United States are the cause of this row, in particular the obligation to inform consumers of the origin of beef and pork. The labels read, for example, "born in Mexico, raised and slaughtered in the United States" or "born, raised and slaughtered in the United States." Canadian officials have argued that the US requirements cost the Canadian pork and beef industries roughly $1 billion annually. The original complaint was filed by Canada in 2008 and the Dispute Settlement Body (DSB) ruled in 2011 that the United States' labeling requirements were inconsistent with its WTO obligations by providing domestic products with more favorable treatment than imported Canadian cattle and hogs. Segregation of the animals was often required in order to track their origins as they moved through the supply chain, and this increased the cost of the foreign goods. The United States appealed this decision and lost in 2012. In response, the United States modified the labels in an attempt to comply with the WTO ruling, changing the labels from vague statements, such as "Product of the US and Mexico" to the more specific labels including the location where the animal was born, raised, and slaughtered.

In summer 2013, a WTO compliance panel was composed at the request of Canada based on the Canadian argument that the new US labels were actually more restrictive and caused additional harm. The compliance panel found that the US requirements were still in violation of its WTO obligations and the United States lost an appeal of that decision in May 2015. In response to Mexican and Canadian threats to impose billions of dollars of sanctions on US products, the US House of Representatives voted in June 2015 to repeal the labeling requirements that were included in the 2002 and 2008 farm bills.[1] A vigorous debate in the US Senate ensued, and as of December 2015, no compromise had been reached.

From a liberal perspective, what does this story tell us about states and the WTO? Countries, both powerful and weak, join the WTO for the extensive benefits provided by open markets and free trade, and research has shown that there is a generally positive record of states complying with rulings issued against them by the DSB. Domestic pressures are ever-present, however, and states try to balance the pursuit of neoliberal economics with the protection of domestic industries and interests. In this case, the labeling requirements were added to please US ranchers who compete with the Canadian cattle industry as well as consumer advocates who claim that shoppers have a right to know the source of their food. In response to WTO rulings, supporters of the requirements urged the US government to find an alternative to repealing the labeling rules. This was the impetus for the US attempts to alter the labels after they lost the appeal in 2012. Democrats in the House and Senate generally support this approach. Other domestic groups oppose the labeling requirements, and have for many years. Those in the US meat industry who buy animals from abroad have argued the rules are costly and unnecessarily burdensome and have gone as far as to unsuccessfully fight the rules in federal court. Opponents see repealing the provisions as the quickest and easiest solution to prevent harmful sanctions from being imposed on the United States, and solving a problem for US meat producers. Republicans in the House and Senate have pursued this approach.

Liberal theorists argue that the United States is trying to appease domestic interests and work within the political structure of the country while pursuing its obligations to the WTO and maintaining its access to two very important foreign markets. It may not be easy or quick, but the importance of trade and cooperation appears to be winning in this case, just as liberals would predict. This case also demonstrates the impact of a liberal supranational institution on resolving disputes. Without the overarching authority of the WTO, the United States would have continued to claim that the labeling requirements did not impact free trade, protectionist policies would continue and increase with retribution from Canada and Mexico, and the states involved would suffer detrimental impacts from a decrease in market access. Liberals argue that the creation of supranational institutions create incentives for states to engage in behaviors they otherwise would not or at the very least find it much more difficult to continue such behavior. Institutions can alter both the costs and benefits of certain behaviors, and in this case, the WTO-guaranteed access to markets creates an incentive for the United States to adhere to WTO regulations. The following sections explain the variations of liberal thought, and at the end of this chapter, we return to the WTO to further illuminate liberal thinking on the behavior of member states.

Roots and Evolution of Liberalism

Like realism, liberalism is a centuries-old tradition that occupies a venerated space in the positivist view of international relations. While it accepts some similar principles with realist thinking, it is the main challenge to realism. As with realism, states are viewed as the unit of analysis, but not all liberals view them as unitary actors. Some liberals assume the state-centric, unitary actor approach, but differ from realists in that they do not believe the constraints posed by the anarchic international environment are debilitating for cooperation between states. Many other liberals focus on the role of domestic factors with one of the primary foci being that of the role of democracy as an influential force in foreign policy. Others look to the influence of individuals including decision-making processes and political views. Hence liberalism can utilize all three levels of analysis: systemic, domestic, and individual. Unlike realists, liberals do not see the world as mired in a constant struggle for state survival. Instead, liberals see a world where cooperation is possible and states pursue policies of mutual benefit, not simply self-interest. It is an approach to international relations that heralds the possibilities of human progress, promotes the spread of democracy, and argues in favor of market capitalism to further the welfare of all.

As explained in Chapter 1, although liberalism re-emerged in the wake of the failure of idealism after the two world wars, its influence was greatly enhanced by the end of the Cold War and the demise of Soviet Communism in the late 1980s and early 1990s. Viewed now as overly optimistic, the resurgence of liberal thought can be seen in the writings of Francis Fukuyama. In 1989, Fukuyama heralded **"the end of history"** as "the universalization of Western liberal democracy as the final form of human government" (Fukuyama, 1989, 4). From his perspective, history has an endpoint, not in a catastrophic sense, but in an evolutionary sense. The liberal, democratic, capitalist society under construction by the European powers is the closest to achieving this endpoint. He points, in particular, to the failure of fascism and communism, as well as the spread of economic liberalization, as the strongest evidence that liberal democracy has won in the sense that no other ideology will vie for the hearts and minds of people. Liberal democracy gives people the security and recognition that they want and need and thus will triumph against any ideological foe. The true "end of history" is still a long way off, as evidenced by terrorist threats around the globe, continuing conflicts in Iraq, Afghanistan, and Syria, the resistance to the implementation of democracy by outside force, and financial crises that have plagued the global economic order since 2007. The failure of liberal leaders to capitalize on the events of the Arab Spring has left even Fukuyama less hopeful about the progress of liberal democracy around the world, but his ideas encapsulate liberal thinking on the benefits of spreading democracy and capitalism. No one said that the progress towards "the end of history" would be easy or quick. The world has clearly undergone some major shifts since the two world wars. Although we see conflicts around the globe, no great power wars have occurred for more than 60 years. For liberals, change is incremental and this evolution towards a more peaceful world will occur incrementally. This is evolution, not revolution. As you will see next, these ideas emanate from the central assumptions of liberalism.

Central Assumptions

There are different variations of liberal thought, but all liberals share certain central assumptions.

- Both state and non-state actors are important actors in world politics.

- Individuals and domestic actors matter.
- Interdependence among actors modifies behavior.
- Cooperation is possible and beneficial as international relations is a positive-sum game.
- Human beings can learn, adapt, and progress and they possess a rationality of thought.
- There is more to international relations than security concerns; economic, social, and environmental issues matter.

Liberal theorists do not solely focus on the state. States remain the unit of analysis, but they are not the only influential actors in global politics. As stated above, individuals matter, as do the domestic influences on their behavior. In this sense, liberals and neoclassical realists share a common thread. Recall that neoclassical realists believe that systemic forces are filtered through unit-level variables, such as public opinion, bureaucracies, political parties, and legislators. In contrast to realists, however, liberals place significant importance on external non-state actors. Not only do they influence the behavior of states, but they may operate as independent actors. International organizations (e.g., the UN, NATO, the EU), nongovernmental organizations (e.g., environmental or human rights groups), and multinational corporations (MNCs) have an important role to play in the functioning of world politics.

Following from the influence of both state and non-state actors, liberals believe that interdependence among these actors helps to modify behavior. This is a key tenet related to the discussion of the WTO that began this chapter. The process of **globalization** is binding the world more closely together economically, politically, culturally, and socially. Economic ties, technological advancements and their consequences, international and nongovernmental organizations, and MNCs create cross-cutting concerns for people and their states. For example, international trade increases the economic health of a nation, thus states engage in trade and created the WTO to promote the benefits of trade. The cross-cutting concern is economic growth and following the rules set forth by the WTO promotes that growth and helps resolve disputes between parties. This peaceful conflict resolution spills over into other areas of concern because states do not wish to damage their economic health by engaging in conflict over other issues that would result in trade sanctions or war. Hence behavior is modified in other areas in an effort to continue to reap the benefits of economic trade. All impacts of globalization are not positive, however, as transnational criminal organizations and terrorist groups use it as a rallying cry to advance their activities, but as stated above liberals see an evolutionary process towards a more peaceful world and thus impediments on this road to progress are expected.

As a consequence of this increased interdependence, cooperation is seen as beneficial and mutually advantageous. This results in states pursuing reciprocal cooperation. Liberals are not blind to the conflict in the world, but they see far more cooperation than conflict and they believe humans can learn and adapt to changing rules of global politics. They do not deny the realist claim that people and states are self-interested, but they argue that cooperation is possible even in such an environment because humans are capable of rational thought and of making progress. **Complex interdependence** (see below) makes cooperation attractive for several reasons. First, states can benefit from this cooperation, satisfying their self-interested nature. States can accept that the benefits can be mutual—other states can experience them too—and that does not diminish the benefits to themselves. World politics is a positive-sum game, in that benefits are not a fixed-sum and all states can mutually (although not necessarily equally) reap the spoils. Second, cooperation comes from a reliance on one another. There are problems in the world that one state cannot fix alone. For example, the six-party talks on North Korea's nuclear program, the P5+Germany coalition that negotiated a nuclear deal with Iran, environmental treaties, and human rights conventions all require cooperation among states for mutually beneficial outcomes. Third, liberals identify a moral interdependence among democracies. Democracies will cooperate because they share certain norms and values, and at the heart of this argument is that democracies will not wage war against each other. This argument is discussed further below.

While realists focus their energies on security and survival through military power, liberals argue that those are not the only important issues to address. Economic, political, social, and environmental issues are also important. If states focus on cooperating in areas of mutual interest, they will fare much better than states solely relying on preserving and enhancing their own security. North Korea is a good example of this argument. Long considered a pariah in the international system, North Korea focuses exclusively on building its military

Prisoner's Dilemma

might—ballistic missile and nuclear weapons development, suspected biological and chemical weapons programs, maintenance of over one million active military personnel and millions more as reserve forces, thousands of tanks, armored vehicles, and pieces of field artillery, and hundreds of submarines, combat aircraft, and helicopters. Estimates of the percent of its budget that North Korea spends on its military vary widely, with North Korea claiming around 15% to South Korea claiming it is upwards of 40%.[2] The military buildup continues despite severe economic problems, a GDP per capita that is one of the worst in the world, a crippling drought and food shortages, and a starving population. Instead of engaging in cooperation and reaping the benefits of being a productive member of the international community, North Korea continues to be the subject of economic sanctions in response to its violent and aggressive behavior. The communist state is not a member of the WTO or a signatory of the Chemical Weapons Convention, it withdrew from the Nonproliferation Treaty (NPT) and is consistently listed among the most harshly repressive regimes in the world. Its overemphasis on military power has created a suffering population and state that remains a threat to international stability. Liberals argue that North Korea would be better off decreasing its focus on military might and engaging the international community on issues of trade, security, and environmental degradation, as maintaining its status as a rogue state is not working in its favor.

While these are central assumptions of liberalism, there are variations of liberal thought. There are also sub-theories that explain a specific argument or phenomenon that fall under the different variations. Figure 3.1 demonstrates the variants and sub-theories that are explored in the following sections. We highlight the evolution of liberal thought and explore the contributions of some of the great thinkers of this tradition. The criticisms of liberalism are also discussed and the chapter ends with an application of liberal thought to the cases of proliferation and the WTO.

Liberal Internationalism

Liberal internationalism (often just referred to as liberalism and building from the roots of classical liberalism) stems from the work of classical philosophers like Hugo Grotius, John Locke, and Immanuel Kant (see below). This school of thought embraces the assumptions that

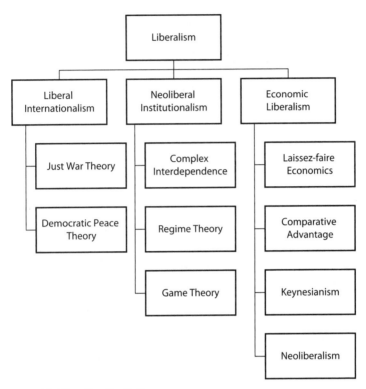

FIGURE 3.1 Liberalism Family Tree.

cooperation is possible even in the face of self-interest, individuals possess rational qualities, and humans can adapt and progress in their social lives. For classical liberals, analysis begins with the individual, and states are to play a minimal role in society.[3] The focus of the state is to ensure the rights of individuals so that they may experience the benefits of their liberty. John Locke's work is perhaps the best exemplar of this thinking. The role of the individual is also critical in economic liberalism, which is discussed later in this chapter. At the heart of capitalist thinking, individuals should be free to pursue economic goals relatively unfettered by government interference. Trade and investment, both domestic and international, should progress without government constraints. This economic thought was dominant in Great Britain and the United States in the eighteenth and nineteenth centuries. The eventual impact of the Industrial Revolution forced modifications in classical liberal thinking. Anything goes, no-holds-barred economic competition proved to have deleterious consequences, and this new strain of liberalism (often referred to as social liberalism) allowed for the state to perform two functions: moderate the harmful effects of uncontrolled competition and use its resources to help individuals pursue their goals. Individuals remain an important component of liberal thinking, however. International relations is more than interactions between states; individuals and the groups and societies to which they belong are important factors in world politics.

Much of the focus of liberalism is the ability to overcome or at least diminish war and conflict and create a peaceful, cooperative environment both domestically and internationally. Liberals agree with realists that states exist in a condition of anarchy, and that war is a defining element of that system. However, just as liberals argue that individuals can live in peace within a state, they similarly argue that states can live in peace in a system of anarchy. As previously stated, liberalism has experienced a resurgence of legitimacy and attention. This is due in no small part to the decline in global conflict. Recent conflicts in Iraq, Afghanistan, Ukraine, and Syria, among others, might lead one to believe conflict is as prevalent and destructive as ever. In assessing conflict, it is important to recall that war has undergone profound and dramatic changes throughout history. Industrial development and advances in technology have created an environment where war is increasingly destructive, culminating in the risk of nuclear annihilation. Despite this, or perhaps because of the destructive power of war, since the end of WWII, during which an estimated 60 million people died, there has been a steady decline in battle deaths. Based on data compiled by researchers Bethany Lacina and Nils Petter Gleditsch of the Peace Research Institute Oslo, through 2008 "deaths caused directly by war-related violence in the [twenty-first] century have averaged about 55,000 per year, just over half of what they were in the 1990s (100,000 a year), a third of what they were during the Cold War (180,000 a year from 1950 to 1989), and a hundredth of what they were in World War II. If you factor in the growing global population, which has nearly quadrupled in the last century, the decrease is even sharper" (Goldstein, 2011). Great-power wars are a thing of the past, and while civil wars and asymmetrical guerrilla wars are ugly affairs, they will not produce the levels of death and destruction seen in previous centuries. Liberals argue that this decrease in conflict is the result of increased interdependence, international institutions, and liberal democracies. The following exploration of some of the great thinkers of this tradition demonstrates how this conclusion is reached.

Pioneers in the Field

Our exploration of liberal thinking begins with the philosopher some refer to as the father of international law and others consider the father of natural law, Hugo Grotius (1583–1645).[4] He wrote the first comprehensive treatise on international law, *The Rights of War and Peace*, published in 1625. Grotius argued that states can and do cooperate in an anarchical environment through the creation of norms and rules upon which they have agreed. Agreement in both political and economic matters comes in the form of practice or formal treaty, and abiding by these agreements encourages cooperation between states. In addition to his discussion of the benefits of cooperation, Grotius was also a main contributor to **just war theory** by showing that ethical standards for war could be based on rational, secular logic. He established rules to protect non-combatants, hostages, and prisoners as well as suggested negotiations and compromise to arrange truces and ceasefires. In *Commentary on the Laws of Prize and Booty* (published after his death), Grotius lays out the existence of a **natural law** and the notion that societies are based on the law of nature, ideas carried through *The Rights of War and Peace*. Natural law is produced by human nature, in that it encompasses actions that are accepted by rational and social beings. These rational and social beings (in other words, humans) pursue two goals: self-preservation and society. As humans possess a social impulse (the need to be with others), our self-preservation instinct is moderated. We do not do anything and everything we desire, as those actions might result in our social isolation. Conversely, our social instincts are moderated by our need for self-preservation. We separate ourselves from those who may be a threat to our existence. We see several of the central assumptions of liberalism highlighted in Grotius' work: the possibility of cooperation, the rationality and adaptability of human beings, and the importance of issues beyond security, namely that of social existence.

The law of nature was adopted by John Locke (1632–1704) in the seventeenth century and is linked to the emergence of the modern liberal state. In his *Two Treatises of Government*, Locke argues that men are free and equal as granted by nature and have rights to such things as life, liberty, health, and property. These rights exist independent of any laws created by society. These arguments lay the foundation for the **social contract**, through which individuals consent to the creation and power of a government to protect their rights and promote the public good. This is the foundation of the state as a constitutional entity. Since the government exists only with the consent of the people, they have the right to change it. Locke does not rule out unelected officials from possessing power in the government, but he does require that the people have sufficient representation to prevent attacks on their liberty. According to Locke, the purpose of government is to protect the liberty of its citizens thus allowing them to live in happiness in the absence of undue influence from others. This guarantee of individual liberty will allow for human progress which in turn will promote advancement in civil society and capitalist economics. The importance of the individual is clear in Locke's arguments, and while his focus was on domestic interactions, this connects to international relations in that these constitutional states will interact with each other based on certain norms and values rooted in mutual toleration.

Immanuel Kant (1724–1804), an 18th-century German philosopher, expanded the notion of constitutional states and their interactions, particularly in relation to war. In his classic work, *Perpetual Peace*, Kant argues that the spread of republican constitutions, through which **republics** (representative democracies) are governed by the rule of law, the need for trade, and a system of international law, would create a "zone of peace" among democratic nations. This is the basis for what is commonly referred to as **democratic peace theory**. The argument is not that democracies will never go to war (clearly they often fight non-democracies), it is that they do not go to war against each other. For the peaceful resolution of disputes, states should form a federation, and Kant argues that this is a natural step is the evolution of human society. This federation would be composed of independent states that are constitutional republics. For the creation of a republican constitution, three foundations are required: "freedom for all members of a society (as men); . . . dependence of everyone upon a single common legislation (as subjects); . . . legal equality for everyone (as citizens)" (Kant, 1996, 370). This type of constitution is required for there to be perpetual peace.

The creation of constitutional democracies would lead to peace for three reasons. First, republics, by their nature, would evince the public will, and humans, as rational and progressive beings, would be loath to commit to war. As Kant writes in *Perpetual Peace*, "as is inevitably the case under this constitution, the consent of the citizens is required to decide whether or not war is to be declared, it is very natural that they will have great hesitation in embarking on so dangerous an enterprise. For this would mean calling down on themselves all the miseries of war" (Kant, 1996, 370). In non-democracies, on the other hand, "it is the simplest thing in the world to go to war" (Kant, 1996, 370). Without the constraint of public consent, monarchies or empires could simply do as they please, while in representative democracies, public opinion must be taken into account. Second, democracies hold broadly shared norms of how political disputes are to be resolved, and these cultural similarities cover both domestic and international conflict resolution. The zone of peace is based on common moral and ethical guidelines accepted by all democracies, and the expectation of reciprocity will lead to mutual attempts to resolve the conflict without resorting to violence. Third, according to Kant, perpetual peace is guaranteed by "the great artist Nature herself" (Kant, 1996, 373). Nature unites states "by means of their mutual self-interest. For the spirit of commerce sooner or later takes hold of every people, and it cannot exist side by side with war" (Kant, 1996, 375). People and their states will naturally seek economic prosperity through cooperative economic arrangements and interdependence. To do so, they will seek peace through mediation as war would disrupt their economic gains.

While critics of democratic peace theory level several aspersions at the argument, not the least of which is that peace between democracies is coincidental not causal (meaning that there are other variables that explain the observed phenomenon), this notion is widely held by liberal theorists and policymakers in the Western world. In 1964, during the resurgence of liberalism, a study by Dean V. Babst reignited the interest in democratic peace theory. Analyzing 116 major wars between 1798 and 1941, Babst found that there were no wars fought between independent nations with elective governments.[5] From this he concluded that it is the form of government that matters not the national character, and that the maintenance of peace is significantly increased by the existence of independent nations with elective governments (Babst, 1964). Further, researchers Zeev Maoz and Bruce Russett (1993, 624) concluded that there is "something in the internal makeup of democratic states . . . that prevents them from fighting one another." According to their analysis, "both political constraints and democratic norms provide reasonably good explanations of why democracies rarely fight each other" but democratic norms provide a more robust explanation (Maoz and Russett, 1993, 636). These findings, and numerous studies since, are the basis for the optimism held by many that the spread of democracy enhances the likelihood of world peace. As mentioned above, conflict has decreased since the end of the Cold War, and subsequently the number of democracies has increased. According to Freedom House, in 1989–1990, 41% of countries were electoral democracies. In 2014, it was 63% (125 out of the 195 countries are elected democracies) (Freedom House, 2015).

What follows from this notion is a normative element of liberalism that is played out in policymakers' decisions about foreign policy. Liberals argue that the greater the spread of democracy, the greater the zone of peace. It is this spread that gives them hope that the process towards world peace is not only possible but that it is currently underway. In addition, since the value being sought is peace, liberal theorists and policymakers alike see promoting the spread of democracy as their responsibility. For example, US president Bill Clinton pursued the strategy of "democratic enlargement" in the 1990s. This strategy included the enlargement of NATO, aid to Russia as well as other newly independent states of the former Soviet Union and Central and Eastern European nations in their development of democracy, promotion of human rights and the rule of law, and restoration of the democratically elected government in Haiti.

Theorists seek the spread of democracy through benign methods, such as continuing the debate and producing scholarly studies. Policymakers seek this goal at times through violence, punishments, and policies detrimental to the population of a non-democratic country. If a democracy wages war against a non-democracy and forces it to accept democratic principles upon its defeat, how entrenched are those values?[6] Democratic peace theory does not hold if the democracies do not share the norms, values, and customs that propel them to seek mediation and conflict resolution. Liberal theorists recognize this and know the process towards world peace will be slow and bumpy. New democracies will need cultivating, some may stumble, others may fail, but this is a process that takes place over a long period of time. As stated above, this is evolution, not revolution.

Neoliberal Institutionalism

The main focus of neoliberal institutionalism (or neoliberalism)[7] is the means by which states and other actors can achieve cooperation. Neoliberals know this will not be easy in an anarchic international environment, but they subscribe to the liberal tenet espousing the capacity of human progress and thus see cooperation as possible and beneficial. Its name is derived from the focus on international institutions as the mechanism for pursuing cooperation. Although cooperation can be difficult to achieve in anarchy, which fosters uncertainty and fear, the increased interdependence which arose after the two world wars has made the creation of international organizations easier to achieve than during any previous point in history. Three interrelated sets of issues emphasize the impact of interdependence. First, the two world wars highlighted the destructive power wrought by states against one another owing to advancements in technology and industrial capacity. As a result, institutions were created in the name of peace and security. The United Nations is the most prominent example of this effort. The UN boasts near-universal membership and it succeeds remarkably well in providing a forum for discussion and cooperation, coordinating aid and humanitarian relief, and acting in the name of peace when the five permanent members of the Security Council (China, France, Great Britain, Russia, and the United States) agree on the existence of a threat and the manner with which to counter it. Clearly the UN has not brought about world peace, but it has facilitated the resolution of conflicts without resorting to war and provided collective security in cases where clear aggression has been committed. In its current form, the organization is only as good as its member states and, as liberals remind us, progress towards world peace is slow and rocky.

Second, interdependence magnifies issues for which cooperation provides the only possible remedy. These are issues that require collective solutions as one state alone would be unable to correct or prevent the negative consequences associated with these phenomenon. Issues of environmental degradation, global health crises, or refugees, for example, cannot be solved by the unilateral actions of a single state. For example, in 2014 the worst Ebola outbreak since the virus was discovered in 1976 occurred in West Africa. This outbreak resulted in more cases and deaths than all the other occurrences of Ebola on record. It is very difficult, if not impossible, to prevent contagious diseases from spreading across borders. Humans are far too mobile and travel far too easily to prevent the movement of the disease. The outbreak began in Guinea, spread to Sierra Leone, Liberia, Senegal, and Mali across land borders, and to Nigeria and the United States by air. The **World Health Organization** responds to outbreaks of Ebola "by supporting surveillance, community engagement, case management, laboratory services, contact tracing, infection control, logistical support and training and assistance with safe burial practices" (World Health Organization, 2015). Countries around the globe instituted additional security measures on travel to contain the spread of the disease and provided emergency response teams and equipment to assist the affected states. Billions of dollars in financial and material aid was sent by governments, NGOs, and private corporations. This was a collective response to a global crisis and containment was only possible with cooperation between states, international organizations, and private citizens.

Third, the interdependence of the global economic system has promoted cooperation in trade and development. The post-World War II focus of the United States and its allies on promoting capitalism and enhancing free trade was supported by the creation of economic institutions, including what are now called the WTO, IMF, and World Bank.[8] The interwoven economic web created by these institutions has greatly benefitted states through increased trade and economic assistance for development projects.[9] Economic interdependence can produce undesirable and damaging consequences, however. In December 2007, the United States entered a recession and dragged most of the developed world down with it (Australia and South Korea were exceptions). The crisis is linked to the damage suffered by global financial institutions when the US housing bubble burst and securities tied to the US housing market were devalued. This became known as the "Great Recession" and was a contributing factor to the Eurozone crisis. The central feature of the crisis in the EU is the fact that some states in the Eurozone cannot finance their government debt without assistance. This crisis has been most pronounced in Greece and debates continue as to whether the heavily indebted country can remain in the EU. The economic crisis that began in 2007 exemplifies the risk when relationships are mutually dependent. Without the risk, however, states would not reap the benefits of cooperation. To assist in this conundrum, neoliberals argue that institutions can moderate the impact of the negative consequences and amplify the benefits.

In addition to international organizations like the UN, WTO, IMF, NATO and hundreds of others, neoliberals also look to international regimes to help coordinate state behavior. Regimes are arrangements that bind states to rules, norms, and principles related to their conduct in given areas such as trade, proliferation, the movement of hazardous waste, and the protection of wildlife and fauna. Regimes are voluntary constructs and states create them to provide a sense of order in international relations. Although voluntary, they do provide a regulatory function and states disobey them at a cost. Thus they are normative structures that interpret and judge international behaviors. As such they have a socially constructed element to them in that the meaning of appropriate behavior in international relations has been determined by those who created the regimes and the regimes allow other states in the system to know the expectations on their behavior. Regime theory is tied to constructivism, which you will read about in Chapter 5.

Pioneers in the Field

Neoliberalism is built upon the foundation of the theory of **functionalism**, a theory pioneered by David Mitrany (1888–1975) as an effort to explain how states could achieve cooperation and collaboration through integration. He reasoned that there is a plethora of technical problems facing society that necessitates collaboration as one individual or state cannot solve these problems alone. This necessity leads to the creation of multilateral arrangements and institutions. Cooperation in one area causes a spillover effect into other areas. If the benefits of collaboration were seen by governments in one area, they would logically seek cooperative solutions in other areas. He further argued that these problems are best addressed by experts rather than politicians. Ernst Haas (1924–2003) is credited with the creation of **neofunctionalism** and this theoretical approach puts politics back into the equation. International organizations will only succeed if political elites see them as serving their interests. The creation of an international institution and the decisions on how it will operate cannot be devoid of political considerations, and they must be seen as serving the interests of the parties or they will fail in their stated objectives. We can see this integration in economic institutions such as the European Union and NAFTA and in security institutions such as NATO. This focus on the interests of the actors makes Haas an early constructivist, an approach that will be fully covered in Chapter 5.

In the 1970s, Joseph Nye Jr. (1937–) and Robert Keohane (1941–) published two influential neoliberal works. *Transnational Relations and World Politics* (1971) focuses on the role of **transnational** actors, both individuals and organizations, while still maintaining that states are the most important players in international relations. Transnational actors include NGOs, MNCs, and employees of governments that form coalitions with likeminded individuals in other governments. For example, Nye and Keohane provide the examples of military officers sharing interests across countries and agricultural officials from various states forming a coalition to improve farming conditions and seek modernization of agriculture. These actors engage in "transnational relations," which are interactions across state borders that are not controlled by central governments (Keohane and Nye, 1971). The focus on individuals in bureaucracies challenged the unitary actor model as proposed by realists, and this challenge would soon be accepted by Kenneth Waltz (see Chapter 2). The conclusion reached by Keohane and Nye is that transnational relations increase interdependence in that societies become more sensitive to the happenings in other societies and as a consequence government relationships are altered.

Complex interdependence is the focus of Keohane and Nye's 1977 book, *Power and Interdependence*. This text, and many that followed, sought to provide additional variables to counter the pessimistic view of interstate relations held by realists. They accepted that international relations was conducted by self-interested actors in a system of anarchy (just like realists). Instead of seeing this as the reason to pursue only power and security, they argued cooperation was still possible and in the best interests of the actors in this type of environment. The sensitivity between states as mentioned above has costs, but the benefits of interdependence outweigh those costs. States will gain more from cooperating than they will lose. Complex interdependence is characterized by multiple channels of contact between states, limited use of force to resolve disputes between states in the interdependent relationship, and a nonhierarchical view of state goals and issues.

In additional to international organizations, a main component of the interdependent relationship is regimes, as briefly discussed above. Stephen Krasner (1942–) defines regimes in his 1983 book, *International Regimes,* as "sets of implicit or explicit principles, norms, rules, and decision-making procedures around which actors' expectations converge in a given area of international relations" (Krasner, 1983, 2).

This term was developed to encapsulate the totality of cooperative endeavors pursued by international actors in any given issue area. Krasner is a neorealist in the sense that he is concerned with conflict prevention and the role of the distribution of power in regime arrangements. While some realists deny the influence or importance of regimes, all accept their existence and would likely accept Krasner's contention that regimes are established in areas where coordination is problematic and the distribution of power is roughly symmetrical (Krasner, 1991). In these cases, weaker states can actually exercise some influence creating a situation in which everyone (not just the powerful states) is better off (Krasner, 1991).

Regime theory is most closely associated with the work of Robert Keohane. He uses the term "institutions" to describe his approach in his influential book, *International Institutions and State Power* (1989a). By institutions he means "persistent and connected sets of rules (formal and informal) that prescribe behavioral roles, constrain activity, and share expectations" (Keohane, 1989a, 3). He identifies three types of institutions that fit this definition. First, formal intergovernmental (IGO) or cross-national nongovernmental organizations (NGO) are bureaucratic organizations that monitor and react to activities and have explicit rules. The United Nations is an example of an IGO and Oxfam is an example of an NGO. Second, international regimes have rules, government agreement, and a focus on a particular set of issues. Examples include the Bretton Woods system established in 1944 and arms control agreements that exist between the United States and Russia. Third, conventions are informal institutions that guide the expectations of actors through implicit rules and understanding allowing for coordination and understanding. Conventions help overcome the Prisoner's Dilemma (see below) by creating incentives not to defect when it might appear profitable to do so. Reciprocity is a convention in that leaders expect reciprocal treatment, favorable responses when they abide by the convention and punishment when they do not. Diplomatic immunity, for example, was a convention for centuries before it was codified into formal agreements. Institutions are important for promoting cooperation because they impact the incentives states face in all issue areas. They allow states to do things that would otherwise be inconceivable, affect the costs associated with different alternatives, and impact the roles leaders believe they should play and their assumptions about the motives and interests of others. It is important to remember that although Keohane accepts that institutions impact state policy, he still maintains the state is stronger in its influence on the institutions (Keohane, 1989a, 3–6).

In both *International Institutions and State Power* (1989a) and *After Hegemony* (1984), Keohane exhibits clear ties to neorealism, more so in the latter than the former. He points out several areas of agreement between neoliberal institutionalism and neorealism. He acknowledges the mutual acceptance of a decentralized international system (anarchy) and the importance of state power. Both groups of theorists believe there is a reality to international politics that can be partially, but not fully, understood. They both believe theories must be tested, thus they share an epistemological approach and a place in the positivist camp. Although still believing in the importance of non-state actors, Keohane argues they are subordinate to states, and understanding the structure of the international system possesses some, although not perfect, predictive power. As such, he accepts the argument that US hegemony allowed for the creation of post-WWII regimes. In fact, American power was required for the creation and maintenance of these regimes. This is the argument of hegemonic stability theory explained in Chapter 2. He argues that institutionalists, those who argue common economic interests lead to a demand for international institutions, are naïve about the amount of power possessed by institutions. Despite these connections to neorealism, he argues neoliberalism is its own school of thought, and he remains in the neoliberal camp through his argument that cooperation can develop through institutions under certain conditions based on overlapping interests. Hegemony is not necessary or sufficient for cooperation, and interests and power are insufficient for understanding international relations. The role of interests and power is supplemented, not replaced, by theories emphasizing the impact of institutions. He argues that the neorealist notion of structure is too narrow and underspecified, ignoring institutional variations that influence world politics. As a consequence, neorealist conclusions are often misleading or wrong. Ultimately, realists have trouble convincingly explaining areas of cooperation where states accept asymmetrical results without considering the impact of institutional arrangements (Keohane, 1984, 1989).

As with our exploration of realist thinkers, this is only a partial list of the influential scholars of neoliberalism. This discussion provides the building blocks of liberal thinking mainly in the political sphere.

The next section addresses the impediments to cooperation and a more focused explanation of why states cooperate. A discussion of economic liberalism follows, completing the set of liberal ideals with capitalism, free trade, and open markets.

Barriers to Cooperation and How States Overcome Them

The section above highlights the fact that neoliberals believe that common interests and concerns enhanced by interdependence will promote cooperation. Despite this, neoliberals recognize that cooperation is not easy. Neoliberals cannot deny the existence of conflict in world politics and they recognize that there is a series of valid reasons why states fail to see the benefits of cooperation. International relations operate in a system of incomplete information. State leaders cannot fully know or understand the interests or motivations of others. Even the staunchest of allies keep secrets and spy on each other. For example, in the 1980s, Jonathan Pollard became the only person in US history to be sentenced to life in prison for spying for an ally: Israel.[10] In this environment of uncertainty and limited information, states fear a cheating partner. States may enter into an agreement and one or more of the partners may defect, meaning a failure to uphold the principles or actions to which they consented, leaving the cooperative states worse off than before the agreement was reached. In addition, states may fear others will free ride on their cooperative arrangements, reaping the benefits without agreeing to any constraints or bearing any of the costs. Hence entering cooperative agreements comes with risk, and states may determine the benefits are not worth the potential costs. While neorealists argue these barriers are insurmountable, neoliberals argue that the reluctance to cooperation can be overcome.

Many neoliberals use **game theory**, which uses mathematical and logical analysis to explain interactions among actors, and to demonstrate the difficulties of cooperating and the means to overcome them.[11] In game theory, outcomes are produced based on the preferences (called utilities) of the actors and they often result in unintended consequences leaving the actors worse off than they planned. The Prisoner's Dilemma is the most famous game theoretical approach to explaining the difficulties of cooperation. It demonstrates how utility maximization results in unintended outcomes. Each player seeks to maximize individual gains and both end up with a result that neither one desired (a suboptimal outcome). The Prisoner's Dilemma begins with two suspects captured by police and placed in separate interrogation rooms. They are each offered a reduced sentence if they rat out the other. The pay-offs vary in different versions of the game, but the punch line is that it is in the best interest of each individual to turn against his or her partner. As a consequence, each receives a penalty worse than if they had both remained silent, but better than if one remained silent while his or her partner did not. Figure 3.2 highlights the pay-offs in this game. If both prisoners cooperate, they would each receive 6 months in prison, the second-best outcome available (with freedom being the first). If they both defect, each receives 10 years in jail, the second-worst outcome (with 20 years in prison being the worst). The rational individual will choose to defect for two main reasons. First, the only way each prisoner has a chance at freedom is to defect on the other. Maximization of individual self-interest sets in and each prisoner defects. Second, distrust and fear come into play as each prisoner does not know what the other is going to do. The lack of information enhances distrust of the other, and each assumes the other will defect. If he or she does not also defect, the sentence will be 20 years in prison (the worst possible outcome). The game is set up so that the only way a prisoner can be saddled with the worst outcome is to cooperate. The dilemma inherent in promoting cooperation in the international system should now be clear. States do not know the true intentions of others and thus the risk of defection is high.

For realists, this demonstrates that the only way for states to protect themselves is to seek power and security rather than cooperative

| | | Prisoner B | |
		Cooperate	Defect
Prisoner A	Cooperate	Prisoner A – 6 months in prison C,C Prisoner B – 6 months in prison	Prisoner A – 20 years in prison C,D Prisoner B – freedom
	Defect	Prisoner A – freedom D,C Prisoner B – 20 years in prison	Prisoner A – 10 years in prison D,D Prisoner B – 10 years in prison

FIGURE. 3.2 **The Prisoner's Dilemma.**

relations. For neoliberals, however, there are multiple methods through which the risk of cheating or defection is lessened, allowing for cooperation to take place with mutual benefits to the parties. In other words, neoliberals have identified ways in which states can overcome the Prisoner's Dilemma. First, in most real-life situations between states the Prisoner's Dilemma is iterated (repeated). While states have in the past disappeared from the map or at least altered their configurations (East Germany, Yugoslavia, and the Soviet Union are some of the most recent), once a state is formed and stabilized it tends to remain. As such, states can expect to have repeated interactions with each other. This helps to decrease distrust through exchanging of information, but perhaps more importantly establishes a reputation for that actor. If a state is known to defect from agreements, other states will be less likely to cooperate with it in the future. There are future costs across issue areas in being known as a cheater and this will serve as a deterrent to defection. On the other hand, there are benefits if a state becomes known as a good partner. There are future benefits to be gained with a positive reputation.

Second, there are strategies that can be employed by actors to increase trust and decrease the likelihood of defection. The most famous strategy of this kind is tit-for-tat. In tit-for-tat, players are instructed to cooperate in the first interaction, regardless of what the other player does, and then mimic the behavior of the other player in subsequent interactions. If the other player defects, you defect; if the other player cooperates, you cooperate. Reciprocity is what leads to cooperation. One of the most cited examples of this approach is the means by which troops engaged with one another in the trenches during World War I. The soldiers adopted a live-and-let live policy. Due to the nature of trench warfare, they faced each other for an extended period of time (thus it was iterated) and their decision to not shoot one another became reciprocal.[12] These were clearly antagonistic parties, but the mutual goal of survival propelled them into a cooperative arrangement.

Third, designing effective and efficient institutions can foster cooperation between states. International organizations, regimes, and law can help states identify each other's interests, motives, concerns, and preferences, provide opportunities for regular discussions on issues, and engage in active joint problem-solving. They help promote transparency between state actors in the hope that if they understand what each other wants and what they are doing to achieve it, distrust will be decreased and collaboration increased. Institutions also provide disincentives for defection. For an institution to be effective, it serves as a means of collecting information about member states and disseminating that information to others (not just other states involved, but nonstate actors as well). This function promotes compliance by member states—if others will know of their defection, they are less likely to do it. If they do, effective institutions provide enforcement mechanisms. These can be carrots, like economic inducements or mediation and arbitration, or they can be sticks, like economic sanctions, diplomatic actions, or military responses. Both carrots and sticks run the risk of failure, but if the institution is designed properly, meaning it addresses a shared interest of the parties, then enforcement should serve to bring the defector back into compliant behavior. Successful institutions also contain a dispute resolution system, such as the DSB of the WTO discussed earlier in this chapter. If mechanisms are in place for states to air their grievances and seek restitution, institutions have a better chance of encouraging compliance.[13]

So far in this chapter we have focused our attention on the political aspects of liberalism. Liberalism began with a focus on individuals and their rights and a limited role for the state. When expanded to the international environment, the focus turned to domestic arrangements that could curtail warfare, namely representative democracies. If the benefits of democratic society in the form of individual liberties and peaceful conflict resolution could expand to the international environment, a peaceful global order could be established. Neoliberals sought the same outcome, but focused their attention on the role of international institutions to promote cooperation. Neoliberals know that this is not a quick process and recognize that not all institutions will succeed in their stated objectives. States have their own interests and neoliberals do not deny that those interests sometimes fail to promote the common good. They do believe, however, that overall, institutions have a positive impact in international relations and their continued use and expansion can promote a more peaceful environment. Criticisms of this approach are discussed below and in more detail in Chapter 4. One critical area that has yet to be fully covered is the liberal economic focus on capitalism, free trade, and open markets. For many people, this is what comes to mind when they think of liberalism. We now turn our attention to the liberal economic order.

Laissez-Faire and Economic Liberalism

As discussed in Chapter 2, mercantilists focus on trade protectionism instituted by states to promote their own power in a competitive global environment. Economic liberals, on the other hand, promote free trade where there are mutual benefits led by the "invisible hand" of the market (meaning limited state interference). These ideas connect to the liberal philosophy discussed above through reliance on rational individuals engaging each other in a constructive, mutually advantageous way. This also takes us back to the foundational liberal thought of John Locke and the limited role for government. Government is created to protect the liberty of the citizens allowing them to achieve their full potential. That potential includes their economic pursuits. Individual economic freedom is emphasized, coupled with virtually unregulated free markets. Liberal economics is the foundation upon which interdependence, integration, and globalization is built.

Pioneers in the Field

Much of the foundational thought of the liberal economic order began in the late eighteenth century with Adam Smith (1723–1790) and David Ricardo (1772–1823). Adam Smith, considered by many to be the father of modern economics, was a Scottish economist with a powerful respect for the regulatory nature of the market and a marked distaste for the potentially abusive role of the state. The abusive state Smith mistrusted was the mercantilist one constructed in the eighteenth century (see Chapter 2). In response, he argued in his famous work, *The Wealth of Nations*, that individuals are in the best position to make social choices, which appear as an "invisible hand" guiding the economy and promoting the general welfare. Smith recognized that people are self-interested, but in the system of **capitalism**, that self-interest is prevented from unhindered expansion. The nature of competition in a capitalist system constrains both producers and consumers. Producers will offer reasonable prices or be priced out of the market by their competitors (those who produce the same goods). Consumers also face competition from other consumers who want or need the same products, thus preventing prices from being driven too low. Both consumers and producers make rational choices that serve their interests in this system and this is what Smith called the "invisible hand." Although an individual in this system, "neither intends to promote the public interest nor knows how much he is promoting it" but "he is in this, as in many other cases, directed by an invisible hand to promote an end which was no part of his intention" (Smith, 1964, 400). The invisible hand of the market guarantees the most efficient allocation of resources and in doing so enables peaceful commercial interactions between states.

Although Smith is most often associated with **laissez-faire** economics, he did believe the state had responsibility for a limited number of roles, specifically developing and sustaining a legal system and providing for national defense. Individuals cannot perform these functions, but for individuals to prosper and reach their potential, they are necessary. Thus, state intervention is required in a limited way. Economic and political affairs are independent, with economics assuming a superior role because it is governed by natural laws and thus does not require interference from the state. Smith also believed that the market should create righteous people, those concerned for the poor. Only with this concern for others will a society flourish producing a happy people. This argument was made in his other significant book, *The Theory of Moral Sentiments* (1759). Contrary to mercantilists, Smith opposed the tariff policies pursued by states to enhance their power.

Similarly, English economist David Ricardo was a staunch proponent of free trade. As a member of the British Parliament, he was in the minority on this subject. Ricardo demonstrated through the law of comparative advantage that free trade increases efficiency and is mutually beneficial. The law of comparative advantage postulates that people and states should produce the goods they are most efficient at producing, based on their available resources, and trade for all others. The goods they trade for are ones that cost more to produce and are thus economically inefficient. Economists call this opportunity cost. From this perspective, the logical and rational choice is to give up producing the products that are made inefficiently in a state and make agreements with other states that produce them efficiently.[14] Trade is thus a positive-sum game—all states can benefit through the free exchange of goods and services. This is not without its political challenges. This argument was used to oppose the **Corn Laws** in England in the 19th century, and the discussion at the beginning of this chapter concerning the WTO ruling against the United States and its labelling requirements also highlights the political battles that come with pursuing trade at the expense of domestic industries.

As negative consequences of unrestrained competition became apparent in the 19th century, economic liberalism underwent significant changes specifically tied to the role of the state. John Stuart Mill (1806–1873) argued that capitalism had deleterious consequences in Europe in the 18th century. Mercantilist also decried the economic policies of the 18th century, but for reasons of unfair competition and disproportionate power (see Chapter 2). For economic liberals, the problems inherit in the capitalist system were related to inequality and its societal impact. Smith discussed this concern in *The Theory of Moral Sentiments*, but it was Mill, in *Principles of Political Economy with Some of the Applications to Social Philosophy* (1848), who expanded these ideas and made them a guiding force in liberalism until the 20th century. Poor factory conditions, child labor, and a general inadequacy of social welfare prompted Mill to argue for a more activist, but still limited, role for states to correct the failures of the market. He continued to promote decentralization and only advocated for as much interference as was necessary to promote the general welfare, in particular, in the areas of education and assisting the poor. Mill published the book the same year as Marx's *Communist Manifesto* and you will read more about the inequalities produced by capitalism in Chapter 4.

The 20th century ushered in the period of **Keynesianism**. John Maynard Keynes (1883–1946) developed this strain of liberal economics with, like Mill, a concern for the negative consequences wrought on society by unfettered markets. His ideas were particularly popular during the Great Depression and lasted into the 1970s. Keynes was a major player in rebuilding Western Europe after World War II and creating the Bretton Woods system of new institutions to regulate the economy (see Spotlight). He used the Great Depression to highlight the fact that the invisible hand of the market does not always work and that individual self-interest will not necessarily lead to a common good. He wrote in 1926, "Nor is it true that self-interest generally is enlightened; more often individuals acting separately to promote their own ends are too ignorant or too weak to attain even these" (Keynes, 1963, 312). As such, the arguments that the market is self-correcting, adjusting prices and interest rates to correct any deviation from full employment, are overstated. When uncertainty prevails, individuals can and will make unwise decisions; and, even when they make rational decisions, the outcome may be collectively destructive. Keynes coined the term **paradox of thrift** to describe when a society is faced with recession or depression and individuals are faced with unemployment. If a person fears unemployment, one rational response is to save money and spend less. If the job is then lost, there is money in savings to fall back on. This approach is a self-fulfilling prophecy of sorts. Spending less slows the economy, and as purchasing falls, so does production and employment. A spiral ensues of decreasing employment, purchasing, and production, and the economic catastrophe that was feared comes to pass. Keynes also feared the impact of market speculation, which is predicting the value of a tradable good, like stocks, and making financial decisions based on those predictions. This practice has a substantial calculated risk of losing the initial outlay, but investors take that risk for the possibility of a huge payout if the speculation was correct. This practice holds the potential for catastrophe for each individual investor and the fragile financial market. Although arguing the system was flawed, Keynes did not agree with Marxists who saw the Great Depression as a harbinger of the collapse of capitalism and the rise of the revolutionary proletariat.

To combat the issues posed by the belief in a self-regulating market, Keynes proposed a system that allows for the continued working of the invisible hand, but with state intervention. This is not unlike the conclusions drawn by Smith in the eighteenth century. Private enterprise should still operate unhindered, but state power was needed to direct "the inner intricacies of private business" (Keynes, 1963, 318). Keynes supported the liberal foundation of individual liberty but argued economics should be used to serve society. He believed speculative investing had destabilized the market in the late 1920s and that states had a responsibility to stimulate the sagging economy. As such, he advocated government spending in order to create jobs and promote spending. Keynesian policies, such as states' attempts to sustain wages, stimulate employment, and promote economic growth, were adopted by many states during the Great Depression. This was seen again in the Great Recession beginning in 2007 when banks and financial institutions were bailed out by states to prevent their collapse. This was not without controversy, however, most state leaders believed this was a necessary step to prevent a complete economic collapse. This will be discussed further below.

SPOTLIGHT ON POLICYMAKERS: JOHN MAYNARD KEYNES

John Maynard Keynes (1883–1946), an English scholar, writer, lecturer, and civil servant, was one of the 20th century's most influential economists. His work was essential in the development of macroeconomics, particularly the argument that states should increase spending during times of economic decline (recession) and decrease spending during periods of economic boom, to keep inflation under control. In addition to his theoretical importance, he had profound influence on the economic policies pursued by states. Although the heyday of Keynesianism was the 1930–1970s, his influence is still felt today. The debate continues in theoretic and policy circles between laissez-faire economics and Keynesianism, and this debate plays out in the global economy through the policy choices made by states.

From a young age, Keynes possessed a sense of public duty and in 1906 he began his civil service career in the India Office of the British Military Department. His job in the India Office only lasted until 1908 when he became a lecturer of economics at King's College. This gave him the perspective of an administrator, a new angle from which to look at economics. When he began his job at King's College, his interests were in probability theory and statistics, but he was hired to lecture on monetary theory. Prior to 1914, he had little interest in monetary policy, either intellectually or practically. The British economy was strong, employment high, the gold standard was working, and the promise of free trade permeated public dialogue. The looming specter of war changed all that. A few days before the outbreak of WWI, Keynes was summoned to London and helped end a crisis in which bankers were pushing to prevent the convertibility of banknotes into gold. A rush on gold reserves at the Bank of England had depleted its reserves and the bank chairman asked for permission to suspend payouts in gold. Keynes' compromise was that domestic transactions be restricted but gold payments continue for international transactions. This approach was pursued in great part to prevent the loss of British reputation abroad. Failing to cover international transactions would have severely damaged Britain's ability to conduct business. Keynes blamed the bankers for the crisis and was concerned that the continued reliance on specie payments (converting banknotes to gold) would create inflation (Skidelsky, 2003).

In January 1915, Keynes assumed a position as a junior advisor at the Treasury. In this role, he argued taxation was the means to cover

continued

government spending (in other words, financing the war effort), not inflationary loans. His concern about inflation was based on the balance of payments—inflation would destroy the sterling-dollar exchange and Britain would not be able to pay for imports from the United States. Keynes lost this argument and Britain financed the war mainly through loans (Skidelsky, 2003). As a result, three years into the conflict, Britain was entirely dependent on the United States to finance the war. Britain had to continue borrowing dollars from the United States, and just as this system was on the verge of collapse, Germany unwittingly saved it by declaring unrestricted submarine warfare. This act brought the United States into the war and prevented Britain from having to suspend convertibility to gold, an action that would have signaled to Germany that Britain was in dire economic shape.

Following the aversion of this disaster, Keynes was promoted to head of the division dealing with external finance and his main responsibility was negotiating terms of credit between Britain and its allies. His work led to his appointment as the financial representative for the Treasury to the Versailles Peace Conference. This was not a positive experience for Keynes. He argued for limited indemnities (reparation payments) by Germany, based upon what Germany could actually afford to pay. If the reparations payments were overly burdensome and damaged its productive capabilities, it would not be able to pay. He reasoned that Germany had to be able to make money in order to make the reparations payments. This argument did not win the day and extremely harsh penalties were imposed on Germany that were, as it turned out, more than its ability to pay. In disgust, Keynes left Paris, in what he called "slipping away from the scene of the nightmare," and resigned from the Treasury before the Treaty of Versailles was signed (Skidelsky, 2003, 232). From this experience, he wrote what many believe is his best work, *The Economic Consequences of the Peace*. He denounced the treaty and the men who made it, and predicted economic disaster. Many argue his predictions panned out as Germany suffered debilitating hyperinflation and a growing sense of despair that softened the German population to the rhetoric of Adolph Hitler and ultimately lead to WWII (Skidelsky, 2003).

During the 1920s, Keynes continued to publish and lecture. He focused on further critiques of the peace treaty, British policy, and warned of the causes and dangers of inflation and unemployment. He also advised government officials, including those from Britain, the

continued

United States, and Germany, but his persuasive abilities were diminished since his resignation from the Treasury in 1919. His influence returned, however, after the stock market crash in 1929, as he was appointed to the Macmillan Committee on Finance and Industry (an exploratory committee on how banking practices affect the economy) and the Economic Advisory Council (a council created by the prime minister). On the Macmillan Committee, in addition to examining witnesses, Keynes presented his own ideas about monetary theory and policy, and this "marks the start of the Keynesian Revolution in policymaking. No policymaker after 1930 made the mistake of assuming that all prices were flexible and that, by fixing the exchange at any level one wanted, one secured an automatic adjustment of costs" (Skidelsky, 2003, 426).

In August 1940, almost a year after the German invasion of Poland, Keynes returned to a position at the Treasury. His goal was to convince the Treasury to rethink how it was financing the war. His ideas were based on his booklet, *How to Pay for the War*, published in February 1940. He argued for higher taxation and increased saving, rather than deficit spending and inflation, to curb public consumption of resources needed to support the war effort. There would be compulsory savings to decrease the public's purchasing power to avoid inflation, thus channeling resources to pay for the war. An additional benefit of this plan was that there would be no postwar slump because workers could use those savings when they were made available after the war. Toward the end of the war, Keynes was a major force in the negotiations that established the plan for the postwar economic system, namely the Bretton Woods regimes that included the IMF and the World Bank (at the time called the International Bank for Reconstruction and Development). As the head of the British delegation, he proposed a compromise (known as the "Keynesian Compromise") that allowed states to control domestic economic activities, but created the IMF to manage global financial policies.

At the conference in July 1944, Keynes focused his attention on the World Bank. He wanted an institution that would help avoid the consequences of the overly punitive Treaty of Versailles by providing assistance to both the winners (creditors) and losers (debtors) of WWII. Keynes was forced to accept a compromise with the more powerful United States, the world's largest creditor nation after the war, and thus the World Bank and IMF left the corrective burden on the debtor countries. The Bretton Woods system tied currencies to gold and fixed exchange rates to the US dollar

continued

(Keynes proposed a global currency, but lost that argument), but endowed the IMF with the power to intervene in cases where imbalance of payments occurs. Although the agreement reflected American views and was seen by many in Britain as the sign that London was no longer the financial capital of the world, Keynes contributed to creating the global institutions designed to promote economic stability and development that remain today (Skidelsky, 2003). They are not without their controversies, but more than 70 years later they maintain a prominent place in the global economy.

Keynesian policies were pursued in the early decades of the Cold War as states sought to use their power to stabilize the global market through the Bretton Woods institutions. Some economists refer to the period between 1945 and 1975 as the "golden age of controlled capitalism." The United States and Western Europe saw impressive economic growth that peaked in the 1960s. According to Barry Eichengreen, an American economist, "Critical to Western Europe's success was the security of private property rights and reliance on the price mechanism." But, the "postwar golden age depended on more than just the free play of market forces; in addition it required a set of norms and conventions, some informal, others embodied in law, to coordinate the actions of the social partners and solve a set of problems that decentralized markets could not" (Eichengreen, 2006, 4). During this time, Swedish social democracy developed as did the British notion of "welfarism." In the United States, the government pursued President Roosevelt's New Deal and later President Johnson's Great Society that sought social improvements through anti-poverty legislation, education, and Medicare, among many other programs. These programs were born from high taxation of the wealthy, both individuals and corporations, and state control of money flows.

Thus, the boom of the early Cold War years saw a combination of the invisible hand with domestic and international regulations and norms to promote the smooth functioning of the international economy. Beginning in the 1960s, the system came under attack by those who believed in more classical liberal approaches to the economy and favored growth over stability. In 1971, in what became known as the Nixon Shock, the United States halted the convertibility of the US dollar to gold and in 1973 the US fixed exchanged system was replaced by a floating exchange system. An increase of competition for trading markets, a decrease in corporate profits, oil shocks leading to dramatic increases in the price of gasoline, and stagflation—high inflation and low economic growth—caused Keynesian policies to fall out of favor.

Keynesianism was replaced by the ideas of Friedrich Hayek (1899–1992) and Milton Friedman (1912–2006), both of whom favored limited state involvement in the economy. Hayek argues in *The Road to Serfdom* (1944) that the increase in state encroachment in the economy was a threat to individual liberty. As with many classical liberals, he feared state involvement in economic matters would lead to socialism or fascism, and saw any state intervention as ominous threats to human liberty and creativity. Limitations on government were the only way to ensure both security and freedom, as security would be born from the market. He extolls the virtues of "independence and self-reliance, individual initiative and local responsibility, the successful reliance on voluntary activity, noninterference with one's neighbor and tolerance of the different, and a healthy suspicion of power and authority" (Hayek, 1944, 128). He warns against states printing too much money (leading to inflation), lacking concern for government debt (by overspending on social programs), and interfering in private business. Similarly, Friedman, who won the 1976 Nobel Prize, emphasizes the role of the market in protecting liberty in his book, *Capitalism and Freedom* (1962). He argues that states should only intervene when absolutely necessary and capitalism will ensure freedom through its competitive open market. From his focus on the dangers of inflation, he developed the theory of **monetarism**. The central concern is the supply and demand for money, and that an excessive expansion of the money supply by governments leads to inflation. Inflation is controlled by a regulated money supply (keeping the supply and demand at equilibrium) so the maintenance of price stability should be the main focus of monetary authorities (such as central banks like the US Federal Reserve). Both Hayek and Friedman harken back to the arguments of Adam Smith extolling the value of free market capitalism and limited state involvement.

In the 1980s, neoliberalism emerged based on the ideas of Smith, Hayek, and Friedman, and US President Ronald Reagan and British Prime Minister Margaret Thatcher were its top practitioners. Reaganomics and Thatcherism are built around the same foundations of neoliberalism, but they took different approaches. For Reagan, the biggest obstacle to economic growth was high taxes. In what is known as supply-side or trickle-down economics (or by many critics, Voodoo Economics), Reaganomics pushed for lower taxes out of the belief that they would promote economic growth that would create the revenue needed to pay for public programs. Reagan cut taxes for the top income bracket from 70% to 28% over several years. Simultaneously, Reagan also wanted to balance the budget and engage in a dramatic increase in defense spending. The dramatic reduction in taxes in the early 1980s, however, resulted in decreased revenue and the inability to fund the increase in defense spending, even with a reduction in spending for social and welfare programs. As a result, the United States engaged in tremendous levels of deficit spending creating a national debt of $2.8 trillion, a figure that may seem unimpressive today, but was unprecedented at the time. Reagan also engaged in deregulation of the banking, investment, and energy sectors, and privatization of many industries in telecommunications and transportation. Although a neoliberal ideal, promoting free trade proved challenging for Reagan, as he often pursued protectionism for industries that made up his core constituencies, such as auto workers and farmers.

In contrast to Reagan, for Thatcher, the biggest cause of economic difficulties was the growth of the money supply. She was opposed to high taxes on the wealthy to fund bureaucracy, but her biggest concern was monetary growth (meaning printing too much money) leading to inflation. She was a monetarist, following the approach of Milton Friedman. She tied a growth in the money supply with the rising national debt and undertook explicit strategies for reducing the deficit. She lowered taxes on the wealthy, but raised the national sales tax and increased taxes on oil revenue. She privatized numerous industries, including utilities, public housing, transportation, and oil and steel. She undermined the role of trade unions and sought to cut state spending through reducing the welfare state. Both Reagan and Thatcher (among other world leaders including Canadian Prime Minister Brian Mulroney and Australian Prime Minister Malcolm Fraser) represented the first-wave of neoliberalism. They successfully assaulted Keynesianism and sought to reduce the size and role of government.

Globalization and Liberal Economic Policies in Crisis?

Neoliberal policies coincided with the promotion of globalization, a word that made its appearance in the mid-1980s. The world was becoming increasingly interdependent as free trade and economic liberalism were pursued. Industrialized nations promoted globalization as a means to increase economic growth through capitalism and the spread of democracy. This approach continued into the 1990s, as the Clinton administration pursued free trade, the European Union's single market continued to expand, and many industrializing states in East and Southeast Asia experienced dramatic economic growth. Neoliberalism is often discussed interchangeably with the Washington Consensus, a term coined in 1989 by economist John Williamson. The Washington Consensus consisted of ten policy prescriptions for countries to adopt to improve economic growth, including fiscal discipline, tax reforms, financial and trade liberalization, privatization, and deregulation.[15] The pursuit of these goals was tied to assistance from international economic institutions, such as the IMF and World Bank. This policy advice was aimed primarily at Latin American countries in economic crisis and was considered by many as the proper means of economic development.

Neoliberalism, the Washington Consensus, and globalization experienced harsh criticism in the mid-1990s and it continues today. Anti-globalization protests have been loud and often violent, illustrated by the "Battle of Seattle" in 1999. Rampant human rights violations, environmental damage, underrepresentation of developing countries in global economic institutions, exploitation of resources in developing countries, and recessions in Mexico in 1994, Russia in 1996, the Asian financial crisis in 1997, and the Great Recession beginning in 2007 all raised difficult and yet unanswered questions about the viability of laissez-faire capitalism and the process of globalization.[16] The critical theories presented in the following chapters expand upon these criticisms. Despite the significant disapproval of the impacts of neoliberal polices, debate continues as to the best approach to ensure economic growth among economic liberals. The Great Recession resulted in increased state intervention, as the United States rescued the Fannie Mae and Freddie Mac loan agencies ultimately through nationalization, provided the American International Group (AIG), one of the largest bank insurers in the world, with a roughly $150 billion bailout, and passed the Emergency Stabilization Act that allowed the use of taxpayer money to buy bad assets held by banks and bailout US automakers Chrysler and GM. Many other countries also passed stimulus packages and agreed with the United States to cut interest rates to stimulate buying. While decision-makers believed these steps were necessary to prevent the collapse of the global economy, not everyone agreed. Many politicians railed against these governmental moves because they opposed state intervention in the economy. However, the Occupy Wall Street movement beginning in New York in September 2011 was an unmistakable sign that the 99% were not happy with the outcomes of neoliberal policies. Middle- and working-class Americans were fed up with inequality, lower taxes on the wealthy, unregulated banks and corporations, lack of assistance to struggling families, and political gridlock.

While there are significant concerns about the economic liberal order—capitalism, globalization, and spreading democracy—the debate rages for the simple fact that thus far no alternative has emerged with enough clout to replace it. We discuss in Chapter 7 how the economic aspects of the theories covered in the book collide in the real world. For now, consider the fact that while great debate ensues between liberal free trade and the protectionism espoused by mercantilists, both occur simultaneously in the global economy. This is the nature of theories—there are adherents to each approach discussed in this book (and several others not covered here), and they are in a constant struggle to promote the adoption of policies consistent with their approach.

Criticisms of Liberalism

Although the theories discussed in the book share some common features, they represent competing images of the world. As such, each one has criticisms leveled against it by the proponents of the others. Despite the fact that they share certain features, liberalism's main counterpoint is realism. Realists attack liberalism on several fronts. First, realists take issue with the liberal view of humans as progressive and human nature as positive. This was a main criticism around the time of WWII, but that is no longer the case. The two camps still view human nature differently, liberals with a positive view and realists with a negative view, but both schools of thought have realized that human nature is a complex phenomenon with a capacity for both good and evil. It is the social, political, and historical influences that determine whether humans will be good or bad in any given situation. A related second criticism is that realists believe the utopian and optimistic view of the world held by liberals is unrealistic and unwarranted. For realists, anarchy and the security dilemma are central features of international relations, but liberals believe those elements can be overcome. Liberals argue that the realist insistence on seeing a world of competition, conflict, suspicion, and distrust is a self-fulfilling prophecy. The security dilemma has been overcome in real-world cases and thus using that as a starting point could become a self-fulfilling prophecy of peace, trust, and cooperation. While liberals see a world that is evolutionary—capable of change—realists argue that the world has not changed, in that interdependence is not a new phenomenon and it has failed to prevent conflict in the past, and it is not going to achieve it in the future.

Third, realists are highly skeptical of the notion of a democratic zone of peace, viewing this as overly optimistic. The theory of democratic peace rests on some questionable arguments. While realists accept that there has been an increase in the number of democracies worldwide and, despite some questionable definitional adjustments regarding what constitutes a democracy by proponents of the theory, can accept that democracies have not fought each other, this does not mean that they will not. Historically speaking, there have been few democracies up until the 1990s, and democracies have no trouble fighting non-democracies, undermining the notion that they are more peaceful. Realists also argue that there is no guarantee that existing democracies will not revert to some form of non-democracy, and in doing so make the current zone of peace an historical anomaly.

Fourth, realists criticize liberalism for being overly descriptive. This criticism is two-fold, one is that it lacks theoretical weight and the second is that it is unnecessarily complex. Realists argue that liberalism leans towards simply describing rather than explaining the occurrence of phenomenon. They often point to the process of globalization as an example. This is not a theoretical concept, but instead a process occurring in reality. Realists also argue that theories should be parsimonious, with limited variables chosen to explain patterns of behavior. Too much complexity only serves to undermine the explanatory value of behavior. Liberals point to the fact that classical and neoclassical realism both include multiple factors in their analysis and that a diversity of variables is a valid approach as it gets us to a more complete understanding of behavior in a complex world. Liberals also point out that neoliberalism and neorealism share many attributes in common.

Fifth, critics contend that neoliberals focus too extensively on the role of institutions. Realists argue that institutions only serve the self-interest of states. Thus, institutions are shells in which states interact and have no power to compel behavior or act independently (an issue that will be addressed at the end of this chapter). Neoliberals know, however, that institutional arrangements do not always work and that state interests do not always align with the greater good. Institutions do facilitate cooperation and even the most powerful states often desire cooperative relations, thus to dismiss institutions out of hand would be shortsighted.

Beyond realist critiques, critical approaches expound their own issues with liberalism. Marxism is at its core a critique of economic liberalism. While liberals argue the international system is a positive-sum game where all can benefit, Marxists argue it is about exploitation and inequality. Capitalist profit is based on labor exploitation, and the international institutions of which neoliberals are so fond serve only to perpetuate economic inequalities. Neoliberals make normative assumptions concerning institutions; specifically they argue that despite the challenges and failures, institutions have had, and continue to have, a positive impact in global politics. Chapter 4 fully addresses the approach of economic structuralists, including Marxists, and their competing view of the liberal economic order. Lastly, like realists, liberals face the ontological issue of accepting certain things as truth. In both positivist approaches, the Westphalian state system is accepted without question and the interests of states are given the utmost of importance. The evaluation of the approach is based on the achievement of state interests, but neither realists nor liberals address the ethical issues surrounding those interests.

As with realism, there are various avenues of liberal thought and many liberal theorists with nuanced arguments concerning the functioning of world politics. Some of the criticisms above are leveled at the basic assumptions of the school of thought, while others are specific to neoliberalism or economic liberalism. Consider the arguments of liberals and their critics very carefully as you analyze the behavior of actors in the international system. The following case studies serve to help you assess behavior and the explanatory value of liberalism. As you read these case studies, remind yourself of the realist explanations you read in the last chapter. How do realists and liberals approach these issues? How do they differ and are there similarities in their approaches?

Case Study: Proliferation

Chapter 1 discusses some of international agreements entered into by states to curb the proliferation of weapons of mass destruction (WMDs), specifically the Non-Proliferation Treaty (NPT), the Chemical Weapons Convention (CWC), and the Biological Weapons Convention (BWC). How do liberals explain the creation of these regimes and their widespread membership? The simplest answer, that realists also accept, is that joining these regimes serves state interests in terms of security. Nuclear-weapons states are committed to preventing non-nuclear weapons states from acquiring nuclear capabilities. Likewise, non-nuclear weapons states would like to prevent their neighbors from acquiring them while pressuring nuclear states to eliminate their stockpiles. Almost all states are committed to the elimination and non-use of chemical weapons, and while support for the BWC is lagging slightly behind the CWC, it is safe to say that there is widespread acceptance that use of such weapons in warfare is unacceptable. For liberals, however, it is much more than that. As (neo)functionalists and regime theorists argue, these regimes represent attempts to coordinate behavior to solve a problem no single state can solve alone (proliferation and the use of WMDs), and neoliberals herald the development and use of international institutions to coordinate behavior and promote cooperation. The confidence-building measures included in these agreements promote good relations that can spill over into other areas of mutual concern. This case also represents a real-world example of how liberals argue the Prisoner Dilemma can be overcome. There is a risk for states in agreeing not to develop or use certain weapons. If their partner(s) defects from the agreement, and the sides engage in a military confrontation, the results for the party who complied with agreement while the other(s) was cheating would be catastrophic. The NPT, CWC, and BWC help overcome this fear by containing confidence-building measures while also creating incentives for the parties to comply. The benefits of compliance, including reputation and positive spillover to other issue areas, promotes compliance and cooperation.

The NPT is a significant achievement in multilateral cooperation, with 191 members and widespread compliance. Nuclear weapons states have little to lose in signing the agreement, but their participation gives the treaty credibility. Non-nuclear states join to engage in a cooperative peace-building measure and avoid being labeled as a pariah state. Only five states are not parties to this agreement and there has been considerable pressure placed on Israel, India, and Pakistan to join the NPT to secure near-universal membership. All three are nuclear-weapons states, although Israel's program remains unacknowledged. If that were to occur, only South Sudan (newly independent in 2011 and mired in internal conflict since) and North Korea would remain outside the treaty. Although not without its controversies, it is one of the most widespread and adhered-to international regimes created. In addition, the NPT is used as a confidence-building measure between parties. The International Atomic Energy Agency (IAEA) is responsible for providing safeguards to cheating by verifying compliance through inspections. As neoliberals stress, institutions and regimes help decrease mistrust and suspicion, and safeguards in place in the NPT create confidence in joining, promote cooperation in the area of peaceful nuclear energy, and act as a deterrent to defecting. If a state defects by withdrawal or is caught by the IAEA, its reputation would be seriously damaged. For example, North Korea was already considered a pariah before its withdrawal from the NPT in 2003, but its reputation was further damaged by its decision to forgo its obligations under the NPT.

The CWC reaches the same level of membership as the NPT evidenced by its 192 members. Israel signed the agreement but failed to ratify it, while Angola, Egypt, North Korea, and South Sudan are non-signatories. Its implementation is overseen by the Organization for the Prohibition of Chemical Weapons (OPCW), which receives a declaration from all member states of their chemical weapons stockpiles, production and industry facilities, and other relevant weapons information. To ensure compliance, the OPCW is charged with inspecting and monitoring facilities and activities through routine inspections, challenging inspections (if there are questions of noncompliance), and responding to alleged charges of chemical weapons usage. Punitive measures for violating the obligations of the treaty can be recommended by the OPCW and serious cases can be taken to the UN Security Council and General Assembly. The cost of violating a state's obligations to the CWC are therefore potentially significant and act as a deterrent as well as a means of overcoming the fear of defection. The OPCW was created to enhance the credibility and transparency of the CWC as well as to increase the confidence of the member states regarding the adherence to the provisions by other states.

The BWC has achieved slower and less complete membership due to questions concerning allowing biological agents for peaceful purposes. Despite concerns, the regime has 174 states-parties (plus several states who have signed but not ratified) and 15 states who have not signed. In a series of review conferences from 1986 to 2006, confidence-building measures were established, expanded, and accepted. The measures include reporting requirements on vaccine production, infectious disease outbreaks, and activities related to past and current biological defense research and development. The purpose of these measures is to reduce ambiguities and allow member states to move forward with confidence that the provisions of the treaty are being carried out by all members. The UN Secretary General has a mechanism for responding to allegations of alleged chemical and biological weapons use. This mechanism was developed in the 1980s and is triggered by a request from any member state of the United Nations. Its initial purpose was to investigate and report to UN members any violation of the 1925 Geneva Protocol which bans the use of both categories of weapons, but now works in conjunction with the CWC and BWC.

The use of confidence-building measures, compliance requirements, and potential punishments for violating obligations in the NPT, CWC, BWC, and Geneva Protocol serve to increase trust that agreements are being adhered to and undermine the suspicion members have that others are cheating. These regimes promote cooperation and allow for mutually beneficial outcomes. States engage in joint-problem solving and the positive interactions promote cooperation in other issue areas. The implementation and adherence to the stipulations in these regimes are not without their problems. States have been known to defect, violating the provisions, but condemnation and sanctions have followed. North Korea is a prime example of this, as is Iraq before the 2003 war that toppled Saddam Hussein. Generally, these nonproliferation regimes are viewed in a positive light and neoliberals argue this is exactly the type of state behavior that over time will lead to a more cooperative and peaceful world.

TABLE 3.1 Liberalism and Proliferation

Liberal Thought	Theoretical Tenet	Proliferation Example
Just War Theory	Ethical and moral standards in war should be pursued and the use of certain weapons causes disproportionate damage and the unjust killing of noncombatants.	Weapons of mass destruction (WMDs) are widely regarded as inappropriate for use in war and international conventions and regimes like the Geneva Protocol, NPT, CWC, and BWC are created to prevent their usage and the indiscriminate death of innocent noncombatants.
Neoliberal Institutionalism	Institutions, organizations, and regimes are created to coordinate state behavior and promote cooperation. Interdependence has made the creation of these entities easier.	The NPT, CWC, and BWC were created to promote coordination and cooperation in controlling the spread of WMDs. Interdependence of states has made cooperation in this area easier as states seek to be viewed as good global citizens to reap benefits across issue areas. Creation of standards for WMDs allows states to know the expectations of their behavior.

continued

Liberal Thought	Theoretical Tenet	Proliferation Example
(Neo) functionalism	Cooperation achieved through integration. Multilateral institutions and arrangements are created to solve problems one state could not solve alone. Arrangements must serve the interests of the parties.	Proliferation is an issue that requires collaboration as it cannot be resolved or controlled by one state alone. The NPT serves the interests of both nuclear and non-nuclear states. Cooperation in the area of proliferation spills over into other areas and states avoid appearing as a pariah by agreeing to the provisions of the treaties.
Regime Theory	Regimes represent the convergence of expectations around a given issue and the cooperative endeavors pursued by actors. Regimes impact the costs associated with certain actions and alter the assumptions about the motives and interests of others.	Expectations have converged against the use of WMDs, and with the exception of existing nuclear-weapons states, around the possession of WMDs. The NPT, CWC, and BWC represent a part of the cooperative effort in the area of proliferation. Confidence-building measures in these regimes decrease mistrust and suspicion, while increasing the costs of defection. For example, the OPCW can request punitive measures be placed on a state found in violation of the provisions of the CWC.
Game Theory	Mathematical and logical analysis used to demonstrate the difficulties of cooperating. The Prisoner's Dilemma demonstrates how utility maximization results in unintended outcomes. Neoliberals believe the barriers to cooperation can be overcome.	The NPT, CWC, and BWC are examples of iterated Prisoner's Dilemma games. If states decide not to develop WMDs, they fear the defection of others. All three regimes have compliance mechanisms and confidence-building measures to overcome the fear and suspicion states have of others. The IAEA conducts inspections to provide safeguards against cheating in the NPT. The UN Secretary General has a mechanism for responding to allegations of chemical or biological weapons usage. If caught by either body, damage to a state's reputation will occur, leading to the unwillingness of other states to engage in future agreements. Sanctions may also be imposed damaging the defecting state across issue areas.

Case Study: WTO

The WTO highlights several principles of liberalism; specifically it promotes free trade and places an emphasis on the role of the individual, both central features of capitalism. Classic liberals support this aspect of the WTO as an attempt to prevent unnecessary state interference (i.e., trade barriers) on individual ambitions in a free market. Neoliberals herald the WTO as an institution that serves as a mechanism to promote cooperation and interdependence through trade and development. The workings of the WTO also demonstrate that states pursue more than power and security, as they value the benefits of cooperation derived from interactions through trade and dispute resolution. This does not undermine the idea that state interests matter, a belief held by realists and liberals alike; however, liberals believe that state interests can be protected and pursued through cooperation and mutual benefit. Increased trade promotes economic growth and prosperity for all involved, thus the WTO is an example of a positive-sum game. This is not to argue that states always pursue the mutually beneficial option. As the discussion at the beginning of this chapter demonstrates, competing domestic factions within a society can adversely impact a state's ability to pursue free trade and cooperation. But, neoliberals would remind us that the process of integration can and will have its hurdles to jump. We highlight this through two issues related to the WTO—why states join and why they comply with the rules—allowing us to contrast the explanations of realists and liberals.

Both realists and liberals argue that states join the WTO for their own interests. For liberals, this is true of the powerful and the weak because there are shared benefits from integration and inclusion. Economic data demonstrate that there is a correlation between free trade and economic growth. Since the end of WWII, trade barriers declined to an average of less than 5% in industrialized countries, while in the 25 years following the war, world economic growth averaged about 5% a year and trade grew at an average of 8% a year (WTO 2015b). To understand why this connection exists, recall the earlier discussion of David Ricardo and comparative advantage. All states have resources, but not necessarily the same ones. States should use their resources most efficiently by maufacturing the products that have the greatest cost benefit, and trading for everything else. If states do this, they will be more economically prosperous because they are not wasting resources (natural, human, monetary) by producing goods they are inefficient at producing. If all states adopt this approach, there will be mutually advantageous outcomes—everyone wins with free trade. Since the benefits of WTO membership include access to other member's markets, it is in states' economic interest to join the WTO and abide by its rules. This is why China strove for 15 years for accession to the WTO; why Russia worked through the accession process for 19 years, the longest process in WTO history; and why Saudi Arabia pursued accession for 12 years. All states joining the WTO must meet a multitude of standards, which in most cases requires a lowering of tariff barriers and nontariff barriers, and liberalizing of the banking and insurance sectors.[17]

The case of Saudi Arabia highlights why states choose to join the WTO. Saudi Arabia was never colonized by Western powers, and that history, combined with its vast oil wealth, allowed it to control its own investment and trade systems. With their decision to apply for membership in the WTO in 1993 and through the 12 years of negotiations, the Saudis proved themselves ready and willing to adopt international norms in these areas. The Saudis were not a weak state pushed into WTO membership by great powers, but a state seeking its own interests and internal reform (Clatanoff, et al. 2006). To reap the benefits of membership, "the Saudis liberalized their markets and restructured their legal regimes" and "fostered a more open and balanced economy" creating an environment in which "there will be countless new opportunities for both Saudi and non-Saudi entrepreneurs in a wide scope of business interests" (Clatanoff et al., 2006, 4). Saudi Arabia is the world's 18th-top exporter (the largest oil exporter in the world, with roughly 90% of the country's total exports being petroleum and petroleum products) and the 31st-largest import market in the world. The Saudi GDP has risen significantly since its accession to the WTO, from roughly $328 billion in 2006 to $746 billion in 2014. The kingdom has signed new trade agreements and as of late 2015, it has never been a respondent or complainant in any WTO dispute. As such, the Saudis appear to be living up to the promise of liberal trade policies, economic prosperity, and an increase in cooperative relations.

Compliance with WTO rules and obligations is an aspect of membership that may conflict with a state or individual leader's domestic interests. One could view the WTO as a mechanism to help move states towards producing their most efficient goods. If a state does not produce a certain product the most efficiently, there is often the domestic pressure to protect that industry through trade barriers. Membership in the WTO comes with compliance agreements and market obligations, so if a state constructs barriers to trade to protect a domestic industry, the WTO dispute settlement system will work to lower those barriers and re-open trade. There is a growing literature on compliance with WTO dispute settlement rulings,[18] and generally those found in violation of their WTO obligations act within a reasonable amount of time to correct the infractions (Wilson, 2007). Compliance is not without its problems. Extension of the implementation period is often requested, incomplete measures are taken requiring further WTO action, and some implementation measures are never enacted (Davey, 2009). Compliance tends to happen more quickly in cases where the violation can be rectified through administrative action rather than legislative action (Wilson, 2007). In fact, very rarely do cases reach the level of the labelling-requirement dispute at the beginning of this chapter. Relatively few cases have ever reached the stage in which retaliation has been requested and/or authorized by the DSB, and in those cases the parties have continued negotiations to solve the dispute.

China provides an interesting case. Although the United States would disagree (see Chapter 2), China has a respectable record of compliance with adverse rulings by the DSB, especially in comparison to the United States (Zhang and Li, 2014). So, why does China generally comply with adverse findings in the DSB? China's top priority is economic growth, and as such the country is concerned about its reputation, both as a "credible rule player in the international community" and as a leader in the WTO (Zhang and Li, 2014, 152–153). China does not want to upset its trading partners or damage the legitimacy of the WTO. "Being the central driving force behind economic globalization, the wellbeing of the WTO is therefore imperative to China's long-term objective," its peaceful rise to world power. Thus, "upholding the legitimacy of the WTO and maintaining amicable relations with trading partners" is critical and could be in jeopardy if China fails to comply with DSB rulings (Zhang and Li, 2014, 152). Ironically, China represents a real-world illustration of the arguments of economic liberals—embrace free trade, experience economic growth, cooperate in international institutions, and benefit from globalization.

TABLE 3.2 Liberalism and the WTO

Liberal Thought	Theoretical Tenet	WTO Example
Laissez-faire Liberalism	The role of the individual is at the heart of capitalism. Economic freedom and virtually unregulated free markets are necessary for individuals to reach their full potential. The invisible hand promotes efficient allocation of resources and peaceful commercial interactions between states.	Through trade obligations mandated by membership, the WTO seeks to prevent unnecessary interference on individual ambitions in a free market. Lowering trade barriers and liberalizing banking sectors allows individuals to pursue their economic goals.
Comparative Advantage	States should use their resources most effectively by producing what they are most efficient at making and trade for everything else. Trade is a positive-sum game as everyone can benefit through the free exchange of goods and services.	Saudi Arabia joined the WTO to reap the benefits of free trade. Utilizing their resources efficiently, 90% of their total exports are petroleum products.
Keynesianism	Promote the smooth functioning of the international economy through a combination of the invisible hand with domestic and international regulations and norms.	The WTO promotes the norm of free trade by requiring the removal of trade barriers. Free trade promotes economic growth and the free play of market forces.
Neoliberalism	Promotion of cooperation and interdependence through trade and development. Capitalism is the key to economic growth and development. State interests are pursued through free trade.	The WTO is a positive-sum game as all states can benefit through free trade. Although often domestically risky, leaders generally abide by adverse rulings in the DSB within a reasonable amount of time. China seeks a peaceful rise to world power through economic growth, hence they are worried about their reputation as a trading partner and the legitimacy of the WTO. As such, China has a respectable record of complying with DSB rulings.

Conclusion

The neoliberal focus on international institutions proposes one last element for consideration. How much power and influence can be exercised by the institutions themselves? There is an element of neoliberal research focused on the **principal-agent theory**. This line of inquiry involves how much authority states are willing to entrust to international institutions. States are the principals and they delegate authority and tasks to institutions as their agents. While institutions are controlled by the preferences and ultimately the votes of their members, many develop powerful bureaucracies that operate as if the organization was independent. It is possible that there is widespread belief that these organizations have their own decision-making authority as illustrated through proclamations by political leaders, the media, and the public, such as, "The UN should do something about the crisis in Syria." Perhaps such statements are simply to abrogate the responsibility held by the members, but institutions are generally only as good as their member states. If the states do not want to do something, the institution cannot go it alone. Some institutions, however, are designed for independence. The International Court of Justice, for example, is an independent judicial body affiliated with the UN and was designed to be so. It is possible in the future we will see more institutions designed to act independently and even those designed as supranational organizations that will have actual authority over their members. This is a highly contested idea as sovereignty still reigns supreme in international relations. Consider the following question, "How much power are you comfortable with institutions, such as the United Nations or WTO, having?" Ultimately, would the world be a better place if international institutions could make independent decisions about global order?

The liberal framework of cooperation, interdependence, democracy, and capitalism provides a counter to the realist focus on power and security. The various strains of liberalism help enhance understanding of the role of states, non-state actors, and trade and markets in global politics. The case studies highlight the application of liberal thinking to security and economic issues. The similarities and differences in explanations for behavior between liberalism and realism, plus the three critical theories in the following chapters, are discussed in Chapter 7. The following three chapters introduce the approaches to studying world politics that are critical of these two main theories and have differing ontological and epistemological approaches to interpreting the world around us.

Key Terms

Capitalism
Complex interdependence
Corn Laws
Democratic peace theory
End of history
Functionalism
Game theory
Globalization
Just war theory
Keynesianism
Laissez faire
Monetarism
Natural law
Neofunctionalism
Paradox of thrift
Principal-agent theory
Republic
Social contract
Transnational
World Health Organization (WHO)

For Further Reading

Fukuyama, Francis. 1992. *The End of History and the Last Man Standing*. New York: Free Press.

Kant, Immanuel. 1996. "Perpetual Peace: A Philosophical Sketch." In John A. Vasquez. *Classics in International Relations*, Third Edition. New Jersey: Prentice Hall. Original published in 1795.

Keohane, Robert O. 1984. *After Hegemony: Cooperation and Discord in the World Political Economy.* Princeton: Princeton University Press.

Keynes, John Maynard. 2005. *The Economic Consequences of the Peace.* New York: Cosimo Classics. Originally published in 1919.

Locke, John. 1689. *Two Treatises of Government.* P. Laslett (ed.), Cambridge: Cambridge University Press, 1988.

Smith, Adam. 1964. *The Wealth of Nations.* New York: Dutton. This is a reprint; *The Wealth of Nations* was first published in 1776.

Endnotes

[1] Labeling requirements included in this amendment are for poultry, beef, and ground pork. Labels would remain for commodities such as lamb, seafood, venison, fruits, and vegetables.

[2] North Korea is arguably the most secretive regime in the world, and thus the actual figures are unknown outside the regime.

[3] Liberalism means something different in the US political context and it is important not to confuse them. As an ideological position in the United States, liberals generally seek a larger role for the government in promoting social programs. This is not the same thing as the theory of liberalism in international relations that is built on the principle of a limited role for the government. The state plays a larger role as liberalism evolves over time, and economic liberals, discussed later in this chapter, since the 1980s are akin to those considered conservatives in the United States political context.

[4] Grotius is considered the father of international law even though Jeremy Bentham coined the term in the eighteenth century.

[5] In this study, Babst found that there were several cases that came close to qualifying as wars between independent nations with elective governments: War of 1812, US Civil War, South African War, and WWII. For the reasons why he discounts them, see Babst, Dean V. 1964. "Elective Governments—A Force for Peace." *The Wisconsin Sociologist.* Vol. 3, No. 1: 9–14.

[6] For a discussion of the implications of democracy imposition, see Cederman, Lars-Erik, and Kristian S. Gleditsch. 2004. "Conquest and Regime Change: An Evolutionary Model of the Spread of Democracy

and Peace." *International Studies Quarterly* 48(3): 603–29. Patten, Chris. 2003. "Democracy Doesn't Flow From the Barrel of a Gun." *Foreign Policy* 138 (September/October): 40–44; Pevehouse, Jon C. 2002. "Democracy from the Outside-In? International Organizations and Democratization." *International Organizations* 56(3): 515–49; Mansfield, Edward D., and Jack Snyder. 2002. "Incomplete Democratization and the Outbreak of Military Disputes." *International Studies Quarterly* 46(4): 529–50.

[7] Neoliberalism here refers to neoliberal institutionalism as a school of thought. Later in the chapter, neoliberalism as an economic policy will be discussed.

[8] The IMF and the International Bank for Reconstruction and Development (IBRD) created in 1944 came to be known as the Bretton Woods system. The IBRD is now one of five institutions of the World Bank Group. The WTO emerged from the General Agreement on Tariffs and Trade (GATT) created in 1948.

[9] It is important to remember that not all assistance from international economic institutions creates positive results. Some economic bailouts by the IMF have resulted in unintended negative consequences to the recipient countries.

[10] To read more about Jonathan Pollard's work as an Israeli spy in the United States, see Doug Stanglin, "Jonathan Pollard: Israel's prolific American spy" in *USA Today*, April 1, 2014. He was released on parole in November 2015. http://www.usatoday.com/story/news/world/2014/04/01/pollard-bio-israeli-spy-imprisoned/7161963/.

[11] Structural realists also employ game theory. Common games include stag hunt, chicken, and the Prisoner's Dilemma. For a comprehensive overview of game theory, see Michael Maschler, et al *Game Theory*. 2013. Cambridge: Cambridge University Press. For a collection of essays on the use of game theory specifically by neoliberals, see Kenneth Oye, *Cooperation Under Anarchy*. 1986. Princeton: Princeton University Press.

[12] The most famous discussion of tit-for-tat can be found in Robert Axelrod, *The Evolution of Cooperation*. 1984. New York: Basic Books. A full explanation of the live-and-let live system in trench warfare can be found in Chapter 4 of Axelrod's book.

[13] For more on compliance systems, see Ronald B. Mitchell. 1994. "Regime Design Matters: International Oil Pollution and Treaty Compliance," *International Organization*, Vol. 48, No. 3: 425–458.

[14] Comparative advantage exists even if a country is inefficient at making every product. If country A is better at making everything than country B, country A is still not equally efficient at producing every product. It produces some things better than others. Thus country A should produce what it is more efficient in making, and country B should produce what it is most efficient in making even if B is not as efficient as A. Both will still benefit because they are producing what each is best at making. Absolute advantage exists when country A is better at making one product and country B is better at making another. In this case, the benefits of trade are obvious.

[15] For a full list of policy prescriptions in the Washington Consensus, see http://www.who.int/trade/glossary/story094/en/. Accessed July 28, 2015.

[16] To read more on the criticisms of globalization, see Joseph Stiglitz 2002. *Globalization and Its Discontents.* New York: W.W. Norton; Thomas L. Friedman. 2008. *Hot, Flat, and Crowded: Why We Need a Green Revolution—And How It Can Renew America.* New York: Farrar, Straus and Giroux; and Paul Collier, 2007. *The Bottom Billion: Why the Poorest Countries are Failing and What Can Be Done about It.* Oxford: Oxford University Press.

[17] To become a member of the WTO, states must sign a series of pre-existing agreements including the GATT, General Agreement on Trade in Services (GATS), Trade-Related International Property Rights (TRIPS), Technical Barriers to Trade (TBT), and Sanitary and Phytosanitary Standards (SPS).

[18] See Bruce Wilson. 2007. "Compliance by WTO Members with Adverse WTO Dispute Settlement Rulings: The Record to Date." *Journal of International Economic Law* 10 (2): 397–403 and Xiaowen Zhang and Xiaoling Li. 2014. "The Politics of Compliance with Adverse WTO Dispute Settlement Rulings in China." *Journal of Contemporary China* Vol. 23, No. 85: 143–160. For arguments concerning why states comply with their commitments generally, see Abram Chayes and Antonia Handler Chayes. 1993. "On Compliance." *International Organizations* 47: 175–205 and Beth Simmons. 1998. "Compliance with International Agreements." *The Annual Review of Political Science* 1: 75–93.

CHAPTER 4

Economic Structuralism

"The history of all hitherto existing society is the history of class struggles."

—Marx and Engels, The Communist Manifesto

I n 1999, protestors effectively disrupted and ultimately shut down the World Trade Organization (WTO) Ministerial Conference in Seattle, Washington. The confrontation pitted unlikely anti-globalization bedfellows against the international organization tasked with deciding international trade policy and disputes. On the streets, members of environmental groups and labor unions, representatives from nongovernmental groups, students, and many other anti-business groups formed a coalition that was united in their protests and criticism of the WTO, particularly its lack of transparency. This was the public face of what became known as the Battle of Seattle. Behind the public demonstrations, less developed states were aligning themselves against the more powerful members, particularly the United States. Ultimately, "more than 40 African, Caribbean, and Latin American countries had united in protest against the way poor countries were being bullied by the rich and the way their concerns were being marginalised" (Vidal, 1999). The Doha Round of trade negotiations began two years later (see Chapter 1). The breakdown of these talks over the past 14 years signals that the schism between the wealthy and poor states persists. The failure of neoliberal economic policies to solve the chronic problems in developing states, such as the lack of economic convergence between developing and developed states, the vulnerabilities to external factors faced by developing states, the lack of technology transfers, and the general social inequalities are all important reasons to understand and study the **economic structuralism** paradigm.

The paradigmatic debate between realism and liberalism explained in Chapter 1 was followed by a wave of critiques from alternative perspectives that we cover in the next three chapters. As described in the previous chapter, liberal economic policies assume that all states benefit from free and open trade and less governmental interference in the marketplace (although states may not benefit equally). However, the gap between the have and have-nots in the international system has led less-developed states to question the fundamental economic and political motivations of advanced states. Economic structuralism occupies a theoretical space focusing on how states are arranged or situated in the international system based on their economic standing or level of wealth, as well as how the many are exploited by the few, both within societies as well as between states in the international system.

Proponents of economic structuralism argue that in order to understand how states behave in the international system, one must examine not only the historical economic development of states, but the subsequent political and social relationships between them, particularly the exploitative nature of wealthy states vis-à-vis poor states. Wealthy states' domination of intergovernmental organizations such as the WTO and the World Bank, as well as less favorable terms of trade imposed on developing states, creates what many see as a neo-imperial system. While developed countries may no longer physically occupy states as in the colonial period, the economic ties and IGO policies serve to keep developing and less-developed countries in a perpetual state of dependency, locked into unequal economic relationships with more advanced states. These different levels of economic development cause theorists and politicians alike to debate the merits of the liberal economic model advocated by the wealthy advanced economies, specifically the idea that less developed states should follow the same path to development as the industrialized, capitalist states of the west.

The 1991 fall of the Soviet Union and the end of the Cold War led to the decline of this perspective. However, the Great Recession, the global spread of the Occupy Wall Street movement, the dominance of multinational corporations, the growth and reach of international capital, the depth and scope of global poverty and underdevelopment, as well as recent electoral victories of left-leaning governments in Europe and

Latin America have breathed new life into many of the ideas inherent in this paradigm. Economic structuralism, with its Marxist roots, is essentially a philosophy that focuses on economic and political emancipation and liberation. It appeals to those who are marginalized within societies as well as the have-nots in the international community of states.

Roots and Evolution of Economic Structuralism

This chapter focuses on the evolution of economic structuralism as a theory of international relations beginning with the critique of capitalism offered by Karl Marx and Frederick Engels. We then turn to the contributions of John Hobson and Vladimir Lenin to Marxist-based theories of war and imperialism, followed by the **dependency** and world-systems framework proposed by modern-day scholars. In addition, we highlight the contributions of Karl Kautsky and Rosa Luxemburg, Marxist activists in pre-World War I German politics, to illustrate how these ideas moved beyond a theoretical exercise of academics. As leading members of the German Socialist movement, Kautsky and Luxemburg not only provided intellectual contributions to the paradigm, they also actively fought for the Marxist economic and political goals of their day. We will also explore the work of Antonio Gramsci, who wrote during the interwar period and focused on cultural factors and the concept of hegemony as a way capitalists control the masses. Finally, we offer a critical assessment of economic structuralism and demonstrate how this perspective might have value for states struggling against the impulses of globalization.

Central Assumptions

In spite of its various strands (**Marxism**, neo-Marxism, radical theory, historical materialism), economic structuralists share some key central assumptions. Recall, assumptions are the foundations of a theory that help to clarify the ontological perspective of that theory. That is, assumptions allow political theorists to state clearly their view of how the world works. We focus on the following four assumptions of economic structuralism:

- Economic class is the unit of analysis and the key actor in the international system.
- Economic interests are the primary motivation for states (often referred to as economic determinism).

- The international system is hierarchical based on capitalism, rather than anarchical based on power; thus, global capitalism determines the position and behavior of states.
- International politics is inherently conflictual.

The first assumption is that economic class is the key unit of analysis. From a classical Marxist perspective, in the advanced, late stages of capitalism there are two classes within a society—the capitalist class, or the **bourgeoisie**, and the worker class, or the **proletariat**. In classical Marxism, the primary focus was on the domestic economy and the division between classes within a society. From an economic structuralist perspective, this class conflict is elevated to one between and among states based on national wealth, resulting in three distinct areas. The structure of the international system consists of the **core** and the **periphery**. The wealthy, industrialized countries in the international system constitute the core, while the poorest countries make up the periphery. A third class of states, the **semi-periphery**, represent a group of states that are no longer classified as poor, but have yet to achieve the economic status of a core state. The relationships among these three groups of states are the foci of economic structuralists.

If, as economic structuralism asserts, class is the key of global societies, then economics must be the driving force or motivation in international politics. Whereas realists see the economy as one component of state power, economic structuralists assume that all political behavior is determined by the economic motivations of the elites within a state. Thus, their second assumption asserts that political outcomes or policies are determined by the economic power and interests of elites within states as well as by economically powerful states in the international system. Such actors do not necessarily take into account the national interests of the state. In fact, they would view the state as a vehicle for elites to pursue their personal economic goals rather than the goals of the state. In other words, the state is simply a tool for the dominant class.

Economic structuralists are not as concerned about anarchy as they are about stratification in the international system. Therefore, the third assumption is that there is a hierarchical or stratified international system based on economic standing. Economic structuralists consider wealth as the most important variable and it is the distribution of this wealth that defines the structure of the international system: the wealthiest states on top and the poorest on the bottom. Given that there are far fewer wealthy states than poor ones, the arrangement of states in the international system resembles a pyramid. Developing states that have gained in economic power but have yet to challenge the wealthy states occupy the middle strata (see Figure 4.1). Further, the different classes of states have different, often opposing, economic interests. As we will see, economic structuralists argue that these three groups exist within states as well. For example, within a particular country such as Brazil, there is a core area usually found in the major metropolitan areas where the majority of capital exists and a periphery which is usually the poorest region in the country. The semi-periphery occupies the area within the state where economic development is occurring, but at a level still beneath the core. For economic structuralists, anarchy where power trumps all is not the major concern, rather what is important is

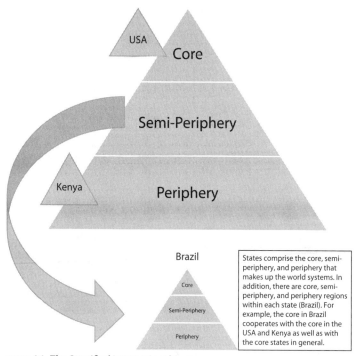

States comprise the core, semi-periphery, and periphery that makes up the world systems. In addition, there are core, semi-periphery, and periphery regions within each state (Brazil). For example, the core in Brazil cooperates with the core in the USA and Kenya as well as with the core states in general.

FIGURE 4.1 The Stratified International System.

the level of economic development among and within states and how it influences or even constrains state behavior.

Economic structuralists also assume the inevitability of conflict within states. They argue that class conflict and exploitation go hand in hand. In economic structuralism, this conflict is transferred to the international system as wars are fought on behalf of the wealthy class (states), rather than for territory, security, or even political ideology. This conflict is structural in nature. The international economic hierarchy is determined by rich states and the hegemon at the international system level and by economic elites and their interests at the state level. Economic structuralists agree with realists regarding the inevitability of conflict and structural nature of the international system. They differ by insisting that the structure arises from economics rather than military measures of power.

Economic structuralism offers a cogent critique of both liberalism and realism focusing on the inequities of an unfettered marketplace on the one hand and the misplaced attention on power rather than economics on the other. Economic structuralists agree with realists about the importance of history, but count on economic history to explain the development of the structure of the international system rather than political history to explain the traditional power structure emphasized by realists. Moreover, economic structuralism is critical of the realist emphasis on the distribution of power and the role of the state. For a realist, the state seeks security in pursuit of its national interests. For an economic structuralist, the state is merely a tool for the wealthy to seek economic gain for themselves. They agree with liberals that the economy is an equally important element of international relations. However, they vehemently disagree when it comes to who benefits within the state (they do not see this as a positive-sum game), who wins and who loses, and the proper role of the state. Economic structuralists view capitalism as the major source of conflict in the international system.

How and why did these assumptions develop? The next section introduces the economic theory of Karl Marx and his role in forging such thinking. In the process, we will see how the assumptions of economic structuralism emerged. We then consider the contributors to the evolution of Marxism as well as the other theories associated with economic structuralism (see Figure 4.2).

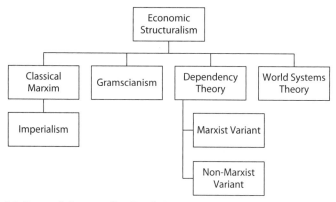

FIGURE 4.2 Economic Structuralism Family Tree.

Classical Marxism and Imperialism

Although the Industrial Revolution brought efficiency to markets and wealth to many nations, not all individuals within industrialized societies benefited from the modern capitalist system. In spite of the promise offered by liberal economic policies, newly urbanized nineteenth-century workers in manufacturing plants in Europe's major cities faced unsafe working conditions, poverty, and malnutrition in crowded tenements. Between 1700 and 1830 in England, the urban population increased from 15% to 34% in cities of at least 5,000 inhabitants. If we consider cities of at least 2,000, these figures rise from 23.1% in 1800 to 42.8% in 1850 and 71.3% in 1910. By 1830, London alone had 1.5 million inhabitants; by 1851 that number reached 2.4 million. Industrialization drove this rapid level of urbanization (Bairoch and Goertz, 1986). The economic structuralist worldview that describes unequal economic relationships between states started as a commentary on living conditions and the plight of the worker, or the proletariat, in the great human migration from farm to factory during the Industrial Revolution where the bourgeoisie, or capitalists, controlled the means of production.

Pioneers in the Field

In 1867, Karl Marx (1818–1883) published the first volume of *Das Kapital,* offering a critique of the dominant liberal and capitalist views of the day.[1] This seminal work was the culmination of critical thinking about the repressive and exploitative nature of capitalism. After first meeting Frederick Engels (1820–1895) in Cologne in 1842, the duo collaborated in writing such works as *The Holy Family* in 1845, *The German Ideology* in 1846, and the *Communist Manifesto* in 1848, as well as helped to establish the **First International** (1864–1876).[2] The philosophy of Marx and Engels resulted from the confluence of several factors. We focus on two here: dialectical materialism and working conditions during the Industrial Revolution.

In his youth, Marx studied the works of Georg Hegel (1770–1831), the German philosopher who argued that societal evolution was a unique process of dialectic progression: that history moves forward in a dialectic manner with new ideas repetitively challenging and supplanting old ones as time moves on. Marx adopted this dialectical process and came to the conclusion that the dominant economic system of his day, capitalism (the thesis), would be challenged by the class struggle of the oppressed workers (the anti-thesis), resulting in socialism, the new economic system (the synthesis). The result is dialectical materialism: a conflict of economics and classes rather than Hegel's conflict of ideas. Marx developed a theory that described the evolution of **epochs** in history based on the **mode of production** or how the economic production within a society is organized. The epochs of economic development started with primitive societies and then moved to slave societies, feudalism, and capitalism. This process would ultimately end with socialism. In each of these epochs, the mode of production defined the social relations within a society: slave to owner, serf to lord, and as a result of the Industrial Revolution, worker to capitalist (in Marxist vocabulary, proletariat to bourgeoisie). These relationships established the economic structure of society such that "the antique state was the state of the slave owners for the purpose of holding down slaves in check. The feudal state was the organ of the nobility for the oppression of the serfs and dependent farmers. The modern representative state is the tool of the capitalist exploiters of wage labor" (Engels 1902, 208–209). Changes in the mode of production led to class conflict, particularly when the class of wage laborers resisted conditions created by capitalism. How might this happen?

Marx argued that human history moved forward as a function of economic development, that is, the path of human history lies in the production process. Each economic epoch consisted of the **means of**

production and **relations of production** that together comprised the **economic base** (or infrastructure) of a society. This economic base, in turn, influenced the **superstructure** of a society, which consisted of laws, institutions, and culture. Marx (1977, 389) wrote that

> In the social production of their existence, men enter into definite relations that are indispensable and independent of their will, relations of production which correspond to a definite stage of development of their material productive forces. The sum total of these relations of production constitutes the economic structure of society, the real foundation, on which arises a legal and political superstructure and to which correspond definite forms of social consciousness. The mode of production of material life conditions the social, political, and intellectual life process in general.

Thus, in each epoch, the mode of production created the rulers and the ruled. Moreover, each mode of production (e.g. feudalism, capitalism) devised methods of creating wealth for the rulers. With innovation, the means of production changed over time, leading to a change in the relations of production. Eventually, existing economic and social relations became obsolete. New relations of production (rules) enabled the dominant class to take advantage of the new means of production. For Marx, the modes of production evolved and changed over time at a greater rate than the relations of production. Thus, class propelled history forward as each epochal mode of production developed inherent contradictions that ultimately led to its collapse.

The socialist revolution envisioned by Marx and Engels would occur in capitalist societies that had already experienced the Industrial Revolution, likely in Britain or industrialized parts of Germany. The working conditions associated with the Industrial Revolution in urban areas served as the second major influence on the philosophy of Marx and Engels. They observed that individuals who once engaged in agricultural production where their own skills, land, and animals provided the sustenance for daily living now worked in a factory using tools they did not own, producing items they could not afford to buy or consume. The worker sold the only thing he owned—his labor—to the capitalist owner of the factory. Marx described the plight of the factory worker in *Wage Labour and Capital* (1970, 20), suggesting that the "labourer becomes worthless. . . . as labour becomes more unsatisfying, more repulsive, competition increases and wages decrease. The worker tries to keep up the amount of wages by working more . . . The result is that the more he works the less wages he receives, and for the simple reason that he competes to that extent with his fellow workers." The former farmer was now an exploited wage laborer. Just as in the previous epoch, the serf sold a portion of his labor to the feudal lord, the labor of the factory worker "is a commodity which its possessor, the wage-worker, sells to capital." By the end of the 19th century, 80% of the active population were wage earners in Britain (Beaud, 2001), a percentage that Marxists undoubtedly believed would eventually make up the alienated masses who were destined to overthrow the capitalist order.

Marx argued that workers added value in the production process but failed to share in the profits. Let's consider how value is added to any product by thinking about a shirt or dress that might be hanging in your closet. What are the costs associated with production? First, there are design costs. The time, effort, talent, and skill of the design entre-preneur constitute the beginning of the production process. Second, there are fixed costs at the factory (lighting, machines, and building costs). Third, there are some variable costs as the price of thread and fabric might change over time. Last, there is the cost of labor. The appli-cation of labor to the raw materials of thread and fabric creates value, what Marx called surplus value. Because the employer has total con-trol of the wage structure, the worker never shares in the profits. She already received the minimum wage necessary to secure her labor.

According to Marx (1990, 342), the capitalist system thrived on the wage labor of the worker, and in fact, would die without it: "Capital is dead labour, that, vampire-like, only lives by sucking living labour, and lives the more the more labour it sucks. The time during which the labourer works is the time during which the capitalist consumes the labour-power he has purchased of him." Ultimately, this situa-tion would lead the wage laborer to experience a sense of alienation as "the more value he creates, the more valueless, the more unworthy he becomes . . . labour produces for the rich wonderful things . . . It produces palaces—but for the worker, hovels . . . It replaces labour by machines—but for some of the workers it throws back to a barbarous type of labour, and the other workers it turns into machines. It produces intelligence—but for the worker idiocy, cretinism" (Marx 2007, 71). The thoughts, beliefs, and attitudes of an individual no longer mattered. The worker became another cog in the factory wheel. Furthermore, this exchange of labor for wages was inherently unequal, with the capitalist class reaping greater benefit than the working class. In fact, Marx contended that this inequity began the moment that humanity moved away from tribal relationships; disparate classes emerged and have remained in existence since.

Having established the realities of the working and living conditions of the wage laborer and the subsequent relationship between the proletariat and the bourgeoisie in the most recent epoch of capitalism, Marx turned to an explanation of the contradictions inherent in the capitalist mode of production. According to his **theory of surplus value**, the subsistence wage that workers earned did not equal what labor was actually worth. The difference between the amount paid and the true value of labor was the surplus, that is, the profit realized by the capitalist owner. As described in the production example above, most costs of production are fixed, leaving labor as the primary variable cost in the process. In order to increase profits, owners suppressed wages more and more over time. The theory also assumed that wages could remain at subsistence levels due to an ever-increasing number of workers available. Eventually this would lead to **underconsumption** in the market, Marx's second contradiction inherent in capitalism. This concept built on the consequences of the surplus value of labor. Over time, fewer and fewer in society would have disposable income due to the subsistent wages paid to the working class. With fewer buyers in the market, underconsumption and over production would occur. Recall that economic liberals claim to solve this problem by suggesting that the invisible hand creates equilibrium regarding supply and demand in the market. Marx directly challenged this with his contradictions to capitalism.

Given these inherent contradictions, Marx derived three laws of capitalism that would eventually lead to its ruin (collapse): the **law of disproportionality**, the **law of the concentration of capital**, and the **law of decreasing profits**. The law of disproportionality addresses the twin problems of surplus and underconsumption. Due to the subsistent wage earned by the worker, the cost of production in terms of labor prices decreases. Increased efficiency leads to a surplus of finished goods, as workers are increasingly unable to purchase what they produced. In the meantime, the increased efficiency in production leads to an increase in profits as the law of the concentration of capital indicated that capital lands in the hands of the few (the bourgeoisie) while there was a parallel increase in the impoverished masses. As this capital and surplus accumulates, there is an eventual decrease in the rate of return, or what Marx referred to as the law of decreasing profits. This creates a disincentive for further investment by the owners of the means of production. Competition culls the capitalist herd so that only the wealthiest and strongest capitalists survive, further concentrating the wealth into the hands of the few. Eventually the exploited workers are laid off, becoming part of the reserve army of unemployed that develop a collective conscious culminating in a workers' revolution—assuming that they are not deceived by religious or nationalist interests. Nationalism and religiosity, according to Marx, were critical functions of the capitalist society and extensions of the economic and social injustice inherent in capitalism. They serve to distract the proletariat from their plight—especially religion, which Marx referred to as the "opiate of the masses."

The influences on Marx and his resulting analysis took place during a time that coincided with great social, economic, and political upheaval in Europe. Like realism and liberalism, much of the theoretical development of Marxism and economic structuralism occurred as a reaction to historical events. The **1848 revolutions** that broke out across Europe seemed to be the start of what Marx and Engels called for; however, state after state defeated the disparate attempts, effectively removing any threat from a truly united—that is, international—proletariat revolution. In fact, there has never been a workers' revolution as Marx envisioned. However, Marx provides a blueprint for subsequent thinkers and leaders to consider, specifically the historical nature of state economic development, the inequities inherent in capitalism, the disparate power arrangements between social classes, the economic nature of power, and ultimately who controlled the factors of production. Specifically, the writings of Marx and Engels influenced the socialist movements in countries all across Europe and North America during the late 19th and early 20th century. Their philosophy encompassed a cadre of arguments that appealed to the working class, the unemployed, and the property-less in a period of rapid economic growth. At the same time, there were demands for democratic reforms with perhaps the most important being the push for universal (male) suffrage and other political rights. Ultimately, the Marxist emphasis on emancipation of the worker fueled those interested in emancipation from the nobility and monarchical rule in Europe.

In the 1870s, European states engaged in a new wave of colonialism, not for the purpose of resettlement or discovery, but rather for the purpose of exploitation. **Imperialism** threw a theoretical bone to Marxist ideology by providing an explanation for the lack of an international proletariat revolution. One of the first to focus on a theory of imperialism was John A. Hobson (1858–1940), an English economist. Although not a Marxist, Hobson provided valuable insight into how imperialism provided capitalists with an avenue of international investment that seemingly cured the inherent ills or contradictions of capitalism perceived by Marx. Capitalists simply transferred the operation to a new market overseas in order to overcome the problems of overproduction, underconsumption, and the accumulation of capital identified by Marx as the holy trinity that would lead to revolution—that is, a domestic workers revolution.

As a reporter, Hobson covered the Second Boer's War (1899–1902) for the *Manchester Guardian* and came to the conclusion that the British diamond merchants manufactured the conflict in order to further their economic interests. He echoed this argument in *The War in South Africa* (1900, 197) stating that British troops were "fighting in order to place a small international oligarchy of mine owners and speculators in power at Pretoria. Englishmen will surely do well to recognize that the economic and political destinies of South Africa are, and seem likely to remain, in the hands of men most of whom are foreigners by origin, whose trade is finance, and whose trade interests are not chiefly British." In his *Imperialism: A Study* (1938), Hobson continued his critique of capitalist states' conquest of new lands for the purpose of occupation rather than settlement and for the purpose of resource extraction rather than migration. The state, in essence, lost control of decision-making to these capitalist financial interests. Hobson contended that it is not rational for states to engage in imperialistic activities and the subsequent wars it is surely to bring; however, the state has become a hostage to financial interests, which in turn have become the "governor of the imperial engine" (Hobson 1938, 59). Hobson concisely argued that the underconsumption endemic to capitalist states was the "taproot of imperialism," that is, the most central and dominant cause of imperialism.

Inspired in part by Hobson's work, Vladimir I. Lenin (1870–1924) applied the idea of class conflict and economic inequality to the international system in an attempt to explain the origins of World War I. In *Imperialism, the Highest Stage of Capitalism,* Lenin (1965, 72–73) outlined how the accumulation of capital reached great proportions, stating that "Firstly, there are monopolist capitalist combines in all advanced capitalist countries; secondly, a few rich countries, in which the accumulation of capital reaches gigantic proportions, occupy a monopolist position. An enormous 'superabundance of capital' has accumulated in the advanced countries." Furthermore, this super-abundant accumulation of capital occurred unevenly among the competing industrialized states, leading to what has been coined the **law of uneven development**.

Lenin agreed with Hobson that this surplus of capital could not be used to improve the standard of living for domestic workers by increasing wages, as this would decrease profits. Because the masses were impoverished and could not purchase any of the surplus inventories, it was necessary for monopolies to export this overripe capital to new markets. This was Marx's law of disproportionality applied to the international system. Thus, capital economies matured and sought land, resources, and more importantly, workers abroad as domestic opportunities decreased. In the process, capitalist states created dependent ones (colonies) that served as investments, new markets, and sources of food and raw materials for these new "metropoles."

According to Lenin (1965, 72), imperialism represented the ultimate form of capitalism, that is, "capitalism is commodity production at its highest stage of development, when labour power itself becomes a commodity." The workers in colonized states became the new proletariat of the international economic system. Thus, capitalist states competed with one another and carved up conquered lands to serve as an outlet for excess capital that eventually led to an unstable and potentially conflictual international system. The potential for conflict was thus two-fold: one was the conflictual relationship between the colonizer and the colonized, and the other was the inevitable conflict among capitalist states for scarce resources abroad. Lenin maintained that the proletariat class would not simply wither away; rather, a violent revolution was required. As for the important consequence of the growth of financial capital in relation to international politics, Lenin argued that it led to competition among wealthy states. This competition drove states to divide the rest of the world leading ultimately to the Great War.

Lenin was not without his critics, evidenced by the writings of Karl Kautsky (1854–1938) and Rosa Luxemburg (1871–1919). After the death of Friedrich Engels in 1895, Kautsky was considered one of the prominent Marxist scholars and he became the leader of the international socialist movement and the major theoretician of the Second International (1889–1916). Kautsky (1970, 44) offered an explanation for the continued dominance and expansion of capitalism, arguing that workers would fail to rise and stage a global proletariat revolution due to the fact that capitalist states could collude to create a system of "ultra-imperialism."[3] He provided a very succinct and limited definition of imperialism stating that it "is a product of highly developed industrial capitalism. It consists in the impulse of every industrial nation to conquer and annex an ever greater agrarian zone, with no regard to what nations live there" (Kautsky 1970, 41). This impulse was driven by the fact, according to Kautsky, that industry expanded quicker than agricultural production, requiring capitalist states to seek agrarian land overseas. Rather than competing with rival states for such land, capitalists can and should develop cartels to jointly dominate in a new system of "ultra-imperialism." This new system of subjugation in the agrarian zones "will only come to an end when either their populations or the proletariat of the industrialized capitalist countries have grown strong enough to throw off the capitalist yoke. This side of imperialism can only be overcome by socialism" (Kautsky 1970, 44). In essence, Kautsky (1970, 46) replaced imperialism for capitalism in Marx's analysis and argued for a continued struggle against "a holy alliance of the imperialists."

Lenin's *Imperialism* was in many ways a rebuttal to the ideas of Kautsky. Lenin (1939, 91) wrote that "the characteristic feature of imperialism is not industrial, but finance capital . . . The characteristic feature of imperialism is precisely that it strives to annex not only agrarian territories, but even highly industrialized regions."[4] A comparison between Lenin and Kautsky illustrates their different interpretations and thus implementation of Marxist philosophy. Lenin viewed imperialism as inevitable while Kautsky saw it as a policy choice for capitalists. Lenin argued that the imperializing capital was a combination of both industrial and finance capital, while Kautsky limited his interpretation to only industrial capital. Consequently, Lenin viewed both the agricultural and industrial regions as areas of imperialism, while Kautsky argued that agrarian zones defined imperialism. As a revolutionary, Lenin's answer was a class approach, while Kautsky's reformist view focused on a national approach; in fact, he denounced violent overthrow as an option. Lenin viewed Kautsky as a bourgeois reformer—and a non-Marxist one at that. Kautsky argued that Lenin was simply wrong in how he defined imperialism, arguing that capitalism can go through a new phase of joint exploitation whereby the finance capitalist in the great powers worked together in their oppression of the proletariat. As a consequence, the great powers could avoid a war, if they so desired.

This schism between the two leading figures in the socialist movement spelled the end of Kautsky's influence and the domination of Lenin. It also led to the primacy of the Russian arm of the movement, while political repression and World War I led to the end of the socialist movement in Germany until its revival in the 1920s. Kautsky's contribution was his interpretation of Marxism as socialist orthodoxy, and today scholars are revisiting Kautsky's arguments and actions concluding that he "was a more consistent revolutionary Marxist than Lenin and the Bolsheviks" (Leier 1995, 373). Kautsky's call for peaceful revolution, a true revolution of the masses rather than a dictatorship of the proletariat and party control like the Bolsheviks, reframe Lenin as the renegade rather than Kautsky (Donald, 1993). We see in Kautsky's interpretation of Marx an argument that resonates with today's generation, with globalization (along with capitalism) as the target of ire among the masses.

A contemporary of Kautsky and Lenin, Rosa Luxemburg argued consistently that the only answer to capitalism and its imperialistic nature was a socialist revolution and not nationalist reform. In fact, she came to disavow both the Marxist revisionist tendencies of many of her reformist contemporaries, such as Kautsky, as well as the bureaucratic and centralized approach brewing in Russia. Like Marx and Kautsky, Luxemburg was an academic by training who was also an active member in the socialist movements arising in Europe. Specifically, she was concerned about the role of the state vis-à-vis the individual, specifically the worker. Consistent with Marxist philosophy, Luxemburg argued in articles and pamphlets that the clash between the proletariat and bourgeoisie was a goal, a necessary one, for the socialist revolution to occur. Thus she believed that there needed to be constant criticism of the socialist movement in order to move it forward. The experiences from the failed 1848 revolutions across Europe were at the forefront of her mind as she argued that the masses turned to national collectivist activity rather than the true Marxist mission of international proletariat emancipation. At the same time, she argued that labor unions and labor movement victories were shortsighted and served to derail the ultimate goal of socialist revolution. She blamed revisionists, those who re-interpreted Marxist philosophy, for leading the masses astray and argued such in her book *Reform or Revolution* (1900).

Luxemburg was also critical of Lenin's approach and views on party organization, believing that such centralization was an anathema to true socialism, an argument similar to Kautsky's. She observed that the dominance of a single party was "simply taking the conductor's baton out of the hands of the bourgeoisie and putting it into the hands of a socialist Central Committee" (Ettinger 1979, *xxxiii*). In 1904, she published *Organizational Questions of the Russian Social Democracy,* wherein she argued, "ultra-centralism asked by Lenin is full of the sterile spirit of the overseer. It is not a positive and creative spirit. Lenin's concern is not so much to make the activity of the party more fruitful as to control the party—to narrow the movement rather than to develop it, to bind rather than to unify it."

Like most other Marxists, Luxemburg opposed German imperialism and entry into the looming war. She advocated more revolutionary tactics and policies in the name of the socialist movement while maintaining an anti-war stance. When the war finally broke out, Luxemburg called for general strikes throughout Germany, but they failed to materialize. In fact, the German Social Democratic Party (SPD) supported the war, signifying that nationalism prevailed over their socialist party platform, a move that devastated Luxemburg. Here she saw the true Marxist call for a united front ignored in favor of state politics. Luxemburg's legacy and contribution to Marxism is her interpretation of Marxism as pure socialism requiring revolution and not merely reform.

Marx, Hobson, and Lenin all argued, in essence, that for all of its faults, imperialism would bring economic development to colonial economies . . . eventually. After all, this was part of the capitalist economic trajectory that first occurred in European states and was simply transported to the rest of the world via imperialism. Once the international working masses grasped their economic plight and the conditions (laws) laid out by Marx were realized, the much-anticipated proletariat revolution would occur and become a global workers' revolution. In the meantime, Lenin co-opted Marxism to fit the political motives associated with the Russian Revolution and the new Marxist/

Leninist philosophy became a model for other socialist movements. In doing so, Lenin and the Russian Revolution hijacked the theoretical development of Marxism, driving the contributions of revolutionary theorists like Karl Kautsky and Rosa Luxemburg to the background.

During the interwar period of the early 20th century, Antonio Gramsci (1891–1937) continued the pattern of theoretician and activism prevalent in the development of Marxist philosophy. Grasmci led several protests in the Italian industrial town of Turin, particularly those against the auto manufacturer Fiat. He questioned why the Italian working class was not revolutionary in the 1920s and 1930s and why they ultimately yielded to fascism after Mussolini came to power in 1922. His answer was that the working class lacked power, while the ruling elites had a monopoly on it—that is, the elites held a hegemonic status within the state. Here hegemony refers to how elites or the dominant class rule in the domestic arena in order to maintain the status quo. Gramsci contended that Marx and Lenin placed too much emphasis on economics while ignoring social and cultural factors; in other words, he argued for the need to put politics back into the equation. This meant that Gramsci's vision of the role of the state was much larger compared to Marx. Accepting that the elite had captured the traditional institutions of government, the concept of the state must be expanded to include "the church, the educational system, the press, all the institutions which helped to create in people certain modes of behavior and expectations consistent with the hegemonic social order" (Cox 2010, 216).

For Gramsci, elites are able to maintain power when the "interests of the dominant class or state are inextricably tied to the interests of subordinate classes, and workers buy into the system even though they are being exploited" (Pease 2012, 81). Thus, elites have basically two options: coercion or consent. In utilizing coercion, elites apply both economic and political power to keep the subordinate classes in line. While this is a powerful tool, Gramsci argued that ideas and culture are even more powerful, leading to his preference for them as the tool of consent. The way to create intellectual hegemony is for the dominant class to formulate and propagate an ideology or worldview that furthers its own interests and then spreads or disseminates this view through the media and education system until the subordinate class accepts (if not internalizes) it.

The acceptance and internalization of the ideology solidified the power of the hegemonic class and subsequently, any opposition was viewed as criminal or illegitimate. Gramsci labeled the congruence between state power and prevailing ideology in society as the historic bloc. In essence, the ruling elite captured the subordinate groups by providing a societal view that went beyond economics and included elements of identity and culture. Here Gramsci tapped into the Marxist concept of the superstructure. Hegemony stemmed from consent rather than from domination and coercion. For any revolution to occur, subordinate groups must create a counter-hegemony based on some alternative or antithetical view in order to challenge the hegemonic class and subsequently, the historic bloc. Thus social movements and other emerging civil society organizations within the superstructure were paramount to mounting a challenge to the ideological hegemony of the ruling elite. Gramsci's emphasis on ideas provides a bridge to constructivism, a paradigm that is addressed in the next chapter.

Economic Structuralism and Dependency Theory

After World War II, liberal economists and government officials wanted to promote economic growth, in part, to fend off socialist and communist political leanings in newly independent states. However, Global South countries began to reject the liberal model of development promulgated by the rich states of the Global North, specifically the diffusion and modernization theories of development both of which included preconceived and linear steps of development. Given their dissatisfaction with these First World ideas about economic development, scholars, intellectuals, and leaders of the Global South sought out alternative explanations and paths to national wealth. They argued that it was unrealistic to expect newly independent countries to develop in the same manner as advanced states in the previous century when they "developed largely free from outside influence, and it would be nearly impossible for a state to recreate the historical structure of environment of the early developed nations" (Wiarda 1985, 135). Furthermore, the vestiges of imperialism and the continued advocacy of liberal economic and trade policies only served to "slow down and to control the economic development of the underdeveloped countries" (Baran 1957, 197). These individuals gravitated toward Marxist philosophy in search of answers and in doing so, moved the radical perspective of Marxism into the systemic theory of economic structuralism. Just as Marx argued that capitalism was exploiting the proletariat class, proponents of economic structuralism maintained that capitalism was exploiting a certain class of states, those located economically in the periphery of the international economic system.

The dependency, or *dependencia,* school emerged in Latin America in the 1950s as leaders and academics attempted to explain why economic growth was slow or stagnant compared to the rest of the West, particularly as their countries could no longer be considered newly independent. Achieving statehood in the 1820s, Latin American countries only lagged 50 years behind the United Sates in terms of independence, yet their economies were light years apart after World War II. In 1870, the per capita GDP in the United States was $1,806 compared to Argentina at $1,311, Chile at $1,290, and Uruguay at $2,181. By the turn of the 20th century, the figures rose to $4,091 for the United States, and $2,756, $2,194, and $2,219 for Argentina, Chile, and Uruguay, respectively. As each decade of the 20th century passed, the per capita GDP in the United States outpaced its South American counterparts by two, three, and almost four times in 1990, until settling back to three times by the year 2000.[5] Thus, dependency scholars pointed to the relationship with Global North states, effectively arguing that "dependent nations were not younger versions of the great capitalist powers; they were equally as old and were the perennial source of their power. Unequal exchange and extractive economies kept dependent countries dependent" (Lomnitz 2012, 350). Ironically, the industrial potential output of these dependent nations as a percentage of the world's total was actually in their favor until around 1860, when the Industrial Revolution took off in Western Europe and the United States (Christian, 2011).[6]

How can this discrepancy be explained? One answer was that in spite of political independence, Latin American countries were still linked economically in a neo-imperialistic fashion to the advanced, capitalist states to such an extent that it stunted domestic economic growth and perpetuated dependency. Dependency is defined as "a situation in which the economy of certain countries is conditioned by the development and expansion of another economy to which the former is subjected" (Dos Santos 1970, 231). Furthermore, dependency theorists argued that these capitalist states purposively cultivated underdevelopment in Latin America in order to take advantage of the raw materials and cheap labor in the region. Capitalist states had a monopoly on technological advancements and finance capital, none of which were transferred to the developing states. Economic advancement of the Global North, therefore, was achieved by exploiting the Global South, keeping these states both dependent and underdeveloped.

Dependency theorists framed their argument in three interrelated ways: first, the general level of underdevelopment in the region was initially a function of the international finance and trade regime dominated by advanced industrialized states, in particular, the United States; second, as a consequence, this exploitative nature of capitalism was the root of poverty prevalent in Latin America; and third, the lack of economic development and resulting poverty was therefore largely due to historical external influences beyond the control of the subordinate economies. A vicious cycle of imperialism, poverty and underdevelopment, and neo-imperialism perpetuated by the Global North kept Global South states in a constant condition of dependency and underdevelopment. Ultimately, dependency theorists pointed to external factors, specifically the history of imperialism and the subsequent economic structure of the international system, as primary reasons for the perpetual state of underdevelopment in Latin American countries.

However, not all dependency theorists agreed on the solutions. For some, the extreme solution was to completely sever the trade link with advanced states and opt for self-sufficiency. For others, altering the terms of trade as well as the type of products exported was the policy prescription. Thus, in the 1950s, many Latin American intellectuals and politicians began calling for measures ranging from the protection of domestic industries to revolution as ways to change the dependent relationship with advanced economies in order to spur economic development and alleviate poverty. By the 1970s, a more reformist arm of the *dependencia* argued for turning the microscope inward to address some of the developmental woes in Latin America. Ultimately, dependency theorists seek to protect domestic markets in order to accomplish two goals: avoid dependent trade relationships and develop domestic manufacturing. We next examine contributors to the dependency school of thought and see how the movement developed its policy prescriptions over time.

Pioneers in the Field

In the years following World War II, several organizations were formed to address the economic development of Global South states. One was the Economic Commission for Latin America (ECLA), a United Nations agency headquartered in Santiago, Chile, led by Raúl Prebisch (1901–1986). Prebisch was one of the first theorists to conceive of states in the international system belonging in either the advanced industrialized core or the agrarian periphery (see Spotlight on Policymakers). The core was comprised of the industrialized states of the Global North that controlled the means of production, but depended on the raw materials and cheap labor in the periphery to maintain their profits as well as their position in the international system. The periphery of the international system consisted of poor states where raw materials were extracted and labor supported the profits and lifestyle of the core states. Prebisch argued that primary products have low-income elasticity. In economic terms, elasticity refers to how demand changes with changes in income. For US consumers, as income increases, their demand for more and more expensive manufactured goods increases. However, the demand for staple products such as coffee, bananas, and other fruits does not fluctuate as much with increases in income.

In order to compete in the international economic system, Prebisch argued that Latin American states needed to alter the structure of their domestic economies by increasing manufacturing while decreasing their reliance on the exports of primary products. Latin American states instituted import substitution industrialization (ISI) policies. The objective was to protect infant industries and thus replace imports from industrialized states. ISI policies spearheaded the shift from a reliance on primary products to manufacturing and the development of industrial sectors within the periphery. Alongside these measures, periphery states needed to develop or strengthen labor unions in order to stabilize and increase wages that had been historically repressed. Prebisch also suggested that states had to stand up to the pressures exerted by multinational corporations (MNCs) seeking low wage environments. By the end of the 1960s, ISI strategies had failed to adequately spur domestic economic development and industrialization. Prebisch was one of the first to call for policy change. He advocated a post-ISI strategy, which included decreasing protectionist measures and developing new exports to compete in the international markets, much like the Asian Tigers and New Industrialized Countries (NICs).

SPOTLIGHT ON POLICYMAKERS: RAUL PREBISCH

An economist by trade, Raúl Prebisch became a leading theorist in the *dependencia* school as well as a leading policy-maker at the state, regional, and global levels. In Argentina, he was the Deputy Director of the Argentine Department of Statistics (1925–27), Director of Economic Research for the National Bank of Argentina (1927–30), Under Secretary of Finance during the Uriburu regime (1930–32), and the General Manager

continued

of the Argentine Central Bank (1932–43). During this time, he was also a professor at the Faculty of Economic Sciences, a university in Buenos Aires. In 1946, Juan Perón came to power and installed a regime calling for a "third way" economically that was neither socialist nor capitalist in nature, while at the same time one that restricted political and civil rights. In this economic and political climate, Prebisch was dismissed from the Central Bank and lost his tenure at the university. However, he was invited to several Latin American countries to provide technical assistance regarding central banks and banking issues in general. Moreover, this is the time when he worked on his own economic theory that would help launch the dependency movement. In 1949, Prebisch went to work for a new United Nations organization, the Economic Commission for Latin America (ECLA, CEPAL is the Spanish acronym) in Chile, eventually serving as the Executive Secretary of the regional organization until 1963 (which evolved to the Economic Commission for Latin America and the Caribbean (ECLAC) in 1984). In 1963, UN Secretary-General U Thant invited him to head up the UN Conference on Trade and Development (UNCTAD), a position he held until 1968. He finished his career as the Director General of the Latin American Institute for Economic and Social Planning (ILPES) in Washington, D.C.

Prebisch came of age during a time of great political and economic upheaval. A student in Buenos Aires during WWI and the Russian Revolution (1917), he was heavily influenced by the conditions in his homeland. His focus on social reform and equity (political and economic) were recurring themes throughout his career. Much like other economists at the time, Prebisch advocated western economic policies aimed at domestic growth. He joined the Argentine public service with a goal of shaping a modern state from within. However, the Great Depression hit hard in Latin America in general and Argentina in particular, causing him to abandon the liberal free trade policies advocated by the United States. Prebisch began to question why economic growth in the poorer countries in the international system did not mirror development in the advanced states. He argued that different rates of economic growth began during the Industrial Revolution and continued in the years following independence in Latin America (circa 1820). The technical advances experienced in Western Europe and the United States failed to trickle down, or diffuse, into Latin America, creating an uneven playing field in the areas of manufacturing and production.

continued

Influenced by the writings of Lenin, Prebisch coined the terms *center* and *periphery,* which later became part of the world-systems lexicon (see below) with *core* replacing *center.* His own theoretical contribution to the dependency literature, *The Economic Development of Latin America and its Principle Problems* (1950), outlined his arguments about the relationship between the interests of the center (advanced economies) and the periphery (Latin American countries). Prebisch questioned and challenged two main precepts of liberal economic thought: first, that trade was mutually beneficial to both trading partners, and second, that the subsequent trade would also reduce the economic gap between the core and periphery. Moreover, Prebisch argued that international economic institutions (IMF and the World Bank) and multinational corporations (MNCs) colluded with the Global North to create an international trade environment that Global South states simply could not penetrate.

Specifically, Prebisch maintained that Latin American states — that is, the periphery—exported raw materials and primary products which were returned to them as finished products with the value added from manufacturing in Global North core states. Furthermore, commodity prices in the periphery states were much more volatile and decreased over time relative to the prices of finished goods. This made the periphery much more susceptible to surpluses in labor, as wages are the most variable aspect of controlling production costs in periphery states. In the core states, on the other hand, labor unions protected the interests of the workers, thus protecting wages and benefits. Ultimately, this created an increasing income gap between the core and the periphery. Hans W. Singer, an economist, independently put this idea of an unequal exchange forth, and the subsequent Prebisch-Singer thesis became a prominent argument in the dependency school.

Prebisch laid the groundwork for future generations of Latin American scholars, as well as other scholars and thinkers dedicated to explaining the economic disparity found around the world. His leadership of ECLA initiated the structuralist school with a focus on reform. Prebisch promoted an alternative economic framework, Marxist in its approach, with more radical policy prescriptions. His arguments can be traced to the *Havana Manifesto* (1949), here he elaborated on his description of the center and periphery and his call for "inward-development."

The framework Prebisch established influenced subsequent theorists and policy-makers as they attempted to explain the current state of underdevelopment in Latin America and other developing states, as well as to prescribe policy alternatives. Paul Baran (1910–1964) and Andre Gunder Frank (1929–2005), for example, developed arguments that were distinctively Marxist. The work of Fernando Henrique Cardoso (1931–) and Enzo Faletto (1935–2003) as well as Peter Evans' work on dependent development took a more reformist approach to the economic woes in the region. The Marxists focused on the deterministic external factors preventing domestic economic development, while reformers (often referred to as non-Marxist or structuralists) pointed to internal factors that Latin American states could, in fact, address.

Marxist Variant of Dependency Theory

In *The Political Economy of Growth,* Paul Baran claimed that it is impossible for any Third World country to break free of its dependent relationships and ascend to an economic status equal to one of the advanced economies. Vestiges of imperialism in which European states "engaged in outright plunder or in plunder thinly veiled as trade, seizing and removing tremendous wealth from the places of their penetrations" (Baran 1957, 142) prevented true independence. This loss of wealth left developing countries devoid of the natural resources necessary for domestic investment, and thus left them unable to follow the developmental path experienced by the European states. In essence, Baran argued that imperialism led to a permanent structural deficit in the developing countries.

Baran's introduced and explained the concept of economic surplus, which he defined as the difference between output and consumption within a state. He divided this concept into three distinct forms: actual economic surplus, planned economic surplus, and potential economic surplus. Actual economic surplus is analogous to the standard definition of economic surplus used in economic theory. In economically developing countries like those in Latin America, this figure tends to be quite small, as actual value of output lags behind consumption. Planned economic surplus represents the optimal scenario under a socialist, state-controlled system. The concept of potential economic surplus is defined as "the difference between the output that *could* be produced in a given natural and technological environment with the help of employable productive resources and what might be regarded as essential consumption" (Baran 1968, 23). The goal for developing states was to tap into this potential surplus; this would require political reorganization and significant changes in current economic relations.

Baran points to several internal "leakages" that developing states must address, namely, "the political and social coalition of wealthy compradors, powerful monopolists, and large landowners dedicated to the defense of the existing feudal-mercantile order" (Baran 1968, 195). Any economic surplus usually wound up in the hands of these landowners. Thus, he argued that there were both external and internal obstacles for economic development and Latin American states need to act as "the gap between the actual and the possible is glaring, and its implications are catastrophic. There the difference is not, as in the advanced countries, between higher and lower degrees of development . . . the difference is between abysmal squalor and decent existence, between the misery of hopelessness and the exhilaration of progress, between life and death for hundreds of millions of people" (Baran 1968, 249–250). His answer was less acquiescence to the demands of the Global North and more revolutionary socialist efforts from the Global South. He argued that the "establishment of a socialist planned economy is an essential, indeed indispensable, condition for the attainment of economic and social progress in underdeveloped countries" (Baran 1968, 261).

Andre Gunder Frank advanced Baran's arguments regarding economic surplus and placed the economic development of Global South in a world-systems context (see below). In *Capitalism and Underdevelopment in Latin America* (1969), Frank argued that issues of dependency could be traced back to the 15th century wave of imperialism. In essence, the Latin American states bypassed the feudal epoch through the imperialistic realities of colonization by Spain. In fact, Peruvian political leader and intellectual Víctor Raúl Haya de la Torre argued in the 1920s that economic development in Latin American states "did not follow the same trajectory that it had in Europe due to the 'feudal' backwardness created by centuries of Spanish colonialism. If imperialism was the last stage of capitalism in Europe, it was just the first stage in Latin America" (Grosfuguel 2000, 355). As a result, wealth had accumulated in the core, contributing to what Frank (1969, 1979) called the "development of underdevelopment" in the periphery.

Frank argued that the underdevelopment of the periphery was, in fact, required in order for the core to prosper. With decolonization, the extent of this underdevelopment only increased. Without influential patrons, periphery states were now economically and politically powerless in the face of the rampant capitalist economic international system. Frank introduces two terms that are analogous with periphery and core in the dependency lexicon: the satellite and the metropolis. Frank (1969, 7–8) outlines a reiterative connection from the metropolis to the satellite arguing that "At each step along the way, the relatively few capitalists above exercise monopoly power over the many below, expropriating some or all of their economic surplus, and to the extent that they are not expropriated in turn by the still fewer above, appropriating it for their own use. Thus, at each point, the international, national, and local capitalist system generates economic development and underdevelopment for the many." In Frank's analysis, we see the parasitic relationship extended beyond the core-periphery originally put forth by Prebisch. In Frank's version, satellite states that are attached to a metropolis are more likely to be underdeveloped. On the other hand, a satellite state is most likely to experience economic growth and development when the ties to the metropolis are the weakest. This is likely to occur during a crisis such as war or an economic depression. Geographic isolation can also contribute to the weak ties between the metropolis and satellite. Frank's historical analysis and description of the global economy is consistent with a Marxist approach and serves to influence future scholarship, particularly the world-systems literature, as we will see.

Non-Marxist Variant of Dependency Theory

From a structural perspective, Fernando Henrique Cardoso and Enzo Faletto (1969) argued that Latin American states were not merely at the mercy of the core, in spite of the fact that much of the historical economic and political development of the international system was beyond the control of periphery states. Rejecting the deterministic view prevalent among Marxist dependency theorists, Cardoso and Faletto maintained that periphery states had several policy options and strategies and needed to look inward to change the core/periphery relationship. These options included land reform, taxing foreign capital to increase monetary flows, and implementing capital controls to stabilize the amount of capital flowing in and out of the state. Moreover, states needed to take a hard look at their own political systems and address the chronic problems of corruption, clientelism, and corporatism endemic in Latin American countries. Cardoso and Faletto also called for the strengthening of domestic institutions such as political parties and rule of law. The results, called "associated dependent capitalism," combined with political reform would provide the economic stability and financial capital necessary for domestic growth in the underdeveloped manufacturing sectors of Latin American economies.

Cardoso and Faletto also contributed a new typology to the dependency literature discourse to provide a description of the path that developing states could pursue: enclave economies, nationally controlled export economies, and new dependency. Enclave economies were characterized by external sources of capital with production controlled by MNCs. In nationally controlled export economies, the source of funding capital and control of production was internal—that is, elements within the developing state maintain control. In the new dependency scenario, the source of capital was external, with the goal of the international MNC dominating the markets in the host economy. Cardoso and Faletto pointed to the national controlled export economies as those with the most promise for the promotion of domestic economic growth and development.

Cardoso eventually became active in politics, ascending to the presidency in Brazil (1995–2003). He was quickly criticized for abandoning his Marxist roots and adopting what seemed to be neo-liberal economic policies. Much like Rosa Luxemburg some 80 years earlier, Cardoso focused on the need to critique Marxism constantly in order to find new ways of governing. He was far more interested in finding a path to economic and political development in Brazil than in maintaining a dogmatic Marxist philosophy. Ultimately, he believed that national governments needed to play a bigger role in order for Latin American states to compete in the economic international arena. The alternative status was as a perpetual provider of raw materials and primary products.

By the 1970s, economic structuralist theorists focused on the state's contribution to the dependent relationship. While Marx, Lenin, and most other theorists addressed financial capital, Peter Evans (1979) identified MNCs as the linchpin that tied foreign capital to local elites in a system he calls "dependent development." He echoed Cardoso and Faletto's argument that the state played a much more active role, particularly when it came to attracting MNCs in the form of direct foreign investment. Thus, a triple alliance existed (MNCs, elite local capital, and state bourgeoisie) that colluded to prevent any form of income/wealth redistribution in periphery states. Because MNCs generally wanted to avoid risk, local elites engaged in activities to keep wages and worker discontent at low levels. This was also the goal of the state. We can think of local capitalism as the stepchild of imperialism, looking for investments that will not compete with foreign capital. Again, Evans argued that it is up to the state to mediate any disputes that might arise; the state must be strong enough and willing to oppose MNCs that threaten the local accumulation of wealth.

We can see that scholars of the two schools of dependency theory point to different obstacles and, thus, offer different solutions. The Marxist school looks to external causes for dependency and underdevelopment and advocates severing the link between the Global North and South, through revolution if necessary. The non-Marxist, or structuralist, school acknowledged the impact of external factors, primarily imperialism, but argued that developing states must look inward for solutions.

World-Systems Theory

Building on the analysis provided by Andre Gunder Frank in his seminal work, *The Development of Underdevelopment,* the concept of a world-capitalist system offers a structural approach to the study of the international system. This historical perspective examines the whole economic system and not just the developing world in an attempt to understand and explain the disparate levels of development and the subsequent social consequences of capitalism found around the world. **World-systems theory** (WST) has Marxist roots in that the driving force of change in the world-system is associated with capitalism and imperialism.

Pioneers in the Field

In an attempt to explain the economic misery of 80% of the world's population, Immanuel Wallerstein (1930–) proffers a Marxist-influenced argument about how states in the international system are arranged and then constrained by the hegemon in what he calls a world-system. Wallerstein traces the development of the current world-system from the 16th century and concludes that the system was and is determined and organized by the world economy. In fact, he argues that this economy "is and has always been a world-economy. It is and has always been a capitalist world-economy" (Wallerstein 2004, 23). This world-economy has a single division of labor; this division consists of the owners of production (ranging from MNCs to Bill Gates to socialist states in today's environment) and the workers.

In this world-system, Wallerstein identifies four key actors: economic zones, the state, social classes, and status groups. First, building on the stratification theme as well as the center-periphery concepts, Wallerstein argues that there are different identifiable economic zones: the core, the periphery, and the semi-periphery. The core, what Frank had called the metropolis, consists of states that are characterized as developed, industrialized, and democratic. These states adhere to the rule of law, provide high wages and levels of social welfare, and are net exporters of manufactured goods relative to raw and primary materials. These are the most powerful states in the world-system and dominate—even exploit—the periphery and semi-periphery. The periphery, on the other hand, consists of generally non-democratic states that pay little adherence to the rule of law. These states are net exporters of primary products and import mainly finished and manufactured goods. As such, wages in the periphery are low, there is little or no organized labor, and citizens have little access to welfare services. Wallerstein also introduces the semi-periphery as an area that occupies an economic space between the core and periphery. Oftentimes serving as a buffer zone between the core and periphery, these states are often controlled by authoritarian regimes, and their imports and exports are a mix of both primary and manufactured goods.

The second actor is the state, whose primary role is to promote the interest of the capitalists, which is simply the accumulation of wealth. Similar to Marxism and dependency theory, Wallerstein views the state as a tool of the dominant class. In a world-system, states make up each economic zone. In addition, Wallerstein explains that the three economic zones are also potentially in existence within each state. In other words, a single state could be made up of a core area, a semi-periphery, and a periphery. For example, a state in the core (state A), could have a beneficial relationship with the core element within another state (state B). A likely scenario is that core state A has economic ties to the elite within state B, which may be a periphery or semi-periphery state. The third actor consists of the social classes within the system. When it comes to social class, Marx emphasized two: the bourgeoisie and the proletariat. Wallerstein identifies four: the owners (capitalists), the workers (either skilled or unskilled), small commodity producers (e.g., blacksmith), and a professional class (doctors and lawyers). The fourth actor, status groups, are defined as the different ethnic, national, or religious groups within the world-system.

As applied to the current economic system, interaction in the world-system is characterized by an unequal exchange of economic activity. Capitalists, supported by the state, extract as much as possible from their own working class. The same exchange then occurs between the core, the semi-periphery, and the periphery. The nature of the system, based on economic class, prevents the emergence of a world empire, as the capitalists in the United States and the capitalists in Germany, for example, relate more to each other than to the property-less in their own states. Furthermore, the goal of this world-system is the accumulation of wealth for the capitalist, and not the expansion of power of the state. While WST provides a descriptive assessment of the international system, critics question whether this is even a theory. They ask, "Does WST help break the cycle of dependency?" and, "What is the prescriptive value?" According to Wallerstein, the answer is the development of a new world-system, one based on more equitable outcomes. He argues that the current world-system lacks the ability to produce enough surplus value and subsequently, profit, to survive. He foresees a split or struggle between two alternative paths: one is a new world-system that replicates many of the current features but it will "not be a capitalist system. It would still be hierarchical and exploitative," while the second alternative is a "system that is relatively democratic and relatively egalitarian" (Schouten 2008).[7] Wallerstein states that it is not possible to predict which path will be taken, only that the present system will not last, as no system lasts forever.

Criticisms of Economic Structuralism

The theories under the economic structuralism umbrella have made several contributions to the field of international relations. For example, this paradigm emphasizes economic considerations, particularly the global impact of imperialism. Moreover, economic structuralism highlights the importance of historical development and the constraints it imposed on countries of the Global South. The role and choices of external actors are important in explaining the economic and political affairs of the less developed states in the international system. This paradigm also helps to explain the role and relationships elites have both between and among the different states in the system. Finally, economic structuralism also introduces normative questions to the discourse, more so than the positivist paradigms of realism and liberalism.

However, while recognizing the failure of modernization and liberal economic policies to spur development in the Global South, critics of Marxism and theories of economic structuralism map out several flaws in the paradigm. First and foremost, critics take umbrage at the deterministic element inherent in all stripes of economic structuralism. Determinism suggests that some external force causes all outcomes. At the individual level, this implies a lack of free will. At the state level, this implies that all domestic troubles related to underdevelopment (poverty, unemployment, lack of domestic industries) are due to forces beyond the control of the state and are, in fact, externally caused. The history of exploitation of the developing countries cannot be avoided or changed, for that matter, leaving the theory with no real prescriptive value.

This fundamental objection leads to several related criticisms. First, all critics claim that the economic structuralist theories go too far in blaming developed, industrialized states in general, and imperialism more specifically, for all the domestic woes in Global South states. In a similar vein, critics argue that the reliance on one variable—economics—to explain all political and social behavior is too limiting. Critics contend that this prevents economic structuralists from adequately explaining conflict that is not economic in nature. For example, they are unable to theoretically explain how the Cold War ended with cooperation between capitalist and socialist states. Nor are they able to explain the conflict between China and India over the Nepal region that, at its heart, is a cultural dispute. Second, the deterministic elements allow states to forego any responsibility for failures of sector development, the emergence of military regimes, poor leadership and policy-decisions, one-party governance, and so on. Third, adhering to a deterministic and external cause marginalizes any local history that might be relevant in explaining the lack of economic development.

Critics are also dismayed with the treatment of the state in this paradigm, which stems from an over-emphasis on the structure of the international system. For example, "Too many writers of this school make the mistake of assuming that since the whole (in this case the international system) is greater than the sum of its parts (the constituent states), the parts lead no significant existence separate from the whole, but operate simply in functionally specific manners as a result of their place in the greater system" (Smith 1979, 252). In other words, dependency theorists and economic structuralists claim what happens within the state doesn't really matter. Furthermore, not all states are alike. While dependency theory has focused on Latin American states that generally have a similar history, the theory does not hold up when addressing other Global South states. The local history of India, for example, paints a different picture of the domestic factors that react to external forces. Thus, not all states will respond the same way to external forces such as imperialism or direct foreign investment. This leads to a reductionist view, another criticism leveled against economic structuralism.

There are methodological critiques of economic structuralists as well. First, there is a lack of empirical evidence to support the claims made by Marxists and economic structuralists. Ultimately, the Marxist revolution never occurred. On the contrary, the middle class in state after state continued to grow over time, rather than shrinking into a mass of alienated unemployed workers. Latin American countries have developed economically, through direct foreign investment and trade; the newly industrialized countries (NICs) are doing even better, as evidenced by the economic growth in India and China. Furthermore, the terms of trade are not as dire as the theory would predict. Ultimately, critics contend that economic structuralism as an approach is "formulistic and reductionists . . . it is formulistic in the sense that it seeks to specify universal laws or processes in blatant disregard of the singular or idiosyncratic. By the same token it is reductionist, since it forces the particular case to express its identity solely in the terms provided by the general category" (Smith 1979, 258).

Case Study: Proliferation

When it comes to nuclear weapons, the countries that are of most concern to economic structuralists generally fall into the category of "have nots." This is a major bone of contention. The nuclear apartheid that exists is simply an extension of the economic divide between the wealthy and poor states in the international system; it is an additional layer in the stratification of states. Here, this stratification adds a dimension of respectability and prestige in that membership in the nuclear club denotes power and technological achievement in the international system. Whether by choice or circumstance, failure to gain entry into the nuclear club inherently places a state in the second-class compartment. The NPT is an interesting case in that of the 191 parties to the treaty, only five are considered NPT nuclear states (the United States, the United Kingdom, Russia, China, and France); thus, 97% of participating states have agreed to a scenario where they can never acquire a nuclear weapon. Conversely, only 3% of the signatory states get to have nuclear weapons.

As outlined in the introductory chapter, those states that constitute the non-nuclear weapon states (NNWS) are further divided into three groups with three distinct goals: those who want them, those who are protected by a nuclear weapons state, and those who don't want them and actually want all others to forego them as well. These states point to Article VI of the NPT that reads, "Each of the Parties to the Treaty undertakes to pursue negotiations in good faith on effective measures relating to cessation of the nuclear arms race at an early date and to nuclear disarmament, and on a treaty on general and complete disarmament under strict and effective international control." Thus, the first area of concern is the compliance status of nuclear weapon states (NWS) with Article VI.

Here, leaders of developing countries make several arguments. First, many of the signatories point to the inherent inequalities within the treaty, which grants a privileged status to nuclear powers. They define this privilege in terms of security, economic power, reputational status, prestige, and regional domination to name just a few. For example, in the Russian case, "the nuclear arsenal underpins its sovereignty and helps it maintain an independent foreign policy. The nuclear sector is the only field where Russia can claim equal status with the United States, so it benefits from the structural impact of nuclear weapons on international affairs" (Lodgaard 2011, 64). For countries outside the nuclear club, like those in the Middle East, where alternative sources of energy are not the primary motiving factor to acquiring nuclear capability, the rationale "involves strong elements of Arab national pride, popular domestic enthusiasm for advanced technology and higher geopolitical status with the Persian Gulf region" (Jackson 2009, 1159). Second, these states point to the false promise made by the NWS and their failure to move toward meaningful reductions in the nuclear arsenals. The "grand bargain" was in exchange for participating in the NPT, NWS would work toward zero.

In reality, the 3% rule over the 97% illustrating that "the treaty more than ever bears unequally on the nuclear and nonnuclear; perpetuates the unequal distribution of security; and reflects an unequal distribution of power" (Bellany 1977, 596). This uneven relationship perpetuates the dependency argument that rich states want to keep poor states underdeveloped and devoid of nuclear capabilities.

A second area of concern for developing states is the peaceful use of nuclear energy for the purpose of energy consumption. According to Article IV of the NPT, NNWS states have the "inalienable right" to "develop research, production, and use of nuclear energy for peaceful purposes without discrimination." Moreover, Article IV allows for the "fullest possible exchange of equipment, materials, and scientific and technological information for the peaceful uses of nuclear energy." Again, there is a deep divide between the "haves" and "have nots." The development of such opportunities for many states is cost prohibitive, and the exchange of technology and materials is ideologically driven. Many NNWS face growing energy concerns that make nuclear-powered energy attractive as a viable and generally safe option.

Iran provides an interesting example. The Iranian leadership claims that it needs to develop nuclear energy for peaceful purposes. Other states, in particular the United States, do not accept this argument. Leaders in the United States argue that Iran has plenty of oil to provide energy and does not need nuclear power. If Iran is genuine in its concern for its energy future, then the United States has been preventing the peaceful development of nuclear energy due to a political conflict with a long-term rival. In mid-2015, the United States (along with the other permanent members of the Security Council plus Germany) came to an agreement with Iran to curb its nuclear program in exchange for the lifting of international sanctions; the deal remains steeped in controversy. Implementation is moving forward, but it provides evidence of the "haves" attempting to control the behavior of the "have nots."

NNWS face three obstacles in acquiring nuclear energy: cost, technological deficiency, and the tension between Article IV and VI of the NPT. The environmental advantages for nuclear power are numerous, but "this magic bullet solution to climate change comes at a security price: the ever-present risk that civilian nuclear energy technology and nuclear materials might be diverted and weaponized to fabricate military atomic weapons" (Jackson 2009, 1157). This fear forces a no-win dilemma on developing states. In the event that such a state had the financial resources to develop peaceful use of nuclear energy, what would stop another state from accusing it of proliferation intentions? When it comes to the NNWS, "any country with significant nuclear technology should probably be regarded as a latent nuclear weapon power" (Jackson 2009, 1157). With such thinking, the countries of the developing world are stymied by the security and economic concerns of the more powerful states in the international community who ponder whether these states will "trade national security for the norm of non-proliferation" (Akiyama and Horio 2013, 158).

In remarks on April 5, 2009, President Barack Obama envisioned a plan that would achieve "peace and security of a world without nuclear weapons" given that the "existence of thousands of nuclear weapons is the most dangerous legacy of the Cold War." He then laid out several policy measures toward this aim: reduction of the number of weapons currently held by the nuclear states, strengthening of the non-proliferation regime via stricter accountability measures, the prevention of nuclear terrorism by tighter controls on materials, and the promotion of safe nuclear power as an energy source. On one hand, he argued that when it comes to proliferation, "rules must be binding. Violations must be punished." At the same time, he acknowledged that all states had the right to the benefits of nuclear energy. As such, he argued that a "new framework for civil nuclear cooperation, including an international fuel bank" needs to be developed so that "countries can access peaceful power without increasing the risks of proliferation."[8]

President Obama had tied Article IV and VI together in what is now referred to as the Prague Agenda. Ironically, North Korea test-fired a long-range missile several hours before President Obama's Prague speech. Five months after the speech, President Obama, French President Sarkozy, and British Prime Minister Brown announced to the world that Iran had an enrichment plant near the city of Qom.[9] Two years later, the world witnessed the March 2011 nuclear accident at the Fukushima Daiichi Nuclear Power Station, the result of a major earthquake and tsunami. The question now is, "how can the peaceful use of nuclear energy be promoted while strengthening nonproliferation and nuclear security" particularly as "Washington faces resistance from potential partners who see tension between the inalienable right to pursue (peaceful) nuclear energy and the norm of nonproliferation" (Akiyama and Horio 2013, 154). Ultimately, some analysts wonder if "a nuclear-weapons-free world is an illogical goal" (Tertrais 2010, 125).

TABLE 4.1 Economic Structuralism and Proliferation

Economic Structuralist Thought	Theoretical Tenet	Proliferation Example
Marxism	The hierarchical international system based on economic class determines the position and behavior of states.	The NPT is another example of how wealthy states dominate and pursue their own interests at the expense of less developed states. Wealthy states make the rules regarding nuclear weapons and the use of nuclear energy. The dominant states also control the international organizations (IAEA) designed to monitor nuclear activity and actively seek to punish states like Iran and North Korea.
Gramscianism	Working-class lack power due to hegemonic power of elites who control not only the wealth but maintain status through the power of ideas. Ruling elite have gained consent from the masses. A counter-intellectual hegemony is required in order for subordinate classes to gain power.	The United States, through the NPT, has garnered near universal consent for the idea of non-proliferation. Even states that might be disadvantaged buy into the treaty. Iran attempts to generate a counter-narrative with its alternative interpretation of how the NPT is administered, that is, it only benefits the wealthy and privileged states in the international system. The NPT is detrimental to those developing states in their pursuit of nuclear energy.
Dependency Theory	Due to imperialism and colonialism, less developed states are in a perpetual state of dependency and underdevelopment. Marxist dependency theorists blame external factors while non-Marxist theorists look internally for states to reform in order to break dependent relationships.	The realities of the NPT perpetuate the client relationship of less developed countries, as they must rely on the dominant states for security. Developing states are also often prevented from pursuing nuclear energy as an alternative source, which negatively impacts the economy of these states.

continued

Economic Structuralist Thought	Theoretical Tenet	Proliferation Example
World Systems Theory	A structural approach that divides the international system into three areas: the core, semi-periphery, and periphery in order to explain the disparate levels of economic development. This division is the result of the capitalist world economy.	The NPT privileges core states by linking economics and military interests together thereby legitimizing their power. It allows core states to falsely develop a safety and security narrative with the net result of chronic and persistent underdevelopment in the periphery and semi-periphery as they are prevented in many cases from pursuing alternative sources of energy as well as nuclear weapons.

Case Study: WTO

One question we examine in this case study is why states join an international organization such as the WTO. From an economic structuralist or dependency view, the state itself has no real choice as policy decisions are made by economic elites within the state. Likewise, pressure from capitalist states and the relationship between the bourgeoisie in both the developed and developing states lead states to join international institutions. According to economic structuralists, a state is a tool of the ruling economic class. As a group, those in the Marxist tradition are generally skeptical of international organizations and view the associated international laws as products of the capitalist, western states. As such, the structure of the international organization itself simply perpetuates the class system as rich states wield more influence, or perceived influence, within the organization.

In the case of the WTO, funding comes primarily from contributions from its members, based on their share of international trade. Thus, the United States and other advanced capitalist states hold more sway through the budgetary process.[10] The United States alone contributed 11.32% of the WTO's 2015 budget. Moreover, these institutions emerged at a time when many of the current developing states were still colonies. With the United States as the hegemon after World War

II and with the demise of the Soviet Union at the end of the Cold War, these institutions also have a pro-democracy, anti-socialist flavor. The WTO is no exception. Here we focus on the Doha Round of trade negotiations in order to better understand how to apply the theories that comprise economic structuralism.

After the WTO ministerial meeting that was interrupted in Seattle in 1999, organizers realized the necessity of focusing on the needs of developing states. Thus, in 2001 the Doha Round of trade negotiations began with a commitment to "make positive efforts designed to ensure that developing countries, and especially the least-developed among them, secure a share in the growth of world trade commensurate with the needs of their economic development."[11] In September 2003, the members met in Cancun, Mexico, where the talks quickly collapsed due to many disagreements, including the issue of farm subsidies. Farm subsidies provided by the US and EU to their domestic agricultural constituents, for example, serve to artificially drive "down global crop prices, unfairly undermining small farmers and maintaining poverty in many developing countries" (Clay 2013). Many of the emerging states have emulated this practice, as evidenced by China's annual agricultural subsidy of $160 billion, far more than granted by the US or the EU. Likewise, Brazil and India have enacted price supports in an effort to protect domestic food prices as well as to avoid price spikes that hit the international system in 2008 (Clay 2013).

By 2004, talks seemed to be on good footing when the United States and the EU agreed to decrease agricultural subsidies while the developing countries agreed to cut tariffs on manufactured goods. However, by the time of the Hong Kong meeting in December 2005, relations between the developed and developing states had deteriorated primarily due to differences regarding agricultural products. Most observers now agree that the negotiations were doomed to fail. Efforts were resumed in 2008 to revive the Doha Round, however, after nine days the talks broke down once again. India and the United States represented the opposing sides of the development debate. The two countries failed to resolve their differences regarding how, other than farm subsidies, best to protect farmers in the poorest countries against surges in imports. The impact of the Great Recession was evident as the WTO reported that global trade was predicted to fall 9%, with developing states hit the hardest.

The **Group of 20** met in Seoul, South Korea, in 2010 and sought to set an agenda for 2011 with the hopes of concluding the Doha Round of trade negotiations. However, by the 2013 meeting in Bali, the WTO was still hoping to come to some agreement that would conclude the negotiations. In 2014, India and the United States finally came to an agreement that paved the way to addressing Global South concerns regarding food security, one of the major issues for developing countries. A majority of these countries trade in primary products, such as agricultural produce, thus they are susceptible to price spikes. India was hard hit by the food price spikes during 2008 and in response instituted a food security program consisting of the acquisition and distribution of food products to the poor, even though this regularly surpassed the WTO-imposed 10% cap on food subsidies. The agreement between the United States and India concluded that this program could continue—what India called the "peace clause." The United States agreed to support the program in the WTO until 2017. Further, this agreement immunized other states from challenges should they need to stockpile food products as well.

While this seems like a victory for developing states, it is only a temporary measure until a long-term solution to food subsidies can be negotiated. Furthermore, the fact that this deal was struck in a bilateral fashion with the United States as the lead negotiator rather than in the multilateral forum that is supposed to be a WTO norm suggests that the hegemon is dictating trade policy. It perpetuates the idea that states occupy a specific space in the international system, a divide that can be traced first to the legacy of imperialism, which created two classes of states, and then to the world capitalist system that maintains the separation of states into the core, semi-periphery, and periphery. This division is simply played out in the WTO arena, with the core states driving trade policy that the semi-periphery and periphery must follow. The alternative is that developing states will be left out of the trade regime. For these states, the concept of free trade isn't all that free—it comes with a significant price.

Conclusion

In this chapter, we provided an overview of the theories that make up the economic structuralism paradigm. We traced the evolution of economic structuralism from Marx to Lenin, from dependency theory

TABLE 4.2 Economic Structuralism and the WTO

Economic Structuralist Thought	Theoretical Tenet	WTO Example
Marxism	Society is divided by class; the state acts on behalf of the bourgeoisie in pursuit of economic interests.	The division of states is perpetuated in the WTO with the wealthy, led by the United States, dictating economic policy for the international system. The international institution is utilized by wealthy states to dominate and take advantage of poor states.
Gramscianism	The dominant class has garnered consent of the masses through its intellectual hegemony. The masses are convinced that their interests match the dominant class.	Through policies and international organizations, wealthy states convinced all states of the benefits of the capitalist system. The issue of agricultural subsidies has led key developing states to question the practices of wealthy WTO members and enact domestic protection policies in an attempt to counter the dominant class. This can be seen as an effort to create an alternative narrative for other developing states to adopt.
Dependency Theory	Less developed countries (LDCs) are linked to industrialized wealthy countries by uneven trade relationships that keep LDCs permanently underdeveloped. MNCs are the primary vehicle used by wealthy states in the postcolonial era to dominate the LDCs.	The LDCs reliance on primary products makes them more susceptible to price fluctuations. The WTO is seen as a defender of developed capitalist states' interests, more specifically the interests of MNCs, and not LDCs as wealthy states have more voting power.
World Systems Theory	A tripolar economic hierarchy exists in the modern capitalist system. The wealthy industrialized core takes advantage of the resource-endowed but poor periphery. The semi-periphery is both exploited and exploiter.	Food security is a major concern for periphery and semi-periphery states. The actions of core states regarding agricultural products through the WTO are viewed as the continued exploitation inherent in the world capitalist system.

to world-systems theory. In the case studies on the NPT and WTO, we provided examples on how to utilize these theories to interpret world events. As you move forward in your study of international relations, you will encounter additional opportunities to analyze current events from the Marxist, dependency, and world-systems perspectives. Economic structuralists as a group focus on the inherent inequalities embedded in the international system and how instruments of the economic elite (the state, MNCs, and international organizations) serve to perpetuate the status quo. Many of the arguments presented in this paradigm speak to the marginalized and disenfranchised, both individuals and states, around the world today.

Key Terms

Bourgeoisie
Core
Dependency (*dependencia*)
Economic base
Economic structuralism
Epochs
First International
Group of 20
Imperialism
Law of the concentration of capital
Law of decreasing profits
Law of disproportionality
Law of uneven development
Marxism
Means of production
Mode of production
Periphery
Proletariat
Relations of production
Revolutions of 1848
Semi-periphery
Superstructure

Theory of surplus value
Underconsumption
World-systems theory

For Further Reading

Frank, Andre Gunder. 1969. *Capitalism and Underdevelopment in Latin America.* New York and London. Monthly Review Press.

Gramsci, Antonio. 1972. *Selections from the Prison Notebooks of Antonio Gramsci.* New York: International Publishers.

Lenin, V. I. 1939. *Imperialism, the Highest Stage of Capitalism: A Popular Outline.* New York: International Publishers.

Luxemburg, Rosa. 2003. *The Accumulation of Capital.* New York: Routledge.

Marx, Karl, and Friedrich Engels. 2008. *The Communist Manifesto.* New York: Pathfinder Press.

Smith, Tony. 1979. "The Underdevelopment of Development Literature: The Case of Dependency Theory." *World Politics* 31(2): 24–288.

Wallerstein, Immanuel. 1980. *The Modern World System.* New York: Academic Press.

Endnotes

[1] Marx worked on *Das Kapital* (The Capital) over the last 25 years of his life, however, only Volume I was published during his lifetime. Based on the notes left by Marx, Frederick Engels finished and published Volumes II and III in 1884 and 1895 respectively.

[2] The First International is the common name of the International Workingman's Association, a workers' party and organization that began in 1864 and lasted until 1876. The Second International was established in Paris in 1889 and lasted until 1916, when the First World War destroyed the association.

[3] "Ultra-Imperialism" was originally published in the Marxist *Die Neue Ziet* six weeks after WWI began in 1914. The essay was later published in English in *New Left Review* No. 59 January–February 1970.

[4] Lenin provides the German interests in Belgium and the French's interest in the Lorraine region in support of his argument.

[5] Data obtained from the Maddison Historical GDP Data available at the World Economics webpage (www.worldeconomics.com) owned and operated by World Economics, Ltd.

[6] In 1750 the Third World's industrial percentage was 73.2% of the global total. In 1880, that figure was 67.3% then 60.9% in 1830 and down to 36.7% in 1860.

[7] Comments made by Immanual Wallerstein in interview with Theory Talk available at http://www.iwallerstein.com/wp-content/uploads/docs/THYTLK13.PDF.

[8] Remarks by President Barack Obama are found at https://www .whitehouse.gov/the-press-office/remarks-president-barack-obama -prague-delivered.

[9] This set off six years of talks ultimately culminating in the Joint Comprehensive Plan of Action in Vienna in 2015 that would lift sanctions in exchange for stricter limits on Iran's nuclear program.

[10] The WTO publishes the annual contributions to the WTO. For the 2015 contributions see https://www.wto.org/english/thewto_e/secre_e/contrib_e.htm

[11] Ministerial Declaration https://www.wto.org/english/thewto_e/minist_e/min01_e/mindecl_e.htm DOHA WTO MINISTERIAL 2001: MINISTERIAL DECLARATION WT/MIN(01)/DEC/1 20 November 2001; Adopted on 14 November 2001

CHAPTER 5

Constructivism

*"It is important to keep in mind that the objectivity of the institu-
tionalized world, however massive it may appear to the individual,
is a humanly produced, constructed objectivity."*

—Berger and Luckmann (2011, 134)

At the height of the Cold War, the USSR had close to 40,000 nuclear
warheads representing a definite threat to US national security. The
approximate US stockpile of 25,000 nuclear weapons constituted a reciprocal risk to Soviet national security. Today, both Russia and the United
States still maintain stockpiles ranging between 1,000–5,000 nuclear
warheads. Furthermore, it is estimated that China possesses 250, France
has close to 300, and England has approximately 225 warheads stockpiled. Among the non-NPT states, India has approximately 90–110,
Israel between 75–200, and Pakistan between 100–120 nuclear weapons.[1] North Korea is believed to possess four to eight short-range nuclear
missiles. To date, Iran does not possess a viable nuclear warhead. Which
of these states is the most dangerous in the international system?
Why? The answer to this question, from the constructivist perspective,
depends a great deal more on a set of norms, beliefs, and ideas one has
constructed about states, or in this case a particular state, rather than on
the structure of the international system.

Emerging as an alternative approach in the late 1980s, constructivism addresses issues in international relations from a different
starting point from either realism or liberalism.[2] Rather than focus
on actors' preferences or interests as a given, constructivists question
the source of an actor's goals. They ask, how are these preferences and

interests formed? Thus, constructivists are more interested with "the issue of identity and interest formation" and the subsequent impact they have on the international system (Wendt 1992, 393). Like most theories or approaches in international relations, constructivists seek to explain change, and how and why it occurs in the international system. In fact, constructivists have a "concomitant faith in the susceptibility to change of even the most seemingly immutable practices and institutions in world politics" (Phillips 2007, 60). Constructivists also focus on how the discourse, attitudes, beliefs, and values about issues such as gender, race, ethnicity, and nationalism inform a state's identity and interests and, in turn, influence the structure of the international system.

Rather than focus on the material structure of the international system like realists (power), liberals (institutions), and economic structuralists (class), constructivists are interested in process, specifically the process of shared ideas and social interaction over time or what is referred to as **intersubjectivity**. In fact, constructivists reject the deterministic feature of the other theories that the structure, defined by power, capabilities, or class, either facilitates or constrains state behavior. For constructivists, concepts such as power and capability only matter to the extent that states have constructed or defined their meaning. It should be clear that language, both the written and spoken word, is an important component in constructivism. Moreover, how a state perceives another, based on norms, ideas, and beliefs, influences its behavior more than how the international system is structured as defined by realists and liberals. One of the core goals of international relations scholars is to understand a state's or other actor's interest and their subsequent behavior. Realists contend that interest in security is driven by the anarchy inherent in the system. Liberals suggest that interests can be achieved cooperatively while economic structuralists argue that interests of the wealthy are achieved through the collusion of elites. Constructivists contend that we are unable to understand interests without examining the underlying ideas, beliefs, values, and norms of the state. This brings us back to the question posed above. Which country with a nuclear weapon—real or potential—is the most threatening? After all, a nuclear weapon in the hands of a friend means something very different than it does in the hands of a foe.

Constructivism and the Third Debate[3]

The end of the Cold War baffled most theorists of international relations. Constructivist scholars Richard Price and Christian Rues-Smit (1998, 265) wrote that it "shook the foundations of international relations theory," while Friedrich Kratochwil (1993, 63) indicated that it was a "crucial test" for neo-realism.[4] Substantively, realists failed to predict the peaceful change at the end of the Cold War, pointing to conflict as the primary vehicle of change to the distribution of power in the international system. Realists argue that the policy of containment was the main contributing factor but they could not adequately explain how the USSR and US escaped the security dilemma and certainly did not foresee the complete internal collapse of the Soviet Union. Liberals argued that the institutions created after World War II and the learned cooperative behavior of the United States and the Soviet Union facilitated the end of the Cold War; however, the lack of strong interdependent economic relationships between the two belie the timing and impact of liberal institutions and regimes. These institutions were in place for years with no significant changes or restructuring that preceded the fall of the Soviet Union. Nonetheless, liberals pointed to détente, the ability of Reagan and Gorbachev to negotiate an arms control treaty (the INF Treaty), and the mitigating influence of international institutions as primary factors bringing about the end of the Cold War. Constructivists, on the other hand, pointed to the changing and evolving ideas that were at the core of state interests and behavior, and argued that attitudes about détente and the changing ideas of the superpower leaders actually fit better into the constructivism paradigm. If competing ideas about Soviet and American identities constructed the rivalry initially, then changed ideas, particularly from Gorbachev's implementation of the policies of *glasnost* and *perestroika*, could reconstruct a new reality.

The existing theories of international relations also fell short on ontological and epistemological grounds. Consequently, we see the emergence of post-positivist or reflective approaches to international relations including constructivism, feminism (see Chapter 6), and critical theory (discussed in Chapter 7). These approaches reject the objective, rational view of realism and liberalism, arguing that subjectivity is called for in addressing how shared norms and issues of identity form state interests and behavior. Recall ontology refers to the study of what exists and the nature of being—that is, what types of objects make up the world. Here, the mainstream theories of international relations assume that the state is the unit of analysis, going so far as to attribute them with individual characteristics. For example, neorealists contend that states are self-interested and rational. Neoliberals also assume that states are fully constituted and behave rationally, although they argue that non-state actors play a significant role in the international system. The **logic of consequences** embedded in rationalism guide neorealist and neoliberals—that is, they engage in behavior that produces the maximum utility and satisfies the actor's interests. Neither theory addresses the process of state formation that might help explain the power distribution in the international system, and in doing so help explain alternative routes of emancipation.

In the case of the end of the Cold War, the primacy of the state as an actor in the international system prevented the major systemic theories of international relations from offering a satisfactory explanation of the undercurrents or source of state change. As we will see, constructivists acknowledge the importance of the state, but for very different reasons. Furthermore, constructivists argue that the **logic of appropriateness** guides actors (i.e., agents), leading them to engage in behavior based on accepted norms deemed legitimate by other agents in the structure. Contrary to the realist view, most states follow norms in the absence of enforcement and threats. Constructivists also suggest that states adhere to norms even without the inducement of economic gain, relative or absolute, which confounds liberals. Ultimately, as the logic of appropriateness suggests, states do what is right or appropriate most of the time due to norms that are deemed legitimate by actors in the structure.

Constructivists ask, from an epistemological perspective, how do we know the things we know? Neorealism and neoliberalism are positivist theories, often utilizing rationalism as their preferred framework. The reliance on the scientific method as the foundation of their substantive claims, according to constructivists, provides a too limited scope of inquiry into the complex issues of international relations. The positivist approach, with its narrowly defined units of analysis, cannot take into account (and measure) concepts such as ideas, norms, and beliefs, factors that are at the core of constructivism. On the other hand, it would be incorrect to classify constructivism as a full-fledged member of the relativist critical theory camp that was the primary foil of the positivist theories of realism and liberalism during the Fourth Debate (discussed in Chapter 7).[5] While it does have more in common with many of the post-positivist approaches, epistemologically, the "true middle ground between rationalist and relativist interpretative approaches is occupied neither by an interpretive version of rationalism, nor by some variety of 'reflectivism' . . . nor by all sorts of critical theories . . . but by *constructivism*" (Adler 1997, 322). So, while constructivists challenge the knowledge claims of positivists and rationalism—that is, realism and liberalism—it pushes critical theory and other interpretative, reflexive, and normative paradigms toward a more empirical approach to the questions that all attempt to address. Ultimately, proponents of this approach suggest that norms and state identity are important factors in understanding "the meaning of anarchy and balance of power, the relationship between state identity and interest, an elaboration of power, and the prospects for change in world politics," all interests to anyone studying international relations (Hopf 1998, 172).

Roots and Evolution of Constructivism

Like many concepts in international relations, a single definition of constructivism is hard to find. According to leading constructivist Emanuel Adler (1997, 322), constructivism is "the view that the manner in which the material world shapes and is shaped by human action and interaction depends on dynamic normative and epistemic interpretations of the material world." Another scholar, John Ruggie (1998a, 856) offers perhaps the most succinct definition by stating, "[i]n short, constructivism is about human consciousness and its role in international relations." The idea here is that society and all types of societal relations do not exist apart from human awareness. What makes society and politics are the people and the individuals, and as such, their ideas and beliefs are important antecedents that must be understood. Thus, "what actors do in international relations, the interests they hold, and the structures within which they operate are defined by social norms and ideas rather than by objective or material conditions" (Barkin 2003, 326). Alternatively, scholar Dale C. Copeland (2000, 189–190) lays out three statements that concisely describe constructivism: "First, global politics is said to be guided by the intersubjectively shared ideas, norms, and values held by actors . . . Second . . . the structure leads actors to redefine their interests and identities in the process of interacting . . . Third, ideational structures and actors . . . co-constitute and co-determine each other." Here, we start to see the major components associated with constructivism.

Martha Finnemore and Kathryn Sikkink (2001, 393), two leading constructivists, contend that constructivism "is not a substantive theory of politics. It is a social theory that makes claims about the nature of social life and social change." In fact, most scholars, including constructivists themselves, agree that constructivism is actually *not* a theory, but rather an approach. This approach provides guidance on what to study (ontology) and how to study it (epistemology). Regardless of whether one considers constructivism a theory or an approach, assumptions or core claims collectively help define constructivism and guide scholarship. As we examine each of these assumptions, we introduce and discuss key concepts important to the constructive paradigm. In doing so, we also compare the constructivist view to the approaches found in the previous three chapters.

Central Assumptions

The central assumptions of constructivism are:

- There is no fixed, determined reality, including the structure of the international system.
- Various agents are important actors in the international system.
- Norms, rules, values, and beliefs of states matter, they are endogenously driven rather than exogenous, and they influence state identity and interests.
- The state (agent) and system (structure) are **mutually constituted**.
- States operate in a structure that is defined in an intersubjective manner rather than in one defined by material factors.

First, as constructivism lies more in the post-positivist camp, constructivists reject the idea of a single, objective reality. They argue that a known, constant reality simply does not exist. Take the concept of anarchy. For realists, this fixed reality of international politics drives states to engage in self-preservation behavior, resulting in a structure of the international system that ultimately determines or constrains state behavior. For constructivists, anarchy is not a fixed or determined reality at all; rather, it is left open to interpretation based upon a state's ideas, interests, values, and beliefs. Ultimately, "anarchy is what states make of it" (Wendt 1992, 395). A state's identity, formed from ideas, interests, values, and beliefs, is not predetermined; consequently, the structure of the international system is not predetermined either. Thus, from an ontological perspective, constructivists are just as interested in process as in structure (favored by realists, liberals, and economic structuralists). A key element in this process is communication, specifically how agents communicate with one another. Hence, language is important. Constructivists take discourse, written and spoken language, as a starting point. This conveys meaning and subsequently is open to interpretation. Constructivists concern themselves with how language is interpreted and argue that the scientific method does not provide a feasible or adequate framework for study. Hence, we need to study social reality (Adler 1997), a social reality that is not predetermined, but constructed through language and the interpretation of a state's values, beliefs, and interests through the linguistic lens.

Second, constructivists argue that a variety of actors in the international system are important, including states. We generally think of agents as actors that have a specific interest and act upon that interest in a rational manner. Constructivists do not take interests as a given; rather, they examine the process by which interests of agents are formed. Let's examine the constructive view of the state first. Many positivists assume that states are rational actors whose interests and even identities are determined by external forces—that is, they are exogenous. In other words, the positivist theories assume that state behavior is a function of either human nature (classical realism and liberalism), how power is distributed within the system (neorealism), or how the wealth of the state determines it international position (economic structuralism). Conversely, constructivists approach state interests from the perspective that we should understand how actors define their interests as well as how states identify threats to their interests. Thus, proponents of constructivism assume that a state's interests and identity are derived internally—that is, endogenously. It is these interests, beliefs, and norms (stemming from identity) that impact and inform the international system.

With that said, most constructivists agree with realists that states are the unit of analysis in the international system; however, the way states act is interpreted very differently.[6] Constructivists also look at what happens within the state, much like liberals. International relations scholar Robert Putnam (1988) argues for a two-level game when analyzing state behavior, particularly in situations where domestic politics and international relations interact. Constructivists agree that it is difficult to separate the levels of analysis—that is, what happens within the state impacts the relations between states in an iterative process. In addition, constructivists believe that the interaction between states and non-state actors is just as important. Constructivists also look at how the ideas, interests, values, and beliefs constitute the social structure *within* states, that in turn influences state behavior in the international system.

Beyond the state, constructivists look to other important agents or actors in the international system, particularly when it comes to promoting norms. International organizations such as IGOs and NGOs, **regimes**, **epistemic communities**, social movements, and even individuals operate as **norm entrepreneurs** and influence both states and the structure of the system. In addition, these agents, including states, "act in society to achieve goals. These goals reflect people's needs and wishes in light of their material circumstances. Every society has rules telling agents which goals are the appropriate ones for them to pursue" (Onuf 1989, 60). The role of rules is further discussed below.

Third, constructivists focus on the origins and evolution of shared beliefs, norms, and interests within the states, as they are integral in establishing state preferences and thus state decision-making. These shared beliefs are part of the **social facts** of the state, that is, their "collective institutional practices" (Ruggie, 1998a, 858) or "the invisible structure of social reality" (Searle, 1995, 4). Examples of such social facts include "linguistic practices, religious beliefs, moral norms, and similar ideational factors. Once constituted as social facts, these ideational factors in turn influence subsequent social behavior" (Ruggie, 1998a, 858). Over time, norm entrepreneurs (see Spotlight) disseminate new ideas within society, resulting in changes to the culture of the group/society that further alter the behavior of the state. This creates a malleable state identity due to the development of new and changing ideas, norms, and beliefs. The state then acts on this new norm in the international system, as do other actors or agents in the international system. In essence, a state's identity becomes their currency in the international system.

Fourth, constructivists also discuss how the agents and the system (structure) are mutually constituted. In essence, the agent and the structure are codependent. They are both dependent and independent at the same time. However, an agent cannot control how other agents in the system interpret this. In other words, "the crucial observation here is that the producer of the identity is not in control of what it ultimately means to others; the intersubjective structure is the final arbiter of meaning" (Hopf, 1998, 175). Thus, just because a state endorses and acts upon a norm important to its identity and interest does not necessarily mean that this norm will become universally adopted. In other words, not all norms become mutually constituted.

Finally, when it does come to structure, constructivists view the states in the system in an intersubjective rather than a material fashion. For neo-realists, the structure of the system shapes state behavior. For example, in a bipolar international system such as the structure of the Cold War, two powerful states in the international system make the rules of the structure that determines the behavior of smaller, less powerful states. For liberals, the actors (state and non-state alike) determine or shape the international system. For constructivists, the causal arrow goes both ways, that is, agents influence the structure and the structure influences agents in a mutually constitutive fashion. Wendt (1992, 406) comments that "it is through reciprocal interaction that we create and instantiate the relatively enduring social structures in terms of which we define our identities and interests." Thus, all types of agents (i.e., international actors) and their relationship (including discourse, actions, and behavior) with each other matter.

We are all subjected to the thoughts, ideas, and beliefs of others. The way we interpret and understand and ultimately add to our own knowledge by reflecting on these shared ideas is called intersubjectivity. It is more than just the exchange of ideas, beliefs, and values between and among people and states; it is how we act and react to them, as well. Constructivists are interested in the intersubjectivity of the system, rather than the material factors that attract realists (power) and liberals (economics). The iterative relationships between ideas and agents (and subsequently the relationship between agents) in the system matter—this is especially true when discussing how change in the international system occurs. For constructivists, this change is predicated on what happens within the state, starting with the ideas and beliefs that are developed into norms that may eventually become adopted in the international system. These norms include either regulatory or constitutive rules. Regulative rules govern existing norms as well as institutions and often develop over time. For example, as the United States moved away from a frontier society, laws were instituted to regulate behavior and protect society—that is, to "order and constrain behavior" (Finnemore and Sikkink, 1998, 891). On the other hand, constitutive rules create new institutions or define a particular set of practices intended as a set of instructions on the prescribed expected behavior. If one has never played Monopoly, for example, the rules of the game still come fully constituted, and they contain a set of practices that are deemed legitimate.

As we can see, separating the core claims and assumptions is difficult as many of the concepts overlap. To help illustrate the key concepts as well as the process of norm emergence and diffusion that is at the core of constructivism (see Figure 5.1), we provide the following example. Prior to World War II, the principles of sovereignty and territorial integrity prevailed in the international system based on the Treaty of Westphalia of 1648. The implication of these accepted principles was that states had free reign within their borders while other states refrained from interfering with each other's internal or domestic politics. The atrocities associated with WWII led to the emergence of new ideas and beliefs about the scope of sovereignty and the international community's responsibility to humanity at large (Step 1). In particular, the United States headed an international effort to enact international covenants codifying human rights in general and the responsibility of states more specifically. Throughout the international system, norm entrepreneurs and transnational actors advocated the protection of individual rights ranging from political to social to economic rights, leading to the emergence of the norm of human rights. For example, in 1961, British lawyer Peter Benenson penned the article "The Forgotten Prisoners" in an attempt to win amnesty for two political prisoners in Portugal. The effort to seek their release, as well as others around the world, led to the creation of Amnesty International. This human rights organization is at the forefront of spotlighting, naming, and shaming repressive states, advocates on behalf of prisoners of consciousness and political prisoners, and works toward ending capital punishment. The acceptance of genocide as a crime against humanity through the efforts of Raphael Lemkin (See Spotlight) is one other example of a norm entrepreneur.

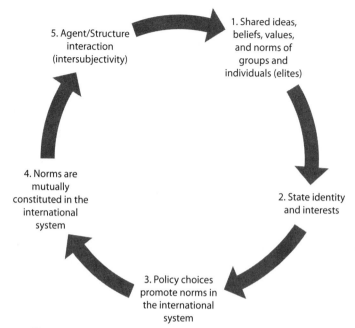

FIGURE 5.1 **The Interactions of the Claims and Assumptions of Constructivism.**

Ultimately, the identity of some states and other agents became synonymous with the protection and promotion of human rights (Step 2). For example, today the Netherlands is identified as a strong promoter of human rights and is home to the International Criminal Court located at The Hague. The Hague is also the site for the International Tribunal for the former Yugoslavia and the Appeals Chamber of the International Tribunal for Rwanda. Beyond states, other agents in the international system work on behalf of human rights, including IGOs, NGOs, and even individuals. Oftentimes, these groups work in tandem, such as the $100 million donation made by international financier and philanthropist George Soros to Human Rights Watch for the purpose of expanding field offices staffed with local citizens. Over time, states engage in policy choices supporting the norm of human rights, for example, sanctioning South Africa over its policy of apartheid (Step 3).

As more and more states adopt the various human rights covenants and treaties, the norm of human rights protection becomes mutually constituted in the international system (Step 4). Finnemore and Sikkink

(1998, 893) argue that the influence of states is "strongest at the early stage of a norm's life cycle, and domestic influences lessen significantly once a norm has become institutionalized in the international system." In the case of human rights, international institutions and organizations lead the way in terms of monitoring, regulating, and even adjudicating human rights claims. The United Nations leads a whole host of intergovernmental organizations aimed at the protection and realization of human rights, including the Office of the United Nations High Commissioner for Human Rights, the Human Rights Council, the United Nations Education, Scientific and Cultural Organization (UNESCO), and the Office of the United Nations High Commissioner for Refugees. Likewise, regional human rights organizations reach just about every corner of the globe. The combination of international law, intergovernmental organizations, and nongovernmental organizations led to the creation of a human rights regime. Through the work of norm entrepreneurs and the various elements of the human rights regimes, a norm emerges in the international system. A tipping point occurs leading to a **norm cascade**, and finally there is the internalization of the norm among states and the system (Finnemore and Sikkink, 1998).[7]

The last phase (Step 5) involves the various agents and the structure reacting and interacting to issues associated with the particular norm. In the case of human rights, we can see how the War on Terror impacted one human rights norm—torture. The United States attempted to alter the internationally accepted definition of torture, and in fact, reframed the argument to suggest that the action was "enhanced interrogation." However, the norm against torture had become so embedded within the international community that a backlash against the United States emerged to the extent that it has lost what little moral high ground it might have had when it comes to the promotion of human rights. The US attempt to redefine torture was not accepted within the international community, demonstrating the power of ideas and norms. Even though the identity and interests of the United States evolved due to the War on Terror and they have even engaged in policy choices in pursuit of their interests, the rest of the international community rejected the new preferred norm of enhanced interrogation promoted by the United States. Constructivism allows us to trace how norms evolve from interests and identities of states and to examine how these norms are either accepted or rejected by the international community. We turn now to a discussion of some of the leading contributors to constructivism.

SPOTLIGHT ON POLICYMAKERS: RAPHAEL LEMKIN

Raphael Lemkin (1900–1959) was a Polish-Jewish lawyer, writer, and activist. He witnessed the atrocities committed by the Ottomans against the Armenians and the pogroms (violent assaults on Jews) in Russia and elsewhere. When Germany invaded Poland in 1939, beginning World War II, Lemkin joined the resistance. After being wounded in the fighting, he fled Europe and eventually found safe haven in the United States via Sweden. He taught at Duke University before assuming a position in the War Department in 1942. In 1945, he became an international law consultant to the Judge Advocate of the US Army and then served as legal advisor to the US Chief Prosecutor in the Nuremberg Trials that prosecuted perpetrators of the Holocaust. Forty-nine members of Lemkin's family, including his parents, were murdered during the Holocaust, thus he had special interest in the proceedings. He is most famous for coining the term "genocide," and he dedicated the remainder of his life to pursuing legal instruments that could be used to prevent additional cases of the atrocity Winston Churchill referred to as "a crime without a name." He was twice nominated for the Nobel Peace Prize, in 1950 and 1952. Physically and mentally exhausting himself in his quest to define, denounce, and prevent genocide, Lemkin died on August 28, 1959, at the age of 59, after collapsing at a bus stop in New York. He was broke and alone. Despite this, and the inconsistent application of the term, the concept and its meaning created an international norm against genocide and other crimes against humanity.

The historical evidence of violence aimed at specific groups of people led Lemkin to seek legal protection for groups of people, rather than individuals, targeted based on their identity. Although Jewish, his identification with the faith was weak, and his concern for targeted groups went beyond that of Jews to mankind in general. Although Lemkin coined the term in 1943, the word genocide first appeared in print in his book, *Axis Rule in Occupied Europe* (November 1944). He formed the word by combining geno-, the Greek prefix meaning race or tribe, and -cide, the Latin suffix meaning killing. He defined his new term as, "the destruction of a nation or of an ethnic group." Further, "genocide does not necessarily mean the immediate destruction of a nation, except when accomplished by mass killings of all members of a nation. It is intended rather to signify a coordinated plan of different actions aiming at the destruction of essential foundations of the life of national groups"

continued

(Lemkin, 1944, 80). In *Axis Rule in Occupied Europe*, Lemkin applied the meaning of genocide to the Nazi campaigns in his native Poland and elsewhere in Europe. In preparing for the Nuremberg trials, Lemkin successfully argued for the inclusion of the word genocide in the indictment against Nazi leaders. While a significant accomplishment, the verdict at Nuremberg only covered crimes committed during a war of aggression. After the trials, Lemkin focused his attention on the new United Nations in his quest for the inclusion of genocide in international law during both peacetime and war.

He undertook an exhausting campaign to persuade the United Nations to draft the Convention on the Prevention and Punishment of the Crime of Genocide, the first UN human rights treaty. Lemkin believed that genocide was not limited to physical killing, but also included the destruction of cultural symbols. Social groups exist because of their common culture, and if destroyed, so too is the group's function. Debates by genocide scholars continue today over the meaning of cultural genocide and if genocide can exist without violence. Many genocide scholars believe it can, but Lemkin argued that genocide had to involve some act of violence. Lemkin was painfully disappointed that the final version of the Genocide Convention did not privilege physical killing over all other activities; he was further dismayed that rather than creating a separate category for cultural genocide, it was included only inherently in Article 2(e) of the Genocide Convention, which forbids "forcibly transferring children of one group to another group." Children are the culture bearers for groups, and thus removing them from their own group equates to an attempt to eliminate a people as a cultural entity. Article 2 of the convention defines genocide, and Article 3 enumerates what acts are punishable under the convention.

Lemkin was known for his tireless, and often annoying, efforts to persuade leaders and national delegations to accept the treaty. He camped out in the hallways of the United Nations, seeking any diplomat who would listen to his pleas. After significant debate and cajoling by Lemkin, the General Assembly unanimously adopted the convention on December 9, 1948. Following the completion of the convention, Lemkin launched another campaign to secure the required number of signatory and ratification states. The treaty received the required number of ratifying states in 1951, and currently there are 146 states who have ratified or acceded to the treaty.

continued

Raphael Lemkin is an exemplar of a norm entrepreneur. He is named in the ranks of other norm creators such as Henri Dunant, who founded the Red Cross in 1863, Eglantyne Jebb, who created Save the Children after WWI, Rene Cassin, who helped draft the UN Universal Declaration of Human Rights and was a judge on the European Court of Human Rights, Aung San Suu Kyi, who initiated a non-violent movement for democracy and human rights in Myanmar, and Leymah Gbowee, who lead a women's peace movement that helped end the Liberian Civil War of 2003. These are all extraordinary people who, with force of will and solitary effort, created widespread acceptance of a moral cause. For his part, Lemkin wrote 11 books, most on issues of international law, and succeeded in bringing not just a new term, but a revulsion against the actions and behaviors behind that term, into international law. As his autobiography, *Totally Unofficial*, makes heartbreakingly clear, Lemkin accomplished this feat without outside support of any kind, often in painful solitude (Lemkin, 2013).

Lemkin would undoubtedly be appalled at the application of the Genocide Convention since his death. The Cold War put a halt to attempts by the great powers to cooperate on issues of human rights and to this day, instead of using the Genocide Convention to promote intervention in cases where a group is being targeted for extinction, great powers have done everything in their power to eschew their responsibilities under the treaty. The most egregious example of this is the 1994 genocide in Rwanda, during which the great powers refrained from using the word genocide to describe the mass slaughter of the Tutsi by the Hutu because the Genocide Convention would have obligated them to do something in response. It is a sad reality that Lemkin did not live to see the first conviction for the crime to which he put a name, as that came in the International Criminal Tribunal for Rwanda in 1998. Although his efforts to pass the Genocide Convention may have thus far failed to prevent genocide, he might take some solace in the knowledge that it has been used to convict and punish perpetrators.

Emergence of Constructivism

As previously discussed, constructivism emerged toward the end of the Cold War as a critique of mainstream international relations theory at a time of great change in the international system. However, there were earlier influences on the paradigm with international relations scholar Richard Ned Lebow even arguing that the father of constructivism was Thucydides, a claim that would surprise most realists. He argued that a deeper reading reveals that Thucydides was concerned with *nomos*, or convention, which can further be interpreted as norms in society. Lebow (2001, 558–559) stated that Thucydides "regarded conventions not only as constraints but also as frames of reference that people use to understand the world and define their interests" and that he "shared the constructivist emphasis on the importance of language, which he thought enabled the shared meanings and conventions that make civilization possible." Further, Lebow argued that Thucydides "implies that civil society is . . . what actors make of it." We can see many of the key concepts utilized by constructivists in the argument put forth by Lebow, specifically, Thucydides' interest in how norms (conventions) inform an agent's interest and subsequent behavior.

Sociologists Emile Durkheim (1858–1917) and Max Weber (1864–1920) provided several points of reference and basic building blocks for constructivism. Durkheim's primary focus was on the creation and effects of social bonds, ranging from an individual's relationship with family to society at large. He believed that these types of social facts could be observed and measured contributing to an empirical analysis of society. His understanding of how social facts constitute an agent, separate from the individuals who make up a society, and then how the agent further influences the behavior of such individuals, contributed to the constructivist emphasis on the argument that agents and structure are mutually constituted. Moreover, his empirical analysis illustrated the causal relationship between social facts and societal outcomes.

Echoing Aristotle's claim that "man is by nature a social animal," Weber (1949, 81) similarly argued that humans are "cultural beings, endowed with the capacity and the will to take a deliberate attitude towards the world and to lend it *significance*. Whatever this significance may be, it will lead us to judge certain phenomena of human existence in its light and to them as being (positively or negatively) meaningful." Weber contended that the knowledge we have of the world can only be known or understood from the particular view point of one's cultural reality. Weber refers to this understanding as *Verstehen*. In other words, one cannot be truly objective regarding what we know about the world, much less the behavior of individuals, because our understanding of the world comes from within our own minds. In this argument, we see the seeds of constructivism, particularly the onto-logical arguments regarding the lack of a known reality as well as the intersubjective nature of humans, culture, and society.

As constructivism is generally considered a product of the 20th century, we look to the arguments presented in the publication of *The Social Construction of Reality* (1966) by Peter L. Berger (1929–) and Thomas Luckmann (1927–) as another early contribution to the development of constructivism. As sociologists, they studied how ordinary people define reality; however, their arguments are easily transferred to the international relations arena. Individuals within a society, through language and discourse, engage in a continuous interaction with one another and eventually create a common knowledge or sets of knowledge about different issues. They argued that individuals created institutions, norms, and rules, and as such, they can be changed. We can infer from this that these institutions, norms, and rules are not immutable and deterministic structures.

In the 1980s, two articles were published criticizing the rational theories (particularly realism), which initiated the sustained development of constructivism as an approach to study international relations. First, John G. Ruggie (1944–) offered a critique of Kenneth Waltz's neo-realism discussed in the influential book *Theory of International Politics* (1979), specifically Waltz's emphasis on structure and the lack of focus on sovereignty (see Chapter 2). Ruggie (1983, 276) argued, "Sovereignty is critical. Unfortunately, it has become utterly trivialized by recent usage, which treats sovereignty either as a necessary adjunct to anarchy or as a descriptive category expressing unit attributes." He further emphasized the importance of including sovereignty, as it "signifies a form of *legitimation*" crucial to a theory of international relations (Ruggie, 1983, 276). Waltz's treatment of international relations highlighted how change must occur at the systemic level and therefore scholars and policymakers must address the issue of anarchy. However, Ruggie argued that what really mattered was the state and the societal changes from within that lead to changes in the system, directly challenging Waltz's conclusions. Ruggie also contributed to constructivism with his work on regimes (with Friedrich Kratochwil in 1986) and epistemic communities (1975).

Second, Richard K. Ashley (1948–) was equally critical of the emphasis realists placed on states and the near exclusion of the role of non-state actors. This perspective doesn't allow for what goes on inside the state. Ashley (1984, 238–239) wrote the "proposition that the state might be essentially problematic or contested is excluded from neorealist theory . . . Despite neorealism's much ballyhooed emphasis on the role of hard falsifying tests as the measure of theoretical progress, neorealism immunizes its statist commitments from any form of falsification." Thus, both scholars took umbrage with the treatment of states; particularly the lack of analysis regarding what took place within the state. Whereas realists, and even liberals, view states as an **atomistic egoist** actor whose interests are formed prior to any social interaction with other states or non-state actors in the system, constructivists delve into the inner workings of the state. It is the social relations within the state that is the starting point for most constructivists.

Much like we saw in realism, liberalism, and economic structuralism, there is disagreement within the constructivist family on a whole host of issues. There are several different schools of thought: **modernist** (neoclassical), **postmodernist**, and **naturalist constructivism** (Ruggie, 1998b). The biggest debate exists between the modernist and postmodernist regarding the appropriate ontological and epistemological foci. A different typology divides constructivism into systemic, unit-level, and holistic forms, which are roughly analogous to the levels of analysis outlined in the introductory chapter. A modernist constructivist can conduct an analysis from a systemic or holistic level of analysis, for example, and the same for postmodernist and naturalists. Those engaged in the unit-level analysis focus on the interests and identities of states, particularly when it comes to foreign policy making and national security strategies. Constructivists engaged in the holistic approach seek to bridge the gap between the systemic and unit-level of analysis. Moreover, within each variant, scholars focused on different concepts, such as states and the structure of the system (structure-oriented constructivism), on norms in terms of norm entrepreneurs, transnational actors, and epistemic communities (norm-oriented constructivism), and finally, on rules (rules-oriented constructivism) (Burch, 2002). All are interested in understanding how social relations and social facts, rather than material facts, influence international relations. We focus on the three different schools of thought and point out the level of analysis and the general orientation of each theorist, where applicable (see Figure 5.2).

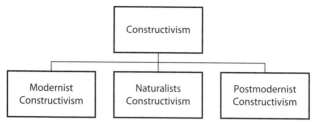

FIGURE 5.2 **Constructivism Family Tree.**

Modernist Constructivists: Pioneers in the Field

On the positivist/post-positivist spectrum, modernists are closer to the positive end and maintain a commitment to conducting studies consistent with the accepted methods in the social sciences. Thus, they want to compete with the rational theories of international relations. Their primary focus is the intersubjective meaning between agents and structure. Nicholas Onuf (1941–) and Friedrich Kratochwil (1944–) are proponents of rules-oriented constructivism and fall into the modernist camp. Both take language as their starting point or foundation in developing the constructivist approach. In his seminal work, *World of Our Making* (1989), Onuf calls for an interdisciplinary approach to the study of international relations, particularly the utilization of social theory prominent in the field of sociology. In order to better understand the world in which we live, analysis must include how individuals, through discourse and shared ideas, create institutions, norms, and identities in a society. He wrote, "In simplest terms, people *and* society construct, or constitute, each other" (Onuf 1989, 36). In addition, to better understand change, analyses need to focus on how humans change their beliefs and norms, which lead to changes in the institutions they create. Ultimately, Onuf (1989) argues that politics is a "world of our making" and not a fixed, static, or objective reality. Like many constructivists, he addresses the issue of anarchy, taking exception to the idea that it has always been a fixture in the international system, as realists claim. After the Thirty Years' War, the replacement of states for the church as the final arbiter (in Europe) instituted in the Peace of Westphalia led to a search for social order. While realists identify anarchy as the ordering principle in this new world, Onuf focuses on the variety of rules (social practices) that are established between people and institutions—rules that are communicated and mutually constituted. Onuf's contribution serves to remind us that constructivism, at its core, is a social theory attempting to explain human behavior in the international relations context.

In *Rules, Norms, and Decisions* (1991), Kratochwil argues that the scientific method is a limiting heuristic (learning) device that precludes an understanding of rules and norms that are prevalent in the international system. He is interested in explaining the source, the formation, and the implementation of such rules and norms and penned what one reviewer called "the closest thing to a manifesto on constructivism in the study of world politics" (Klabbers, 2015, 1195). Kratochwil introduces us to the difference between constitutive and regulative rules, an area that he argues realists fail to distinguish. Constitutive rules operate in such a fashion that they make some behavior impossible and other actions possible. Moreover, Kratochwil contends that we should be examining the source and emergence of these rules and not assume that they are a given. Kratochwil is considered a holistic constructivist in that he attempts to bridge the divide between the domestic and international levels of analysis.

In 1993, Kratochwil offered another critique of neorealism, suggesting that it should be embarrassed at its inability to predict, much less explain, the changes in the international system brought about by the end of the Cold War. Pointing out that the changes occurred due to shifts in the domestic political structure rather than at the international level, Kratochwil (1993, 63) wrote that "neo-realism had no conceptual apparatus for understanding the nature, scope, and direction of change . . . The mass movements brought about sweeping changes through a new conception of empowerment, while the realization of 'powerlessness' of the leading strata point to a crisis in 'power.' Neo-realism as a theory of power, oddly enough, had no way of comprehending either phenomenon." He blames, in part, the failure of realism on the professionalization within the academy that necessitates publications at all costs resulting in research that is neither innovative nor produces a research program that rewards self-criticism or reflection. As an alternative, Kratochwil offers a historical and analytical approach focusing on the rules and norms present in the international system that govern practices and behavior. He posits several queries, including, "What would international relations as a discipline look like if the autonomous sphere of activity was, after all, not constituted by the deep structure of 'anarchy'? . . . What if . . . historical structures were not immutable givens but the result of the practices of actors?" (Kratochwil, 1993, 69). He argues that realism and liberalism cannot answer these questions.

Kratochwil also takes neorealism to task for not paying more attention to multilateralism in the international system, something that post–World War II planners initiated and nurtured. He points out that the norms inherent in a multilateral order, "principles of indivisibility, generalized norms binding upon members, and diffuse reciprocity" are principles that "contradict the central teachings of realism" (Kratochwil, 1993, 70). In this light, the dominant paradigm in international relations is at odds with the policy preferences of foreign policy actors. He also argues that a focus on regimes would help to explain the multilateral approach enacted by the major states after World War II. Ultimately, examining the constitutive rules and norms of society and treating them as antecedents for a particular state's strategy explains state preference and interests far better than a reliance on power as the primary variable of study.

Martha Finnemore (1959–), Kathryn Sikkink (1955–), and Margaret Keck (1949–) are considered modernist, norm-oriented constructivists. Finnemore (1996) examines how international institutions and organizations are able to reconstitute state interests—that is, how such agents can be norm entrepreneurs and influence state behavior at the same time. In essence, she examines the factors that change state behavior making it the dependent variable and international institutions and organizations the independent variables. Since her focus is on the structure side of the agent-structure debate, she is considered a systemic constructivist. She conducts three case studies in her analysis: the International Red Cross, the World Bank, and the United Nations Educational, Scientific and Cultural Organization (UNESCO). Finnemore illustrates how each organization constituted new norms and rules that govern state behavior regarding conduct during war, how states should engage in Third World development issues, and finally how states responded to the charge put forth by UNESCO leading to the creation of science bureaucracies at the state level. Her analysis provides insight into norm development that flows from institutions to states and how these norms, along with the regulative and constitutive rules, become mutually constituted.

In their 1998 collaboration, Finnemore and Sikkink focus on how norms are diffused in the international system. They identify three stages in the life cycle of norm development and utilize two different case studies to illustrate these stages: women's suffrage and the laws of war. First, there is norm emergence where the "characteristics mechanism . . . is persuasion by norm entrepreneurs" (Finnemore and Sikkink, 1998, 895). In the laws of war case study, they point to the efforts of Henri Dunant, a Swiss banker, whose own war experience as a wounded soldier led to the creation of what would become the International Red Cross. As for the women's suffrage movement, Elizabeth Cady Stanton and Susan B. Anthony from the United States and Millicent Garrett Fawcett and Emmeline Pankhurst of England are noted norm entrepreneurs. All of these individuals are important to norm emergence through their promotional work, including the use of "language that names, interprets, and dramatizes" the issues (Finnemore and Sikkink, 1998, 897). Here we see the importance of linguistics and discourse in the norm creation and emergence phase.

Once a critical mass of states adopts a new norm, Finnemore and Sikkink argue that the norm has reached a tipping point. Albeit hard to build a prediction model, their analysis generated two hypotheses: a certain number of states must adopt the norm and certain types of states must adopt the norm. The authors argue that no less than one-third of states must adopt the norm; moreover, states critical to the particular issue at hand must also adopt. Finnemore and Sikkink use landmines as an example and argue that critical states are those involved in the manufacturing and distribution of such weapons. Thus, having a major landmine producer, like Great Britain, accept the norm against landmines goes a long way in reaching the tipping point for the norm cascade to occur.

The second stage of a norm cascade occurs when "norm leaders attempt to socialize other states to become norm followers. The exact motivation . . . where the norm 'cascades' through the rest of the population (in this case, states) may vary, but we argue that a combination of pressure for conformity, desire to enhance international legitimation, and the desire of state leaders to enhance their self-esteem facilitate norm cascades" (Finnemore and Sikkink, 1998, 895). During this stage there are several actors, beyond the norm entrepreneurs, seeking to legitimize the particular norm. States, international organizations (both governmental and non-governmental), transnational actors, and even regimes engage in activities designed at socialization and institutionalization of the norm. In today's environment, human rights NGOs such as Amnesty International or Human Rights Watch use multiple platforms to publicize issues to the general public in order to socialize individuals and states about human rights. During this stage, we start to see a quick succession of state adoption due to a contagion effect whereby states are more influenced by international pressure than domestic movements.

The final stage of norm internalization occurs when "norms acquire a taken-for-granted quality and are no longer a matter of broad public debate" (Finnemore and Sikking, 1998, 895). They caution that the completion of the norm life cycle is not inevitable, as in the example of the United States attempting to redefine torture in the War on Terror. The internalization of norms is a double-edged sword: on the one hand it is a powerful force in the international system as an accepted and legitimate type of behavior. However, the taken-for-granted nature of the norm makes it that much more difficult to discern. This leads to the question of which norms matter and when? It is only when the norm is not taken for granted that we see much debate and discussion. Finnemore and Sikkink demonstrate the constitutive nature of norms and norm development that constructivists argue is at the heart of world politics.

In *Activists beyond Borders: Advocacy Networks in International Politics* (1998), Keck and Sikkink focus on a specific type of norm entrepreneur, or what they call **transnational advocacy networks** (TANs). They suggest that TANs emerge and are influential under certain conditions. First, a variety of actors or agents constitute a TAN, including research groups, advocacy groups, church groups, the media, and unions, as well as the usual governmental and non-governmental organizations. They coalesce and exchange information regarding issues such as environmental matters, women's rights, or instances where "others" are marginalized in society. Second, these TANs tend to emerge when the victims or domestic groups have little or no recourse within their own states and where norm entrepreneurs believe that advocating on their behalf would be useful, if not necessary. Last, TANs engage in a variety of behaviors aimed at alleviating or changing the conditions that create the issue in the first place. Keck and Sikkink argue that a boomerang effect occurs when the TAN pushes citizens in other states to lobby their own governments to action. The issue of female genital mutilation (FGM) serves as one of their examples of how TANs emerge, operate, and ultimately change domestic and international norms. Through the examination of international institutions and organizations (Finnemore, 1996), the process of norm diffusion (Finnemore and Sikkink, 1998) and how TANs combine both organizations and norm diffusion (Keck and Sikkink, 1998), we see how norms, ideas, and beliefs are at the root of the agent-structure debate.

Naturalistic Constructivists: Pioneers in the Field

Alexander Wendt (1958–) is often considered to be in a category unto himself. What makes his approach a "naturalist" one is his adherence to the idea that science provides the best source of knowledge, and in fact, "concedes important points to materialists and individualist perspectives and endorses a scientific approach to social inquiry" (Wendt 1999, 1). Thus, he operates in a more positive fashion than most constructivists, who believe that social and cultural factors more than natural or material factors explain agent behavior. Moreover, Wendt's approach is state-centric given that "states are the dominant form of subjectivity in contemporary world politics" and thus "should be the primary unit of analysis" (Wendt 1999, 9).

Wendt takes as a starting point the work of Kenneth Waltz (see Chapter 2), specifically the material emphasis in the Waltzian description of the international system. While not rejecting material factors outright, Wendt makes an argument for an equally important immaterial and social nature of the structure of the system. Moreover, realists take for granted that the interests and identities of states are known prior to any interaction with other states. Wendt rejects this notion arguing that the "[s]tructures of human association are determined primarily by shared ideas rather than material forces and identities and interests of purposive actors are constructed by these shared ideas rather than given by nature" (Wendt 1999, 1). In fact, Wendt's early articles focus on the concept of identity where he indicates that identities are "relatively stable, role-specific understandings and expectations about self" and these identities serve as the "basis of interests" (Wendt 1992, 397–398).

Wendt (1994) develops several competing state identities: corporate versus social state identity and interests as well as domestic elements of identity versus elements derived from interacting with international society. Wendt describes social identity as "the meaning an actor attributes to itself while taking the perspectives of others" while corporate identity refers to the "intrinsic, self-organizing qualities that constitute actor individuality . . . for organizations, it means their constituent individuals, physical resources, and the shared beliefs and institutions"

(Wendt 1994, 385). In other words, the social identity of a state takes into account the possibility of multiple identities that allows a state to assume a particular identity given a particular situation with regard to another state. For example, a state's identity as a democracy only really matters in its relation to another state. The corporate identity of a state, its fundamental qualities that are encapsulated in its norms, beliefs, and values, leads to its corporate interests. Wendt categorizes these corporate interests as physical security, a desire for predictability in relationships with other actors, recognition by others, and the pursuit of development, generally in economic terms. Moreover, domestic factors and international society influence these corporate and social identities. This supports the constructivist view that interests and identity are mutually constituted in regards to the agent-structure relationship.

This interest in identity leads Wendt to focus on the agents in the traditional agent-structure problem, more specifically the actions of the agents. In doing so, he argues that anarchy is basically in the eyes of the beholder and that the subsequent self-help system identified by realists is in essence a self-fulfilling prophecy. If states believe that anarchy determines the system, then states will engage in the security dilemma. Wendt's position is that the system may be anarchic; this is up to the states, based on their interests and identities, to determine. States create the system they want. However, the anarchic nature of the system does not necessarily lead to a self-help system. He further identifies three ideal types of anarchy based on the interaction of states: **Hobbesian anarchy** characterized by enmity, **Lockean anarchy** with an emphasis on rivalry, and **Kantian anarchy** based on the concept of friendship. According to Wendt, status quo states, those who wish to maintain what they already have, will seek to establish one type of anarchy (Lockean or, ideally, Kantian), while revisionist states will constitute a Hobbesian form of anarchy that fits with their perception of potential conflict. States make what they want of anarchy based on their interests. In turn, the interests of these agents constitute the structure of the system and vice-versa. Wendt doesn't totally reject the concept of power and recognizes that material forces do play a role. He argues that these material forces must be considered alongside the social factors.

Postmodernist Constructivists: Pioneers in the Field

According to Ruggie (1998a, 881), postmodernist constructivists examine the "linguistic construction of subjects" with "[l]ittle hope held out for a legitimate social science." Finnemore and Sikkink (2001, 395) state that "postmodernist constructivists reject efforts to find a point from which to assess the validity of analytical and ethical knowledge claims. This stance makes it possible to deconstruct and critique the knowledge claims of others but makes it difficult to construct and evaluate new knowledge claims." Ultimately, postmodernists reject the scientific method and deem it inappropriate for the social sciences. Their focus is on the effect of language and discourse on the formation of ideas, values, and beliefs of agents and structure. At the same time, they question the rational theories arguments regarding power and anarchy. We focus on the contributions of two postmodern constructivists: Richard Price (1964–) and Christian Reus-Smit (1961–).

Like Finnemore and Sikkink, Price (1995, 75) examines the evolution of the norm regarding the nonuse of chemical weapons (CW) suggesting that the "existence of a stigma against using CW was a necessary condition for the nonuse of CW." Using what he referred to a genealogical approach, Price argues that only a historical analysis offers insight into how this norm developed rather than why—that is, the focus is on how historical events forged the interests and identities of states. An integral part of the genealogical approach is analyzing discourses and power where the former "are theoretical statements that are connected to social practices" (Price 1995, 87). Here, we see the importance of language and linguistics to the post-positivist approach. By tracing the history of chemical weapons and the reaction of states and organizations, Price discovered that the association of CW to poison and later to biological weapons is an important, but not sufficient, factor in the CW taboo. He also examined the discourse regarding the evolving technology associated with CW concluding that the technology itself is not immoral; "their moral value was understood to depend upon how they were used" (Price 1995, 90). In essence, new technologies, including CW, are what states make of it, to borrow from Alexander Wendt. Ultimately, Price concludes that more than anything else, the use of CW would violate the Hague declaration that was viewed as legitimate among the member states. Thus, states were hesitant to go against this norm more than any revulsion against CW. Price points out that these results are not feasible under the realism paradigm that relies on mutual deterrence to explain nonuse. Without employing a historical analysis, Price (1995, 77) argues that it would not be possible to address the following: "How could bombing with CW be more feared than bombing with conventional weapons, and how was it that such categories came to be constituted in the first place?"

In 1998, Price addresses another type of weapon—landmines—and questions how, rather than why, the norm of abandoning landmines and adhering to the ban evolved. Realists look at this query and find that states would either use or forego any particular weapon based on its utility, in this case, in achieving a national security objective. It is one thing to convince a state not involved with the production and distribution of landmines to adhere to the ban; however, how does realism explain "why relatively insecure states—such as Angola, Cambodia, and Croatia and the Taliban regime in Afghanistan—have committed to banning mines . . . The support for a comprehensive ban treaty by 122 nations confounds realist expectations" (Price 1998, 614). Price also argues that liberal theories are unable to adequately explain participation and acceptance of the norm as they "treat interests as exogenous and privileges the state as the key site of agency, whereas in the case at hand the key impetus for normative change lies in processes engendered by transnational and non-state sources of agency that generate interests" (Price 1998, 614).

In this critique of the two dominant positivist paradigms, we see the consistent constructivist themes focusing on the source of state interests and the role of transnational actors. Where Finnemore focuses on how international institutions influenced states and Keck and Sikkink focus on transnational advocacy groups, Price (1998, 615) looks at them both in an effort to understand how they influence "security policies of states by generating international norms that shape and redefine state interests." Here, we see the constructivists' emphasis on the intersubjectivity that occurs in the structure.

Christian Reus-Smit also takes a historical approach as he attempts to explain how norms and rules translate into governing institutions. In *The Moral Purpose of the State: Culture, Social Identity, and Institutional Rationality in International Relations* (1999)[8], Reus-Smit traces governing institutions from the Greeks to the Italian city-states to the monarchies in Europe and argues that we need to understand the connection between the social identity of a society and the governing practice and institutions that they create, something he refers to as "constitutional structures." Again, this is something that realism and liberalism cannot address given their positivist framework. We see the familiar constructivist argument that social reality and facts are the starting point for understanding political outcomes. Reus-Smit focuses on the historical and discursive elements in the development of norms—that is, how language facilitates intersubjectivity, which then leads to institutions within a society. This is the only way to explain the different types of institutions created by the vastly different types of societies and, in turn, how these institutions influence society.

In 1998, Price and Reus-Smit posited whether critical theory (see Chapter 7) and constructivism taken together constituted a "dangerous liaison"? Here they make an important contribution to the ontological and epistemological debates, specifically the call for even the most critical of theories to engage in more "conceptual elaboration and sustained empirical analysis" (Price and Reus-Smit 1998, 264). After reviewing the factors that led to the emergence of constructivism and the ontological propositions familiar at this point, Price and Reus-Smit address the nexus between constructivism and critical theory. First they comment on the critical theorists critique of the positivist nature of some constructivist research and warn that this "is a precarious strategy at best—either it can be turned easily against the critics themselves, or denying that, then it is not clear what the critics can say about the improvements they offer. One could equally indict some critical theorists for parallel sins using the same technique of guilt by word association" (Price and Reus-Smit 1998, 270). In essence, the authors believe this infighting only serves to hurt both critical and constructivism in the long run and look for ways to bridge the theoretical, and primarily, ontological and epistemological, divide.

More specifically, Price and Reus-Smit (1998, 271) investigate whether constructivism, in their engagement with mainstream theories of international relations, "have abandoned or transgressed certain principles of critical international theory." They examine how constructivists utilize evidence and the limits of interpretation, whether they adhere to law-like generalizations (a violation in the minds of critical theorists), and the extent to which constructivists engage in the scientific method. They find that even in engaging with the mainstream theories, "constructivism need not be inconsistent with the development of a broadly defined critical theory of international relations" as they "have built on ontological assumptions and drawn on conceptual frames and methodological techniques that have their origins in critical social theory" (Price and Reus-Smit 1998, 283). In fact, the authors contend that the constructivist engagement has enhanced its research

program and even facilitated interdisciplinary dialogue and theoriz-
ing. Moreover, they argue that constructivism can make a positive
contribution to critical theory itself and refute the belief that such a
relationship constitutes a "dangerous liaison."

Criticisms of Constructivism

Constructivism appeals to many introductory students, and seasoned
scholars alike, due to the fact that it seems to make sense. As individuals, we can easily relate to the notion that as our ideas and beliefs
evolve and change over time, so do our preferences. Applying this to
the system of international relations is not that big of a leap. The idea
that states are not destined to a future determined by factors outside
of its control is also intellectually satisfying. The deterministic qualities of realism and liberalism leave most states in the international
system as nothing more than pawns in the game of big power politics.
Furthermore, constructivists opened a dialogue focusing on the source
of actor's beliefs, values, and preferences. In spite of its appeal, there are
critics from both the rationalists (realists and liberals) as well as from
some of its post-positivist brethren.

First and foremost, critics argue that constructivism is simply not
a theory of international relations; rather what they provide is a framework on how to study politics. Constructivists' response to this critique is that they "find the pursuit of a general theory of international
relations an absurdity" (Reus-Smit 2013, 230). As pointed out in the
chapter, most constructivists themselves base their research agenda on
a set of assumptions about how to study international relations and
focus on the ontological and epistemological elements to guide their
queries. However, Alexander Wendt argues that he indeed developed
a constructivist theory in *Social Theory of International Politics* (1999),
utilizing accepted methodological standards in the field.

Second, the rejection of the idea of a known reality allows constructivism to get away with not testing any verifiable hypotheses. If
everything is subjective, what is there to test? Furthermore, along with
subjectively comes the problem of relativity. How do we know right
from wrong? How do we judge actions? Critics contend that constructivism has made a lot of hay by criticizing the assumptions of realism
and liberalism as well as their conclusions, but have generally failed
to develop their own substantive assumptions about how the world

196 INTERNATIONAL RELATIONS THEORY

works. Realist scholar John Mearsheimer (1994), in particular, argues that constructivism and post-positivists in general have yet to offer any policy prescriptions on a whole host of issues, including the mechanisms for peaceful change.

Third, critics focus on the abstract and normative nature of many constructivist concepts. For example, realists argue that norms are simply another name for interests. A state can easily veil its interests in the lexicon of norms and values. Likewise, international relations scholar J. Samuel Barkin (2003, 335) argues that constructivism is simply liberal idealism with a new name stating, "constructivist theorists are, in fact, predominantly liberal idealists." Indeed, constructivism shares with liberalism a focus on norms and institutions as well as a faith in logic of appropriateness. Both realism and liberalism also take umbrage with the inability to adequately measure some of the key concepts of constructivism: ideas, beliefs, values, and norms. Moreover, constructivism lacks a connection to any political philosophy; "consequently, the normative commitments that give realism, liberalism, or even Marxism the degree of internal coherence for them to serve as distinctive rival approaches to the study of IR are absent from constructivism" (Phillips 2007, 67).

Fourth, while constructivists focus on agents, liberals contend that it is institutions that matter and constructivists do not go far enough in acknowledging the importance of these institutions. However, as we see in the work of Finnemore and Reus-Smit, constructivists often engage in how institutions are formed and sustained. Fifth, realists and liberals alike criticize constructivism's naïveté regarding the importance of power in the international system. As indicated, constructivists focus much more on the social elements and less on the material factors in international relations. The one major exception is Alexander Wendt. This perceived deficiency allows critics to question how constructivism can offer any guidance to those interested in national security, war, and other international issues that require a discussion of power.

Case Study: Proliferation

The question posed at the beginning of the chapter speaks to the nature of the constructivist argument. Which country that currently has a nuclear weapon is the most feared? A rational assessment would lead one to point to the United States or Russia given their still large nuclear stockpiles. However, North Korea and Iran are viewed as the most dangerous states in the international system due to their respective pursuits of nuclear technology. On the subject of proliferation, constructivism points to the advancement of a nuclear taboo brought about by changing norms regarding nuclear weapons. This nuclear taboo evolved within and among the community of states, which the NPT theoretically serves to reinforce. The fact that North Korea remains outside of the agreement (along with Pakistan, India, and Israel) contributes to the perception that non-member states pose a significant security risk to the international system as a whole. Constructivism helps to explain the development of the nuclear taboo as well as the pariah status of North Korea and Iran. Thus, the nuclear proliferation case offers an illustration of constructivism in a couple of ways: norm development and the identity of states.

Why hasn't a state utilized a nuclear weapon since August 1945? Realists argue that deterrence prevented a nuclear holocaust between the superpowers during the Cold War. Liberals assert that international organizations help to mitigate conflict in the international system. However, these explanations do not answer the following: Why didn't the Soviet Union or the United States deploy nuclear weapons in any of their other conflicts, such as the USSR's long war in Afghanistan or the US war in Vietnam? Nina Tannenwald (2005, 2007) presents a compelling argument that a nuclear taboo evolved based not on security or economic concerns or even deterrence, but rather on the idea that nuclear weapons were simply too destructive and devastating for civilized societies to entertain. She argues that the nonuse of nuclear weapons is more than a norm and that the term taboo denotes "a particularly forceful kind of normative prohibition that is concerned with the protection of individuals and societies from behavior that is defined or perceived to be dangerous. It typically refers to something that is not done, not said, or not touched" (Tannenwald 2005, 8). When it comes to nuclear weapons and proliferation, the "subjective (and intersubjective) sense of 'taboo-ness' is one of the factors that makes the tradition of nuclear nonuse a taboo rather than simply a norm" (Tannenwald 2005, 9). Note that this taboo is not a legal norm; rather it is considered a de facto norm, as the prohibition of the use of nuclear weapons is not codified in international law. The question then, is, how did the taboo develop, and why do states comply?

This nuclear taboo emerged during a time that might be considered the height of US hegemony, a time when the US actually opposed such a norm due to its Cold War security concerns. Thus, theories focusing on hegemony and power fail to explain how the idea that utilizing a weapon that would ensure security should be shelved could even emerge, much less become the norm in the international community. The norm against nuclear weapons developed in stages (van Wyk et al. 2007; Tannenwald, 2005).[9] From 1945 to the 1970s, the international community faced the realities of nuclear testing by the major powers as well as tense international confrontations such as the Cuban Missile Crisis that, along with the memory of the use of atomic weapons in World War II, provided the framework to consider nonuse. The passage of the NPT in 1968 delivered the legal framework in that it codified the prohibition against the proliferation of nuclear weapons, but not the nonuse. The 1995 extension of the NPT contributed to the nonproliferation regime to the extent that most states are signatories and deem the regime to be legitimate.

However, the end of the Cold War and then 9/11 altered the nuclear landscape to the extent that new concerns emerged absent the traditional great power rivalries. In its stead were the threats from regional conflict and non-state actors, namely international terrorist groups. While the United States was not successful in redefining torture in the War on Terror, their role as a norm entrepreneur vis-à-vis nuclear proliferation is a different matter, as "the US was instrumental is constructing and institutionalizing new meaning and norms relating to nuclear weapons, such as the establishment of the Proliferation Security Initiative (PSI) and the Global Threat Reduction Initiative (GRTI)" (van Wyk et al. 2007, 30). Likewise, Tannenwald (2005, 2007) points to the activities of the United States as a norm entrepreneur, in particular, their promotion of the idea that the use of nuclear weapons was not consistent with civilized societies.

Given the acceptance of the nuclear taboo by the international community at large, what explains the continued pursuit of nuclear weapons by Iran and North Korea? Here, constructivism offers additional insight, beyond the security and power arguments provided by realists. This analysis requires us to delve into not only domestic politics, something realists are loath to do, but to the source of how Iran's and North Korea's self or corporate identity developed. Constructivists point to the social facts that have led to the identity and perspective of these two rogue states, as well as the intersubjective relations with the international community in general and the United States more specifically. Nuclear weapons constitute a social fact—that is, they "illustrate, among other things, states' commitment to their constructed social purpose, namely maintaining power and prestige (i.e., identity), and dominance (i.e., identity *and* interests)" (van Wyk et al. 2007, 23). This compels Iran and North Korea to pursue nuclear technology in spite of the universal norm regarding nonproliferation and the perception by most of the international community that they are pariah states.

For Iran, the pursuit of nuclear technology and weapons is a rational policy choice given several realities: its regional insecurities vis-à-vis Iraq and subsequent desire for regional hegemony, the history before and after the rule of Shah Mohammad Reza Pahlavi, and the presence of the United States in the region. Ironically, the United States and its allies supported the development of nuclear technology in Iran during the Shah's regime (Whyte 2011). Iran, an original signatory of the NPT, ratified the treaty in 1970 in order to purchase nuclear power plant technology from the United States. This support obviously changed with the Iranian Revolution of 1979, when the US withdrew any support—and more importantly, material—for a nuclear program. Iran's desire to acquire nuclear weapons goes beyond a security concern, as it would bring "honor and prestige" as they attempt to "play a leading role in the Persian Gulf region . . . Becoming the first nuclear-capable Muslim nation in the Middle East would allow them to enhance their appeal to Muslims across the region, despite sectarian differences" (Sherrill, 2012, 43). Perhaps even more important, having nuclear capabilities would be a symbol of Iran's independence from Western dominance. As most universal norms are viewed as driven by western states, particularly in the aftermath of World War II, the acquisition of nuclear weapons would raise Iran's stature not only in the Middle East, but in the rest of the developing and non–aligned states in the system. In essence, Iran is attempting to promote an alternative norm of noncompliance. As Sherrill (2012, 44) comments, "They want to parade their nuclear arms in front of friends and adversaries."

If this is the case, then why did Iran agree to a deal in 2015 in which they consent to ending their pursuit of nuclear weapons in exchange for lifting of economic sanctions? The deal, between Iran, China, France, Germany, Great Britain, Russia, and the United States, requires Iran to reduce its stockpile of enriched uranium and the number of centrifuges it has to produce the uranium over the next 10–15 years. To ensure compliance, the agreement has an inspection regime conducted by the International Atomic Energy Agency (IAEA). Although the deal remains tenuous, we must consider how this impacts Iran's identity. Iran's reason for agreeing could be one of two options. First, Iran could be moving towards norm-consonant behavior, in that they have come to realize after decades of economic sanctions and pariah status, it is actually in their best interest to abide by the norm of nonproliferation. Second, Iran could be looking to follow the path of another pariah state, North Korea. In October 1994, North Korea and the United States negotiated the Agreed Framework, which called for the eventual elimination of North Korea's nuclear facilities in exchange for assistance in their energy sector (the building of proliferation resistant nuclear power plants). The agreement broke down in 2003, when North Korea announced its withdrawal from the NPT, followed in 2005 by their declaration that they had developed nuclear weapons, culminating in their first nuclear test in 2006. Many argue that the Agreed Framework allowed North Korea to develop its program in secret, actually assisting in the very thing it was intended to prevent. Thus, it is possible Iran is pursuing its norm of noncompliance through the façade of compliance.

Likewise, North Korea flouts international norms with its attempts to acquire nuclear weapons. Again, utilizing a constructivist framework allows scholars to go beyond the obvious security arguments offered by realists and the rationale most asserted by policymakers and pundits. North Korea's corporate identity "is based on the so-called *Juche* idea, which means that the state will maintain its *Chajusong* (independence) through self-reliance" (van Wyk et al., 2007, 33). This manifests in the state as they construct policies designed to protect its citizens from the west, and from the United States specifically, "which it regards as a country of 'western barbarians' and as 'imperialist'" (van Wyk et al., 2007, 33). Thus, due in large part to ideational factors, North Korea has pursued a nuclear program with the ultimate goal of demonstrating to the rest of the international community that it deserves respect. The continued discourse and standoff between the United States and North Korea perpetuates the latter's belief that the United States is bent on regime change on the peninsula.

Constructivism provides a framework to look beyond the material factors obvious to the issue of nuclear proliferation. It allows us to understand how and why a nuclear taboo developed in the face of national security concerns; concerns that would otherwise suggest that there were no weapons off limits. Likewise, constructivism helps to explain why countries like North Korea and Iran continue to seek nuclear technology as history, identity, language, and discourse come together to construct a state's interest that is contrary to what realism or liberalism would predict.

TABLE 5.1 Constructivism and Proliferation

Constructivist Thought	Theoretical Tenet	NPT Example
Modern Constructivism (Norm-oriented)	Modernists examine how rules, norms, and structure influence the intersubjectivity of the agent-structure relationship. Norm-oriented constructivists focus specifically on how norms are constituted through norm entrepreneurs and transnational advocacy networks and adopted by states in the international system.	The development of the norm of non-use of nuclear weapons is explained as a consequence of the nuclear taboo. After the end of the Cold War and the events of 9/11, the United States acted as a norm entrepreneur in arguing that the use of such weapons was not consistent with civilized states.
Naturalist Constructivism	Adheres to the scientific and systemic approach to the study of international relations, yet argues that social and cultural factors as well as state identity are as important as material factors. Naturalists agree with other constructivists that interests and identities of states are not fixed or known.	The pursuit of nuclear weapons by Iran and North Korea is explained in part by the development of state identity based on power and prestige. Iran's identity is also tied to their desire for hegemonic status in the Middle East and as a model of defiance vis-à-vis the United States and other signatories of the NPT. North Korea's nuclear pursuits are consistent with its desire for respect in the international community and to demonstrate to its own citizens that it can stand up to the United States and other "imperialist" states.

continued

Constructivist Thought	Theoretical Tenet	NPT Example
Postmodern Constructivism	Postmodern constructivists focus on how language and discourse influence the development and formation of ideas, norms, values, and beliefs of agents as well as the structure of the international system. Thus, they look at the historical process, through the lens of language and discourse, to explain policy outcomes.	Over time, the language used to describe nuclear weapons changed from concepts of power and prestige to weapons that were deemed immoral. This change in discourse helped to change the norms associated with nuclear weapons and helps to explain why most states willingly join the NPT

Case Study: WTO

As was discussed in the introductory chapter, international trade often pits wealthy and poor countries against one another. The WTO is designed to even the playing field and allow developing countries to reap the benefits of the liberal trade regime. Like the NPT, the WTO constitutes a set of norms developed over time between and among states. The free trade norm, in particular, serves to promote economic development, but it is also considered to have a "peace dividend", as trading partners rarely engage in violent conflict due to the potential for economic loss. Thus, the idea that free and open trade leads to not only economic development but also peaceful international relations has been a norm that the United States and other liberal states have promoted since the end of World War II. This dual benefit of the free trade norm is one of the hallmarks of the WTO. The statistical evidence confirms the increased openness to trade. In 1980, less than 30% of the countries in the international system had open trade policies (Sachs and Warner, 1995); however, by 2000, this number had climbed to 73% (Wacziarg and Welch, 2008).

Constructivists argue that liberalism and other positivist theories cannot address two specific paradoxes: First, China's identity as a developing country in the WTO on the one hand, versus its powerful identity in terms of economic and military power on the other (Khan, 2004); second, the seemingly abrupt change of position from opposing a multilateral trade regime to support among the coalition of developing countries (Ford, 2002). When it comes to the China case, constructivism allows us to examine how identity informs policy decisions, while in the latter case, we will see how collective ideas regarding free trade become institutionalized as norms. Ironically, "many [developing] countries unilaterally liberalized and became vocal advocates for stronger multilateral rules. They sought to hoist developed economies with their own petard by highlighting protectionism in developed countries" (Ford, 2002, 116).[10]

Before proceeding to these two questions, we must first address how constructivists explain the development of the free trade norm. Several mechanisms have contributed to this norm: the hegemonic and soft power of the United States, the successive rounds of GATT, domestic economic and social coalitions, and an increasing acceptance by most countries of the liberal free trade regime. While accepting these factors, constructivists are more interested in how the idea of free trade was initially diffused across the globe and then internalized and adopted by states. One study attributes this diffusion to the influence of US-trained economists, specifically their ability to "influence policy through the dissemination of ideas, leading to changes in the preferences of voters and policymakers" (Weymouth and Macpherson, 2012, 672). These US economists act as an epistemic community by influencing and shaping the perceptions of key policymakers. More specifically, these experts were able to share the norm regarding the economic and social benefits of trade openness first developed among themselves through graduate training. Over time, the greater the number of economists in a country, the more likely and the more quickly that country adopts policy reforms in line with the norm of free trade. This study helps to illustrate the constructivist argument that ideas emanating from norm entrepreneurs, in this case an epistemic community of US-trained economists, inform public policy in an intersubjective manner, resulting in the emergence and development of a new norm. Here, we have new and changing economic ideas leading to trade liberalization.

In 2001, China had the fourth-largest economy in the international system. In addition, it was the sixth-ranked country in terms of military expenditures behind the United States, France, Japan, the United Kingdom and Germany.[11] In the aggregate, China's economic and military power suggests that it is a powerful country regionally and globally. Thus, China's entry in the WTO the same year as a developing country is perplexing. How can this be explained? On a practical level, China can point to its large population to demonstrate its developing country status. For example, when examining its economy, China's per capita GDP between 1996 and 2001 was $5,574, compared to $49,781 for the United States. In the 2011–2015 time period, these figures rose to $7,594 and $54,629 respectively. In terms of military expenditures, China spends $75 per capita compared to $2,140 for the United States. Moreover, the United Nations classifies China as a developing country, albeit one with upper-middle income based on its per capita GNI.

From the constructivist point of view, the answer lies in China's identity and subsequent interests as a developing country. The WTO does not define what constitutes a developed or developing country, rather upon accession members announce for themselves. There are obvious advantages to the developing country label, specifically certain rights which allow such countries longer transition times, often referred to as "special and differential treatment", as well as technical assistance in efforts to adhere to WTO trade policies.[12] Herein lies China's interest in self-identifying as a developing country. Entering the WTO as a developing country provides China with a "normative shield to uphold its economic interests" as it engages in trade negotiations (Khan, 2004, 17). Beyond this advantage, China sought to join the WTO to satisfy additional economic interests, primarily to protect its ability to access Western markets and compete within the EU and NAFTA frameworks. In this manner, the Chinese identify with other developing countries that are concerned with competing in the international trade regime.

The view and role of these developing countries in the free trade regime provides an opportunity to highlight how constructivism can help explain political behavior that belies the positivist theories of international relations. During the early rounds of GATT, developing countries exhibited a strong tendency to reject the terms of trade put forth by the industrialized states in general, and the United States more specifically. By most accounts, developing countries would be at a great disadvantage under the new free trade norm developing under the guidance of US hegemony and the pressure exerted by GATT, as they would have to abandon protectionist policies aimed at spurring internal industrial growth and preventing imports from glutting the domestic market. Since the end of World War II, developing countries spent a great deal of energy forming an identity as "the protectionist Other to a Self of predominantly developed country traders" (Ford, 2002, 122). Over the years, the developing countries forged groups such as the Group of 77 (G77) and developed manifestos such as the New International Economic Order (NIEO) in order to pursue favorable trade policies. Moreover, GATT reinforced this identity "as 'protectionist Other,' with provisions for discretionary special and differential treatment" (Ford, 2002, 123). The reversal of this position on the part of developing countries, thus, is difficult to explain utilizing the realist or liberal paradigm.

Constructivist theory, once again, focuses on the interests of the states and how these interests alter the ideas put forth by developing countries in regards to trade protectionism. During the Uruguay Round specifically, developing countries became alarmed by the increasing attempts by the United States and the EU to enact protectionist policies in certain industries and more importantly, in the area of agricultural products. In an ironic turn, developing countries called for trade liberalization while developed countries, long advocates of trade openness, attempted to engage in protectionism. What emerged were coalitions of both developed and developing countries, such as the Cairns Group, that called for trade liberalization in the agricultural sector. The developing countries were willing to make sacrifices in the service and tech sectors in order to "secure a stronger multilateral regime. This action was due to a variety of material and ideational reasons" (Ford, 2002, 127). The Cairns Group and other coalitions began to hold GATT's feet to the fire regarding adhering to rules and regulations set forth in the trade regime and sought to prevent developed countries from utilizing their economic clout to sway GATT rulings. Here, we see that constructivism helps to explain the change in policy preferences on the part of developing countries that realism and liberalism alone cannot explain. Moreover, constructivism helps to explain how ideas and interests combine to alter a state's policy position.

Conclusion

As we have seen, constructivists argue that ideas and identities are the starting point for the "world of our making" rather than material factors such as military or economic power. In this chapter, we traced the emergence and evolution of constructivism, focusing on its position between positivist and post-positivist approaches to international relations as well as its take on the ontological and epistemological elements

TABLE 5.2 **Constructivism and the WTO**

Constructivist Thought	Theoretical Tenet	WTO Example
Modern Constructivism	In the area of international political economy, modern constructivists not only examine how individuals and norm entrepreneurs aid in the development of international norms, but also look at how international institutions regulate and enforce norms as well as develop norms that are adopted by states. They argue that states respond to both ideational and material factors in the policy-making process.	In attempting to promote and regulate the norms of the free trade regime, the WTO accepted China into the organization in 1995. At the same time, constructivism helps to explain China's decision to ascend as a developing state based on its identity and interests. In economic terms, China identifies as a developing state, in spite of its military prowess. WTO rules allow special dispensation for developing states as they enact free trade policies.
Postmodern Constructivism	Rejecting the rational actor model and material factors as the sole motivating factor for state behavior in regards to the economy, postmodern constructivists trace how states and institutions develop ideational norms by examining their discourse, language, and actions.	Developing states initially resisted the norm of free trade based on their identity and interests. By tracing the actions and discourse of wealthy advanced states, particularly regarding the attempt to protect their own agricultural interests, postmodern constructivism helps us understand how and why LDCs altered their own preferences regarding the free trade norm and their support of the norms institutionalized in the WTO.

of theory. Constructivists look at the norms, beliefs, and values within societies in order to understand how a state's interest develops and furthermore, how these interests are then pursued in the global arena of international politics. While some constructivists focus on the norms or rules and others focus on the structure of the system, all constructivists examine the interaction between the agents and structure in order to better understand how states behave in the international system.

As you read the next chapter on feminism, you will encounter elements of constructivism again as these two approaches share an emphasis on ideas and norms.

Key Terms

Atomist egoist
Hobbesian anarchy
Epistemic communities
Intersubjectivity
Kantian anarchy
Lockean anarchy
Logic of appropriateness
Logic of consequences
Modernist constructivism
Mutually constituted
Naturalist constructivism
Norm cascade
Norm entrepreneur
Postmodernist constructivism
Regimes
Social facts
Transnational advocacy network

For Further Reading

Adler, Emaneul. 1997. "Seizing the Middle Ground." *European Journal of International Relations*. 3(3): 319–363.

Checkel, Jeffrey. 1998. "The Constructivist Turn in International Relations Theory." *World Politics*. 50(2): 324–348.

Wendt, Alexander. 1992. "Anarchy is What States Make of It: The Social Construction of Power Politics." *International Organization*. 46(2): 391–425.

———. 1999. *A Social Theory of International Politics*. Cambridge: Cambridge University Press.

Zehfuss, Maja. 2002. *Constructivism in International Relations*. Cambridge: Cambridge University Press.

Endnotes

[1] Data gathered from the Arms Control Association at www.armscontrol.org.

[2] Some constructivists identify themselves as part of the critical theory paradigm (see Chapter 7) which includes other critical international theories such as post-modernism, feminists, and neo-Marxists (Price and Reus-Smit 1998).

[3] Recall we outlined the four debates in the introductory chapter. Note that many scholars refer to the debate between positivists (rationalists) and post-positivists (reflectivists) as the Third Debate. These scholars do not view the inter-paradigmatic debate between realists, liberals and economic structuralists as one of the major debates in international relations.

[4] Kratochwil included the demise of the Soviet bloc and the reunification of Germany as additional tests of neorealism.

[5] As discussed in more detail in Chapter 7, critical theory attacked positivist theories stance on their immutable view regarding the structure of the international system and perhaps more importantly, offering policy prescriptions based on this stance (Cox, 1981). Moreover, critical theorists brought a normative approach to the study of international relations leading the positivist theorists to question their claims due to a lack of perceived empirical analysis.

[6] This is particularly true of constructivists who call for a systemic approach to the study of international relations (e.g., Wendt).

[7] A more complete discussion of the life cycle of norms is provided later in the chapter.

[8] Many of these ideas were initially published in "The Constitutional Structure of International Society and the Nature of Fundamental Institutions" in *International Organization* in 1997.

[9] Van Wyk et al. (2007) present the development of the norm against nuclear weapons in four distinct phases while Tannenwald (2005, 2007) traces the nuclear taboo through two stages.

[10] The phrase 'hoist by one's own petard' is found in Shakespeare's *Hamlet* and is defined as being hurt, damaged, or destroyed by one's own plot to hurt another.

[11] Military expenditure data is information from the Stockholm International Peace Research Institute (SIPRI), http://www.sipri.org/research/armaments/milex/milex_database/milex_database.

[12] This designation is not absolute, however, as the Generalized System of Preferences (GDP) allows the preference giving country to accept or deny certain benefits to a self-described developing country. The Generalized System of Preferences is a program where developing countries are given preferential treatment in the form of lower trade barriers for certain products in order to gain access to markets in developed countries.

CHAPTER 6

Feminism

"Representation of the world, like the world itself, is the work of men; they describe it from their own point of view, which they confuse with the truth."

—Simone de Beauvoir

Would it be more peaceful if women ruled the world? This is a common question asked of students in introductory courses in international relations. Feminists are more likely to ask, "Where are all the women?" In other words, given the percentage of females within each country, why are there not more women in positions of power? Harvard professor Swanee Hunt addressed this very question in a 2007 essay in *Foreign Affairs* titled, "Let Women Rule." Referencing studies by the World Bank, NGOs, and academics, Hunt concluded that indeed the world would be more peaceful. In countries where there are higher numbers of women in parliament, there are lower levels of corruption. Women holding elected office are positively correlated with greater levels of economic competitiveness. Surveys indicate that women are more trustworthy, have higher moral and ethical standards, and generally have a broader definition of security, one that goes beyond the security of the state. Women in positions of government are also more likely to address the needs of those marginalized in society, a product of their previous experiences in the NGO and non-profit arenas.

Given this evidence, Hunt asks, "Where are the women leaders?" She argues that women are not eager or willing to run for political office for several reasons: the perception that politics is a dirty game and a man's world, societal expectations of the traditional female role of wife and mother, and sexist political roadblocks including threats of physical violence. Consequently, potential female political leaders gravitate toward NGOs and other outlets that have less structural impediments for women. Hunt suggests several areas of reform ranging from recruitment and training strategies to campaign finance reform to quotas at every level of government. Still, today there are only 50 female elected heads of state or government in the international system comprising 26% of the 193 member countries of the United Nations. In the business sector, only 23 women (less than 5%) are CEOs of all the companies that make up the Fortune 500. As part of the women's movement, feminists fought for equal representation in positions of leadership, both in government and business. Yet, they continue to ask, "Where are all the women?"

We start to see more women elected to positions of power in government after World War II, but are they more peaceful? In India, Indira Ghandi became the first female prime minister in 1966, serving in that role until 1977 and again from 1980 until her Sikh bodyguard assassinated her in 1984. Under her leadership, India went to war with Pakistan in 1971. From 1969 to 1974, Golda Meir served as the leader of Israel and guided her country during the aftermath of the massacre of eleven Israeli athletes at the 1972 Munich Olympic Games and then led Israel in the 1973 Yom Kippur War. In 1979, voters elected Margaret Thatcher as the United Kingdom's, in fact Europe's, first female prime minister. A staunch defender of Europe against communism and a close ally of President Ronald Reagan, Thatcher hardly embodied the popular image of a feminist. The woman known as the "Iron Lady" reportedly told President George H.W. Bush, "Don't go wobbly on me," urging resolve when Saddam Hussein invaded Iraq in 1999. Women like Ghandi, Meir, and Thatcher demonstrated to many observers that once in power there was little difference in behavior between men and women. In fact, their behavior in office aligned with the realist perspective, particularly the primacy of national interests and concerns regarding the distribution of power. In addition to the development of feminism as a critical theory of international relations, we also see feminists influenced by the liberal, Marxist, and constructivist paradigms creating an approach to international relations that is complicated and complex. Moreover, feminism is both a social movement and a theoretical approach creating blurred lines between the two. Thus, feminists are more likely to be engaged in the political process as activists than the theorists discussed in the chapters on realism, liberalism, and constructivism.

What is feminist theory? According to scholar Christine Sylvester (1994, 9), it "is about studying gender—its stories, shapes, locations, evocations, and rules of behavior—usually in tandem with other modern subject statuses such as class, race, age, religion, region, and so on." Another prominent feminist scholar, V. Spike Peterson (2004, 36), argues in order for a study or approach to be considered feminist it must be "*critical* of masculinism and gender hierarchy." Thus, feminists ask very different questions. For example, do women really behave differently than men in positions of political or economic power? If so, what does this suggest about policy outcomes? Other feminists argue that a more appropriate question is whether the international relations discipline, as well as the practice, is biased. Specifically, does the way that the discipline thinks about international relations have a masculine bias? Another group alters the causal arrow and asks how international politics impacts the lives of women.

Thus, feminists challenge the traditional concepts and theories of international relations suggesting that realism and liberalism offer an incomplete picture of the international system, one that is defined by a masculine perspective. They are particularly interested in the roles assigned to men and women in the international system given the constructed ideas regarding what is considered masculine and feminine within a society. At the heart of the discourse about gender is identity, which in turn is influenced by societal norms, values, and even taboos. Beyond the policy outcomes that might be different with the inclusion of more women in positions of power, international relations feminists also direct their critique at the discipline itself, arguing that international relations scholarship is dominated by men and consequently it is biased by the male perspective on how the world works.

In this chapter, we trace the development and evolution of feminism as a theory or approach of international relations. We start by exploring feminism as a social movement where we identify the distinctive waves beginning in the 19th century. We conclude this section with an example of a 21st century feminist policy maker, Swedish Foreign Minister Margot Wallström. We then turn our attention to feminism as international relations theory. Here we highlight the ontological, epistemological, and methodological questions posed by feminist international relations scholars as for many feminists this is at the heart of the debate as to what constitutes feminist international relations theory. We then outline the central assumptions that drive the feminist approach. The next section examines the various strands of feminism, as there is no single feminist theory, but rather feminisms that make up the feminist family tree. In doing so, we explore the contributions of the pioneers in the discipline. We point out the critiques of feminism as well as trace the very public debates with liberal international relations scholars Robert Keohane and Francis Fukuyama. We close the chapter with the case studies on nuclear proliferation and the global trade regime.

Feminism: A Movement

The term feminism conjures up many different ideas and images. Feminism is interdisciplinary, obscuring the lines between the humanities and social sciences. It is a theory, as well as, a movement. In fact, it is difficult to separate feminism as an academic discipline and feminism as a movement as those engaged in activism are also often engaged in developing feminism as an international relations theory. Thus, we start by looking at feminism as a social movement, one that has had three distinct waves. The abolitionists and suffragettes that focused on voting rights during the 19th and early 20th century are retrospectively referred to as the first wave of feminism. The "second feminist wave" emphasized female liberation in the private as well as public sphere in the 1960s through the 1980s.[1] The 1990s witnessed what Rebecca Walker (1992) coined "third-wave feminism" which called for female empowerment that went beyond political and economic equality. More recently, there is a discussion on whether a fourth wave of feminism, coinciding with the election of Barack Obama in the United States, is underway.[2]

The first wave of feminism occurred during the 19th and early 20th centuries in the United States and Europe with a focus on women's suffrage, working conditions for women and children, as well as educational rights. These early feminists sought equality in the public sphere, specifically, the right to vote (McLaughlin, 2003). Those involved in the first wave looked back on the efforts of individuals like Susan B. Anthony (1820–1906) and Elizabeth Cady Stanton (1815–1902) and other suffragettes as well as those involved in the abolitionist and temperance movements for inspiration. Women in the movement like Anthony, Stanton, Alice Paul (1885–1977), Carrie Chapman Carr

(1859–1947) and Anna Howard Shaw (1847–1919) were overwhelmingly white, middle-class, and well-educated women, although members of the black abolitionist movement such as Maria Stewart (1803–1879), Sojourner Truth (1797–1883), and Frances E. W. Harper (1825–1911) often participated in events (Krolokke and Sorensen, 2006).[3]

In Europe, first wave liberal feminists found guidance in the writings of Mary Wollstonecraft (1759–1797). Her book, *A Vindication of the Rights of Woman* (1792), was published in the wake of the French Revolution and called for educational reforms for women as a means of liberation. The key for Wollstonecraft was that all of society would benefit, not just women. During this time, a Marxist-inspired feminism was taking shape among union workers in the United States, within the leftist socialist parties in Europe, and in communist Russia. Similar to their liberal counterparts, this group sought equal opportunities for women but focused primarily on the plight of working-class women within the familiar class struggle indicative of the socialist movement (Krolokke and Sorensen, 2006). These first wave feminists were ultimately successful in fulfilling the dreams of those at the Seneca Falls Convention in 1848 when women were granted the right to vote with the 19th Amendment in the United States in 1920. In England, women were granted full voting rights in 1928, expanding the 1918 law that limited the right to vote to women over 30 years of age. The realization of the right to vote for women embodied the larger quest for rights of citizenship.

By the 1960s, the women's liberation movement emerged and ushered in the second wave of feminism. This wave relied on more radical methods of activism in their efforts to achieve economic, social, and political equality for women, partnering with and oftentimes obscured by the anti-war and civil rights movements. In the United States, Betty Friedan's *The Feminine Mystique* (1963) influenced second-wave feminists.[4] She explained that women were afflicted with "a disease of confinement, unhappiness and loss, a product of seclusion in the home and a life centered on children or husbands" (McLaughlin, 2003, 9) or what Friedan labeled 'the problem that has no name'.[5] This problem was identified as a malaise that afflicted white, middle-class, and well-educated women, many who became second-wave feminists. However, other female voices were emerging, representing far different groups who argued that Friedan and other white feminists ignored the realities of non-white women. For example, African-American feminists such as Angela Davis (1944–) and bell hooks (1952–) called for an understanding of the differences not only between men and women, but also between women of color and women in general.[6]

The event that was the symbolic beginning of the second wave was the protest against the 1968 Miss America Pageant. In 1969, additional groups joined the protest "to show how women in pageant competitions were paraded like cattle, highlighting the underlying assumption that the way women look is more important than what they do, what they think, or even whether they think at all" (Krolokke and Sorensen, 2006, 8). The message during this wave was that not only were women oppressed in the public sphere particularly when it came to equal pay and property rights, but they suffered inequality in the private sphere as well. Consequently, feminists began to focus on issues related to reproductive rights, domestic violence, as well as the role and value of domestic labor (McLaughlin, 2003). For this generation of feminists, "the personal is political."

This second wave was bolstered by efforts of several international organizations to focus on women's issues. The United Nations Conference on Women (1975) and the declaration by the UN of the Decade for Women (1975–1985) signaled that the lives of women all over the world were important (Thorburn, 2000). The internationalization of the feminist movement attracted a diverse set of women beyond privileged white women; women of color and women from developing states became more and more active leading to an expansion of interests beyond equality at the polls. For these new activists, **gender** was tied to other issues associated with identity politics such as class and race. Thus, this second wave witnessed the evolution of feminism from its liberal roots to many different types of feminisms such that the question no longer was are you a feminist, rather it was what kind of feminist are you? (Wood 1994; Krolokke and Sorensen, 2006).

The symbolic start of the third wave was the Clarence Thomas Supreme Court confirmation hearings in 1991. Law professor Anita Hill's sexual harassment claims were front and center during the hearings. The appointment of Thomas to the high court in spite of the corroborated testimony of Hill energized a new generation of feminists. The third wave of feminism of the 1990s was driven by a younger generation of women, benefactors of the efforts made by first and second wave feminists, who embraced their sexuality and called for female empowerment. Individuality became the focus of this generation, particularly in the area of sexual orientation as gender moved beyond a binary categorization into a more fluid status. At the same time, the feminists of this generation reclaimed what the previous generation would consider a trapping of femininity: lipstick. In fact, many third wave feminists embraced a number of artifacts that were previously deemed as evidence of women's objectivity including high heels and low cut blouses. This new feminism was coined 'grrl feminism' in the United States and 'new feminism' in Europe and collectively this new movement eschewed formal organization in favor of a portable brand of feminism (Krolokke and Sorensen, 2006; Baumgardner, 2011; Rampton, 2015).

In 1989, Kimberlé Crenshaw, a law professor, argued that the feminist critique was hindered by the traditional conception that subordination and subjugation occurred on a single axis and that "this single-axis framework erases Black women in the conceptualization, identification and remediation of race and sex discrimination by limiting inquiry to the experiences of otherwise-privileged members of the group" (Crenshaw, 1989, 140). She described this as a problem of **intersectionality**, a problem that can't simply be fixed by adding Black women or any other group to an already existing structure. This insight of intersectionality provided a bridge to the next wave of feminism.

Many observers believe that a fourth wave of feminism has emerged since the 2008 election of President Barack Obama focusing on and embracing the multiple axes of identity identified by Crenshaw. Feminists argue that oppression does not occur independently; rather multiple forms of oppression are generally interrelated (e.g. racism, sexism, and homophobia). This wave is also defined and facilitated by technology, primarily social media where a global community of feminists regularly "call out" attitudes and behavior that devalue and oppress women. Although some debate whether a new era of feminism can be defined by technology alone, feminist scholar Jennifer Baumgardner (2011, 202) argues that the "fourth wave exists because it says that it exists. I believe the Fourth Wave matters, because I remember how sure I was that my generation mattered." While the third wave focused on individuality and looked inward for empowerment, the fourth wave has sought to bring politics back in and in doing so, embraces the political process. Women that were born during the second and third waves of feminism, women who have enjoyed the political and economic gains brought about by the previous generations, are now engaging in the political process and practicing feminism in the political, economic, and social arenas (see Spotlight) in ways that previous generations never experienced or perhaps imagined.

SPOTLIGHT ON POLICYMAKERS: MARGOT WALLSTRÖM

Margot Wallström (1954–) is a Swedish diplomat and politician in the Social Democratic Party. She was appointed minister of foreign affairs in October 2014. Previously, she served in the Swedish government as a member of parliament (1979–1985), minister for consumer affairs, women and youth (1988–1991), minister for culture (1994–1996), and minister for social affairs (1996–1998). She held several positions in the European Union's commission, including the European commissioner for the environment (1999–2004) responsible for the EU's environmental policy and the European commissioner for institutional relations and communication strategy (2004–2009). From 2010–2012, she was the first to serve as the UN secretary-general's special representative on sexual violence in conflict. As foreign minister, she made headlines by announcing that the Swedish government would pursue a "feminist foreign policy." In some circles this was met with disdain and ridicule, while others applauded the notion, even if there was significant confusion about what it actually meant. Wallström has not only strived to explain the meaning of this approach, but has taken actions, controversial as some may be, to put this feminist approach into practice.

In an interview with Al Jazeera in June 2015, Wallström explained that a feminist foreign policy is not a list of views or positions, but tools that can be used to promote the rights of women and girls around the world. She explained the principles of the approach as the "Three R's"—rights, representation, and resources. The strategy seeks to ensure that women have the same legal rights and normative framework in all countries, representation in decision-making bodies, and development assistance resources directed at women's projects (Patel, 2015). In a speech at the United States Institute of Peace, Wallström argued that a feminist foreign policy is like any other visionary foreign policy, seeking peace, justice, human rights, and development. These goals are unachievable if global society fails to address the discrimination, exclusion, and violence inflicted upon women. She explained that gender equality is not simply

continued

a goal in itself, but "a precondition for achieving our wider foreign, development and security policy objectives" (Rupert, 2015). In fact, according to researcher Valerie Hudson (2012), "the very best predictor of a state's peacefulness is not its level of wealth, its level of democracy, or its ethno-religious identity; the best predictor of a state's peacefulness is how well its women are treated."

In addition to internal equality, Wallström argues that women must hold positions in foreign policy establishments in governments around the world as well as international organizations. The UN has been working for women's rights for decades. The Economic and Social Council established its Commission on the Status of Women in the first year of the UN's existence; 1975 saw the proclamation of International Women's Year and the first World Conference on Women; 1976–1985 was the UN decade for Women; 1979 saw the General Assembly adopt the Convention on the Elimination of All Forms of Discrimination against Women (CEDAW); and in 2000 the UN passed its first resolution (UNSCR 1325) calling on governments to prevent violations of women that occur during conflict and ensuring a role for women in the pursuit of peace and security. Several additional meetings of the World Conference on Women were held and gender issues are explicitly pursued in the UN's Millennium Development Goals. Despite this progress, women remain largely outside the process of peacemaking. Wallström argues that there are plenty of highly skilled women who should be engaged in peace negotiations around the world, but "from 1992 to 2011, fewer than four percent of signatories of peace agreements and less than ten percent of peace negotiators were women" (Rupert, 2015).

In less than six months, the practice of a feminist foreign policy set off a series of crises and created confusion over unclear objectives between Sweden and other countries. Wallström's feminist approach was questioned her first month as minister of foreign affairs when a suspected Russian submarine encroached in the Stockholm archipelago (a breach of Sweden's territorial waters) prompting a response from Swedish armed forces. Arguments abounded that there is no place for a feminist foreign policy in issues of territorial security, a claim bristled at by Wallström. She contends that a women-focused approach is applicable in all areas of foreign policy, stating, "To say it's not relevant in such situations is to suggest that women don't think we should have a defense force and that is just not true" (Rothschild, 2014). Problems arose again

continued

when Sweden recognized the state of Palestine on October 30, 2014 becoming the first EU member in Western Europe to do so. Wallström pushed for the recognition as confirmation of the Palestinian right to self-determination and the correct course of action under international law. Although Israel recalled its Ambassador to Sweden and had harsh words for the Scandinavian country, Wallström argued that recent wars in Gaza and the radicalization of the Palestinian youth necessitated this move that she claimed would promote the peace process and negotiations to end the Israeli occupation.

Arguably the most pronounced crisis came with Saudi Arabia beginning in February 2015. In a speech before the Swedish Parliament, Wallström stated that the royal family exercises absolute power in a country that violates the rights of women, including forbidding them to drive. She also criticized the public flogging of blogger Raif Badawi as medieval. The Saudis accused Wallström of interfering in their internal affairs and criticizing Sharia Law and Islam, and in response recalled the Saudi Ambassador and ceased issuing visas to Swedish business travelers. The Gulf Cooperation Council, the Organization of Islamic Cooperation, and the Arab League condemned Wallström. The crisis took a new turn in March when Sweden decided not to renew its bilateral arms agreement with Saudi Arabia, a lucrative buyer of Sweden's arms exports. This move was a clear example of feminist foreign policy in action as it would be difficult to argue a feminist policy would support arms sales to a nation that violates and abuses women. While Wallström admitted to a misunderstanding and the Swedish government made clear she had not intended to criticize Islam, she did not back down from her statements and offered no apology for her remarks.

Wallström embraces the argument of Joseph Nye (see Chapter 2) in contending that foreign policy should be a mixture of hard and soft power, a concept Nye labels "smart power" (Nye 2009d). Pursuing a feminist foreign policy promotes soft power through its engagement in humanitarianism, but Sweden has not ignored elements of hard power in the name of territorial defense. In 2014, Sweden dedicated about $4 billion to international aid efforts, and the country spends .97 percent of its GDP toward aid (for perspective, compare that to the United States at .19 percent of GDP for aid) (Rothschild, 2014). Simultaneously, in late 2014, the increase in tension between Russia and the West prompted Sweden to increase its military budget, and despite the row with Saudi

continued

Arabia, Sweden continues to be one of Europe's largest per capita arms exporters. Wallström sees no contradiction between the pursuit of both hard and soft power, stating, "Sweden has been a world power because we have acted constructively to find political solutions and because of our aid policy and contribution to achieving global development" (Rothschild, 2014). She is not alone in this approach, as other policymakers such as Hillary Clinton, Samantha Power, and William Hague, have focused on women, peace, and security. Wallström is unique however in that she has labeled her approach as "feminist." Others might have pursued feminist objectives, by shied away from using the term to avoid any negative connotations that come with it. Wallström proudly and unabashedly talks the talk, and walks the walk.

Roots and Evolution of Feminist International Relations Theory

We now turn our attention to feminism as an approach to international relations. Similar to the previous theories, there is no single feminist theory. The variety of feminist approaches intersects with several of the previous theories such that there are liberal feminists, Marxist feminists, and constructivist feminists to name just a few and the feminist variant often shares theoretical assumptions with its counterpart. For example, feminism agrees with the realist assumption that conflict is inevitable (however for very different reasons as we will see). Liberal feminists value the role of the individual consistent with liberal theoretical assumptions. Likewise, feminists share with Marxists the idea that society is divided between the privileged, economically as well as by gender, and the oppressed. It is appropriate, then, that feminism is the last approach discussed in this book as it often combines with each of the previous theories, yet offers a very different perspective on how the international system is constructed and operates.

While feminism was well-established within the humanities and social sciences disciplines, it has been a relative late-comer to the "malestream" field of international relations, a discipline categorized as a "gender free zone" for seven decades (Pettman, 2004).[7] However, the third debate within the international relations discipline "opened up a flicker of intellectual space, giving feminists room for thought and articulation" (Zalewski, 1993, 15). In addition, female international relations scholars were coming of age at this time, influenced by the activism of the second wave of feminism (see above). As such, in the late 1980s and early 1990s, feminist panels at academic symposiums and conferences sponsored by international organizations signaled the beginning of an alternative, gendered approach to the questions and issues within international relations. These included the *Millennium: Journal of International Studies* conference at the London School of Economics in 1988, a conference at the University of Southern California in 1989, and one at Wellesley in 1990 (Peterson, 1998; Wibben, 2004). The *Millennium* conference resulted in the publication of a special issue on "Women and International Relations" which is commonly viewed as the start of the feminist program in international relations (Sjoberg, 2009). Gender conferences sponsored by the UN such as the 1995 women's conference in Beijing and the declaration by the UN of the Decade for Women also facilitated the emergence of feminist scholarship. Finally, the publication of several groundbreaking books by first-generation feminist scholars Jean Bethke Elshtain (1941–2013), Cynthia Enloe (1938–), J. Ann Tickner (1937–), and Christine Sylvester (1949–) attempted to break into the male-dominated discipline of international relations.[8]

These feminist scholars confront the same ontological, epistemological and methodological questions as their realist, liberal, economic structuralist, and constructivist colleagues. Ontologically, feminists problematize the role of the state much like all of other theories; they also, of course, question how to theorize about gender. In the first case, feminists range from conceiving of the state as the central actor in the system to the state "as a set of patriarchal practices that support, yet silence, the structural disadvantages that women face" (Hansen, 2009, 21). As we will see in more detail later, when it comes to gender, the ontological debate ranges from the use of gender as a dichotomy variable used to express biological differences to a socially constructed differentiation of masculine and feminine to a combination of both. Feminist scholar Gillian Youngs (2004, 77) argues that traditional approaches to international relations "takes the *appearance* of a predominantly male-constructed reality as a given" and consequently "[F]eminism requires an ontological revisionism: a recognition that is necessary to go behind the appearance and examine how differentiated and gendered power constructs the social relations that form that reality."

In terms of epistemology, some feminist scholars offer an additional variable, gender, in empirical analyses, which contributes to studies in the rational or positivist tradition. At the same time, other feminists take a more normative position like their constructivist and critical theorist counterparts arguing that in order to understand outcomes in international relations, scholars must look beyond the state level of analysis and take into account the fact that the experiences of women and men are fundamentally different. Thus, as a primarily post-positive approach, feminism shares many ontological and epistemological positions with constructivism specifically that identities are constructed, with feminism focusing on the constructed roles of women in the theory and practice of politics. These epistemological differences lead to the categorization of feminist scholarship into three perspectives: **feminist empiricism**, the **feminist standpoint**, and **feminist postmodernism** (Harding, 1986; Hansen, 2009). In our discussion of the family of feminist theories, we follow this epistemological categorization (see below).

Methodologically, feminist scholarship includes both quantitative and qualitative analyses with the former more likely to appear in positivist, rational studies where scholars attempt to explain the relationship between gender and state behavior. For example, in the area of peace studies and the causes of war, researchers might ask, "whether there is a correlation between the level of gender equality in a given country on the one hand and this country's likelihood of going to war on the other" (Hansen, 2009, 20). One of the criticisms of this approach, particularly from other feminist scholars, is that the study of gender requires more than to "add gender and stir" to the current models of conflict. Feminist scholars engaged in examining gender as a socially constructed artifact in the post-positivist tradition utilize a wide range of qualitative methods including case studies, ethnography, discourse analysis, fieldwork and interviews (Sjoberg, 2009). Ultimately, there is no single feminist methodology. According to feminist scholar J. Ann Tickner (2006, 20), the uniqueness of feminist scholarship lies in its "distinctive methodological perspective or framework which fundamentally challenges the often unseen androcentric or masculine biases in the way that knowledge has traditionally been constructed." Regardless of the ontological, epistemological, and methodological differences, feminists all share several central assumptions.

Central Assumptions

- Gender matters and is the primary unit of analysis.
- International relations are characterized by **patriarchy**, and masculinity is privileged with power in the international system.
- Issues in international politics are ranked in gendered fashion.
- The nature of international relations is essentially conflictual and has a masculine bias that ignores women.

The first assumption is that gender matters and is the primary focus for feminists. In other words, "a shared assumption of feminist research is that women's lives are important" (Tickner, 2006, 25). It is important to differentiate between the terms *gender* and *sex* here with the former more closely associated with the social construction of what is meant by masculine and feminine and the latter used to differentiate biological differences. More specifically, we can think of gender as having a "symbolic meaning that creates social hierarchies based on perceived associations with masculine and feminist characteristics" (Sjoberg, 2009, 187). In our everyday lives, we generally use these terms interchangeably focusing on categorizing individuals into two groups based on the perceived physical form of the individual—male and female. In essence, we engage in what is referred to as **dimorphism** whether we are aware of it or not (Shepherd, 2009).

Therein lies the problem, according to most feminist international relations scholars. Individuals are socialized from an early age to form opinions about the masculine and feminine behaviors associated with each physical form. Traditionally, masculinity is associated with power, autonomy, and aggressive behaviors that are highly valued in most societies while femininity generally denotes weakness, sensitivity, passivity and nurturing behaviors that have less value. The characteristics of femininity and masculinity vary from place to place and from time to time. That is, what is deemed feminine in one country at a specified time in history may not be deemed so in another country so that femininity and masculinity are culturally and temporally relative. Furthermore, the meaning of feminine and masculine is important only to the extent that they relate to each other; what is meant by feminine is only understand in comparison to what is meant by masculine. Gender should not be thought of as synonymous with women; on the contrary, feminist scholars argue that gender is equally about men and masculinity.

Second, feminists argue that the key concepts in the traditional study of international relations are characterized by patriarchy that is inherent in the international system resulting in masculine privilege. Early studies in political science revealed that "women and their experiences were rendered invisible by the traditional focus on public events, public figures, and politics understood as competition for power" (Peterson, 1992, 192). Feminists agree with realists about the importance of power in the international system. For feminists, gender is about power and they argue that gendered relations influence policy outcomes at the domestic and international level. In addition, feminists don't necessarily disagree with realists that the system is characterized by anarchy; it is anarchy, however, that is male dominated. Thus, like realists, feminists are interested and concerned about power in the international system, but for very different reasons.

In fact, feminist scholars strive to mitigate if not eliminate the binary nature of international relations in general. This bifurcation of individuals based on sex or gender has denied women access to political, economic, and social arenas of decision-making and by "categorizing men and women oppositionally, and equating masculinity with humanness, Western philosophy has denied all women—and others stigmatized as feminine—the privileged states of being fully 'human'" (Peterson, 1992, 193). The international relations discipline is rife with dualisms that serve to perpetuate gender inequality: male/female, masculine/feminine, subject/object, public/private, agency/passivity, and reason/irrationality. Feminists also argue that men are privileged in the private sphere leading women to become subordinate at home as well as in the workplace. However, most feminists do not seek to privilege women over men; rather they strive for equality in all areas of life by eliminating gender discrimination. When feminists engage in gender studies, therefore, they are not only addressing women's issues, but also how women interact with men and vice-versa.

The third assumption of feminism is that issues in the international system are ranked in a gendered fashion, that is, there is a gender hierarchy. This is due to the fact that, until recently, most of the actors in the international system have been men. When we look at conflict, politics, and economics, decisions are based on the experiences of men by men. Issues that are traditionally championed by women, the "low politics" issues of healthcare, education, child care, and even the environment have been deemed irrelevant, particularly by realists. Like their liberal counterparts, feminists argue that the theory and practice of international relations have overemphasized concepts such as anarchy, security, sovereignty, power, and hierarchy. The goal of feminism is not to simply add women, but rather to uncover or expose the field of international relations as one that is and always was gendered.

The last assumption addressed here is that like realists and economic structuralists, feminists view the international system as generally conflictual with an inherent masculine bias that ignores not only women but issues important to women when it comes to war. The study of conflict has long occupied center stage in the field of international relations. As such, most theories address the nature of war and the means necessary to mitigate conflict. Feminist theory addresses several aspects of conflict: traditionally, in practice men make decisions to go to war, and traditionally in the discipline men have focused on the study of war, primarily from the state and system perspective. In both instances, the input of and effect on women has traditionally been ignored. Feminists argue that the positivist theories in international relations not only ignore the devastating effect of conflict on women and other marginalized populations, but fail to recognize women's level of agency during conflict such that their contributions are either ignored or undervalued.

Family of Theories

The first thing to remember is that there is no single feminist theory of international relations. There are various feminisms that often overlap, so it should be clear that these categories are not mutually exclusive. Moreover, many feminists resist any one particular label of feminism. As previously mentioned, sociologist Sandra Harding (1935–) developed an epistemological typology of feminist scholarship that helps to differentiate between the various strands of the feminist approach: feminist empiricism, feminist standpoint, and feminist postmodernism (Harding, 1986).[9] Within each of these categories, there are additional schools of thought that are highlighted (See Figure 6.1).

Feminist Empiricism

The first generation of feminist international relations scholarship emerged in the 1980s and focused primarily on critiquing mainstream

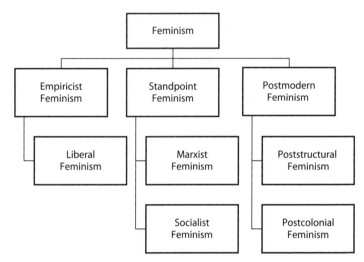

FIGURE 6.1 **Feminism Family Tree.**

theories, specifically the gendered nature of the discipline. Feminist empiricism is most consistent with the positivist approach to international relations as these scholars accept that a known reality exists and believe that we gain knowledge based on experience. In addition, feminist empiricists place their faith in the scientific method as the means to make sense of all knowledge. They also argue that including more women researchers can solve the male-centered nature of the study of international relations. This would remove any male bias, the "entrenched misogyny and androcentrism" inherent in international relations as a discipline and "with more at stake, women are more likely to notice (and prevent) androcentric bias than men. This feminist empiricism is the philosophical underpinning of liberal feminism, the aim of which is to 'add women and stir'" (Zalewski, 1993, 15). This is also one of the major critiques of this variant of feminism.

The idea that the primary difference between men and women is biological is the key characteristic of **liberal feminism** and well as **difference feminism**.[10] However, the conclusion of each is quite different. Liberal feminism or traditional feminism adheres to the liberal philosophy espoused by John Locke and others about individualism and equality. Liberal feminists focus on the question, "Where are the women?" Thus, they focus on underrepresentation of women in positions of power, particularly in terms of political office, international organizations, and business. In other words, liberal feminists examine how the state, and its various functions, is gendered. They argue that women and men are equal based on their shared humanity; as such, women should have the same rights as men. However, states have traditionally been gendered toward men in terms of voting and property rights and "women have been excluded from many of the most important public spheres of modern social, political and economic life" (Whitworth, 1994, 75). In line with the primacy of the individual in liberal philosophy, liberal feminists are also interested in how conflict and economic issues impact the lives of women as well as how women act during times of war and peace.

Liberal feminist scholars argue that women have always played a role in international relations and world politics, just in ways that were obscured due to the primacy of conflict and diplomacy as topics of interest. Women are engaged in the invisible work within societies: factory and agriculture labor, wives of diplomats, prostitution, sex slaves, comfort women, and home domestics (Enloe, 1989, 1993, 2000).[11] Society must remove all obstacles, legal and institutionalized, in order to overcome these gendered stereotypes, end sex discrimination, and realize gender equality. In doing so, liberal feminists argue that the inclusion of women will add to the talent pool of any given state, particularly in the area of politics, diplomacy, and economics. However, liberal feminists do not expect that the inclusion of women in positions of power will necessarily or fundamentally change the nature of the international system. In fact, they expect that women will solve problems facing states in the international system in very similar ways to men. The examples of Indira Ghandi, Golda Meir, and Margaret Thatcher in the introduction to this chapter help to illustrate this point. As leaders, they handled and utilized power in the same manner as their male counterparts. For liberal feminists, women in positions of power are not any less committed to the tenets of the modern state system: sovereignty and territorial integrity.

In contrast, difference feminists conclude that the biological differences between women and men are significant and meaningful. This variant of feminism emerged in the 1980s and 1990s and attempted to reclaim the feminine characteristics that were deemed as less valued. This view of feminism valorizes these feminine qualities, which they argue are distinctly different than masculine qualities. They contend that women are naturally more nurturing and caring and such qualities should be glorified, valued, and utilized in specific areas of global politics. The argument here is that women's unique abilities will transform the international system. Liberal feminists reject the notion that there are any unique feminine qualities, ones that have women morally and ethically superior to men, that women can bring to bear on issues of diplomacy, foreign affairs and economic issues. Liberal feminist international relations scholars contend that there are no essential biological differences in men and women that will lead to different, masculine or feminine, policy outcomes.

The Feminist Standpoint

The feminist standpoint takes the position that due to their historical and now structural subordination in terms of patriarchy, women have a unique view or standpoint on how the world works and knowledge in general. Sociologist Sandra Harding (1986, 26) writes that the feminist standpoint "argues that men's dominating position in social life results in partial and perverse understandings, whereas women's subjugated position provides the possibility of more complete and less perverse understandings." Harding is quick to point out the potential pitfalls of this position, specifically, that there cannot possibly be just *a* feminist standpoint given the different class, race, and culture of women found around the world. Critics of feminist standpoint argue that this position attempts to privilege women over men. International relations feminist scholar, J. Ann Tickner (2006, 26) argues that approaching international relations from "the standpoint of women's lives, particularly marginalized women, leads to more robust objectivity, not only because it broadens the base from which we derive knowledge, but also because the perspectives of 'outsiders' or marginalized people may reveal aspects of reality obscured by more orthodox approaches to knowledge-building" (Tickner, 2006, 26). This suggests that real differences exist between men and women, not merely based on the obvious biological grounds (as in the case of difference feminism), but on the basis of their very different experiences (due to a combination of sex and gender). Furthermore, these differences impact the dissemination of knowledge with men traditionally determining which knowledge matters. Harding (1986) argues that this is one of the main problems with malestream science—its claim of objectivity. She argues that knowledge is socially located and is laden with the experiences of the knower and this has traditionally reflected experiences of men, that is knowledge has been "inextricably connected with specifically masculine—and perhaps uniquely Western and bourgeois—needs and desires" (Harding, 1986, 23). The feminist standpoint is that this perspective is incomplete, "partial, distorted, and reflects only the interests of men and masculinity" (Zalewski, 1993, 16).

Consequently, the feminist standpoint encompasses a whole set of feminisms that are critical of masculinity and the inherent masculine bias in the international system. The radical, Marxist, and socialist feminists discussed below all agree that men have a monopoly on knowledge and collectively ask, "If knowledge is a social construct and reflects only the interests of men . . . would the world look fundamentally different, would our perception and understanding of it be very different, if knowledge was produced from different realities, different versions of the world—from women's experiences" (Zalewski, 1993, 18)? This is a key difference between feminist empiricism and the feminist standpoint. Empiricists argue that men and women are the same; while the feminist standpoint believes that there are indeed true differences between men and women, differences that are primarily socially constructed.

Radical feminists, prominent during the second wave of feminism, argue that the oppression and discrimination of women is fundamental and occurs before race and class discrimination. Proponents of this position seek to eliminate both patriarchy and sexism, which they view as inextricably linked. As men are the beneficiaries of a patriarchal society, they are viewed as the agents of oppression and discrimination. Applied to global politics and international relations, radical feminists argue that the "masculine worldview emphasizes conflict and neglects cooperation" (Whitworth, 1994, 78). A foreign policy based on a radical feminist perspective would replace the concept of power with empowerment and expand the definition of security beyond the male-centered philosophy of national or state security to include the issues of development and environmentalism (Whitworth, 1994). Some radical feminists are similar to difference feminists in that they see the qualities of the female sex as playing a role in transforming global politics and providing for a more peaceful international system. Others reject the notion of biological determinism, arguing instead that the social constructs of masculine and feminine perpetuate the gender hierarchy in domestic and international politics. If males are taught aggressive behavior and females are taught nurturing and conciliatory ones, then women need to "lean in" in order bring these feminine characteristics to the decision-making table.[12] Radical feminism made its mark more in practice, as part of the second wave of feminism. The radical feminists from an academic perspective are generally today's standpoint feminists.

Socialist and **Marxism feminism** are often lumped together as both address the patterns of oppression inherent in the male-dominated capitalist system and the subsequent impact on the lives of women. However, there are true differences between the two. Marxist feminists view women's inequality as a function of the capitalist system; therefore, they advocate changing the economic structure of the international system. While Karl Marx did not address the "women question" directly, Frederick Engels did in *Origin of the Family, Private Property and the State* (1902) where he traced the oppression to the impact of the class system on the family unit. In pre-capitalist societies, women and men were equals. Although labor divisions existed, the contributions made by each were viewed equal in value. With the capitalist system emphasis on private property, inequality soon followed as ownership was passed down based on paternal lineage. Capitalism also demanded more and more labor with women bearing important responsibilities: reproduction in order to provide more labor and production in the home in the form of unpaid labor. Women were still performing most of the same functions as they did in pre-capitalist societies, however, in the new capitalist system they were not paid for their work while men were paid for theirs, and thus her labor had less value. In fact, Marxist feminists argue that the capitalist system strives to maintain this form of household labor in order to perpetuate the capitalist mode of production (Chowdhry, 1994). The solution, in line with traditional Marxist philosophy, is the socialist revolution, however for the feminist it must include an anti-patriarchal focus as well.

One of the major concerns for feminists is the proclivity of the male-centered Marxist view to dominate the feminists' perspective producing an "unhappy marriage" such that "either we need a healthier marriage or we need a divorce" (Hartman, 1979, 1). Marxists have traditionally focused on the "woman question" of how the capitalist system oppresses women and not the "feminist question" which addresses how women are oppressed by men. A Marxist philosophy that considers how to marry the "struggle against patriarchy and the struggle against capitalism" is required" (Hartman, 1979, 24; see also

Bryson, 2004). Today, Marxist feminists focus on how to address the marriage between Marxism and feminism as well as the unique features of women's oppression in the capitalist system. In 2005, *Science & Society* published a special issue on Marxist-feminist thought. The purpose was to refute the claim that an understanding of the vagaries of globalization was possible without an understanding of Marxist philosophy, especially how globalization impacts women. A reliance on identity politics alone is insufficient to "theorize exploitation and oppression, including the exploitation and oppression of women, outside the framework of Marxist theory" (Gimenez and Vogel, 2005, 5).

Socialist feminists examine oppression stemming from patriarchy as well capitalism. Dual systems theory suggests, "that both capitalism and patriarchy operate as separate, related, and at times opposed systems of oppression" (McLaughlin, 2003, 51; see also Hartman, 1979). This strand of feminism focuses on how women are generally omitted from economic decision-making and ultimately are the most vulnerable economically. In contrast to Marxist feminists, socialist feminists argue that oppression of women occurred before the onset of the capitalist system but that capitalism determines the current nature of patriarchy. They point to the male dominance within societies, or patriarchy, in addition to capitalism, as a major source of oppression. Socialist feminism is distinct from the Marxist variant in "its view that autonomous structures of gender, race, and class all participated in constructing inequality and exploitation" (Gordon, 2013, 22). Also in contrast to Marxist feminists, socialist feminists do not call for a revolution or even a socialist economy; rather they work toward "a just economy" that provides political equality and economic well-being and this "would have to emerge from a democratic process" (Gordon, 2013, 22). In many ways, the theoretical development of socialist feminisms has been co opted or captured by the emergence of postcolonial and poststructural scholarship (see below).

Feminist Postmodernism

Proponents of feminist postmodernism are critical of both empiricism and standpoint feminism, specifically that feminist empiricism fails to adequately account for power and has an underdeveloped understanding of how knowledge is constructed (Zalewski, 1993). They are also critical of the liberal feminist agenda of simply integrating women into both the practice and discipline of international relations. They view this as naïve as it "ignores the structural features of social and political action" (Whitworth, 1994, 77). Furthermore, they reject the standpoint feminist position that accepts that the masculine and feminine differences in international relations have been distorted to the extent that the masculine is privileged. Postmodernists suggest that the standpoint feminist position is "committed to an essentialized view of woman which, despite its adherence to the social construction of knowledge, seems to attach itself to a notion of truth to which only women are privy" (Zalewski, 1993, 16). Postmodern feminists argue that the categories of masculine and feminine, like anarchy, are what we make of it, that is, they are social constructs. Like all feminists, proponents of this perspective focus on women's liberation and emancipation.

Like its postmodern counterpart, feminist postmodernists question the existence of any universal truths and focuses on relative truths instead. Postmodernism also rejects the idea that scholarship must be objective, arguing that it is impossible to separate the researcher from the subject (see discussion of Postmodernism in Chapter 5). Like the other major theories of international relations, postmodern feminists seek to explain power in the international system. They argue that power exists not only in the state as realists and liberals contend, and not only in the dominant classes as economic structuralists believe, but "it is also present in symbols, language, and knowledge" (Chowdhry, 1994, 166). Just as there are variants of postmodernism, there are also different strands of feminist postmodernism. We focus on two here: **poststructural** and **postcolonial feminism**.

Poststructural feminists investigate how the use of language in the political, economic, and social arenas impacts women, specifically when it comes to the dissemination of knowledge. Men have traditionally been the arbiters of what knowledge was important and relevant, particularly in the public domain. Those who construct language have a monopoly of power over others. For example, in a seminal research project, peace researcher Carol Cohn (1987a, 1987b) examines the language of the nuclear strategic sector, specifically technostrategic language inherent in the industry and its influence. She argues that the language and terms used in the industry serve to desensitize those who are involved; in actuality, it develops a chasm between image and reality. Terms such as "clean bombs" and the "peacemaker" and the domestication of weapons, such as "silos" and

"Christmas tree" to denote the stages of liftoff, and the friendly language of nuclear weapons as enemies "exchanging" warheads belie the devastation they are intended to bring. Cohn employed a post-positivist epistemological approach, one that focused on an analysis of language, to a predominant topic in international relations—security. In doing so, she demonstrated the gendered nature of the nuclear industry as well as the power of language and discourse to mold behavior at the individual level, including her own. "As I learned to speak, my perspective changed. I no longer stood outside the impenetrable wall of technostrategic language and once inside, I could no longer see it. I had not only learned to speak a language: I had started to think in it" (Cohn, 1987a 23). We will revisit the gendered nature of nuclear weapons in the case study on proliferation.

Another variant of feminist postmodernism is postcolonial feminism.[13] Proponents of this view argue that white, western feminists ignore important factors, namely race, ethnicity, culture and colonial history in how women encounter discrimination and inequality within societies. Postcolonial feminists argue that Western feminists have constructed an experience that in no way relates to women in non-Western societies. Postcolonial feminism challenges the traditional paths of development and modernity arguing marginalized members of societies tell a very different story based on their very different experiences. For example, the study of gender and development (GAD) is enhanced by insights from postcolonial feminism "through such concepts as representation, 'othering' and the silencing of Third World women's voices" (Marchand, 2009, 922). Another area of research for postcolonial feminists is the issue of sports, gender, and development (SGD), an initiative of the United Nations to engage women and girls in sporting events as a vehicle to enhance female emancipation and empowerment. Funding by multinational corporations headquartered in the Global North is increasingly utilized in SGD programs in Third World countries.[14] While the underlying motivation of the MNC may be to enhance their corporate image, "a postcolonial feminist IR lens would view such activities with an eye to the historical presence of corporations in development, and would also consider neocolonial interests and privilege in world politics" (Hayhurst, 2011, 537). We examine the role of postcolonial theory in more detail in the concluding chapter. We now turn our attention to leading scholars in feminist international relations theory.

Pioneers in the Field

The first generation of feminist international relations scholars emerged during the second wave of the feminist movement striving to establish a feminist agenda within the discipline. These pioneering women also fit the demographics of the majority of activists in the second wave of feminism: white, educated women in the West. They challenged the traditional ontological and epistemological focus of the field and entered the fray of the third debate (see Chapter One). These scholars contended that the traditional state-centered and positivist approach to the discipline, particularly the realist paradigm, was exclusionary in nature and failed to address the questions important to women, activist and scholar alike.

Second-generation feminist scholars moved the dialogue beyond the central question of "where are all the women" in both practice and the discipline to "make gender a central analytic category in studies of foreign policy, security, and global political economy not at the level of abstract theory but through the exploration of concrete historical and geographic contexts" (True, 2003, 2). This generation of feminist scholars attracted women from not only the West, but from the postcolonial world as well as, bringing additional foci to the feminist agenda. The advent of the second-generation of feminist scholars coincided with the emergence of constructivism in international relations, a perspective that shares ontological and epistemological sensibilities (Locher and Prügl, 2001). Scholars utilized atypical methods such as ethnography and participant observation hoping that the research "will help to improve the lives of the women they study as well as expose hierarchical exploitative social structures upon which states and their security policies are built" (Tickner, 2006, 30).[15] Second generation feminists also identify with the third wave of feminism, particularly regarding their shared interest in female empowerment and understanding how the political, economic, and social arenas are gendered. We discuss three of the pioneers from the first generation of feminist international relations scholars highlighting their respective ontological, epistemological, and methodological approaches as well as highlight several of the second-generation scholars below.

Jean Bethke Elshtain was a political theorist that resisted being labeled as a particular type of feminist, although fellow scholar Christine Sylvester (2002) indicates that she blended standpoint and postmodern feminism in her influential book, *Women and War* (1987). Her first book, *Public Man, Private Woman* (1981) tackled the very issue that was prominent in the activism of the second wave of feminism: the schism between the public and private sphere and the role of gender. The political sphere, she argued, is identified by masculine characteristics and thereby privileges men over women. She dove into the deep end of the international relations pool by addressing the core concept of war in her next book. Her post-positivist approach, however, kept her out of the exclusive malestream of international relations scholarship. In *Women and War* (1987), Elshtain introduced two myths that represent the traditional roles of men and war and their subsequent appropriate roles in war: 'Man the Warrior' and 'Woman as Beautiful Soul'. She shattered these myths with narratives that reveal the true nature of war and its impact on men and women. An additional reason her work was generally shunned by the international relations establishment was the inclusion of her own experience as she wove her maturation as a feminist into part of the narrative. Thus, the methodological gulf between her work and the prevailing international relations scholarship at the time left Elshtain's contribution, ironically, hidden from the field. In addition, her arguments ran afoul of radical feminists who argued that even in the private sphere, women were oppressed. Elshtain disagreed with this assessment and consequently "feminists accused her of every sin in the book, including labeling all feminism 'radical,' failing to acknowledge patriarchy, and refusing to see problems in the heterosexual family" (Sylvester, 2002, 22). The importance of Elshtain's work lies in the fact that it was the first to break into the hallowed topics of war from a feminist perspective by a trained academic and she served as a role model for subsequent international relations feminist scholars.

Cynthia Enloe began her career as a comparativist concentrating on Southeast Asia. She came to the study of gender as a nationalism scholar focusing on identity politics. Ontologically, Enloe problematizes both the state and gender. She is critical of the notion of the state as the primary actor in the international system, arguing instead that to truly understand military relations or any other phenomena, one must peel back the state-level veneer and examine voices that otherwise have been silenced. This is a recurring theme in most of her research. Ultimately, she is interested in power, specifically where it is situated and who has control of it. She also addresses one of the major concepts in international relations—war. From an epistemological perspective, Enloe's research is difficult to situate into a single framework. The question that motivates her research is, "Where are the women?" As such, this seems to point toward the empiricism feminism identified by Harding (1986). However, her analysis quickly adopts a post-positivist approach consistent with the feminist standpoint. Enloe argues that international politics is not exclusively male; it is just that the discipline of international relations has not provided the full picture. This is due to two things: only men asking the questions, and subsequently, men asking the wrong questions, or rather, questions that only men are interested in pursuing such as the proper role of the state, how states solve the problems of anarchy, and whether sovereignty protects states from intervention.

Enloe produced a trio of books focusing on the intersection of women and war. In *Does Khaki Become You? The Militarization of Women's Lives* (1983), Enloe applies her interest in identity politics and nationalism to military studies. Like Elshtain's *Women and War*, there is a biographical element that is not found in traditional international relations scholarship (Sylvester, 2002). It is with this publication that Enloe enters into the field of feminist international relations theory. In *Bananas, Beaches and Bases: Making Feminist Sense in International Politics* (1990), Enloe exposes where women really are and tells a very different tale of women and international politics. In the preface to the first edition, Enloe (1990, xi) writes "I got an inkling of how relations between governments depend not only on capital and weaponry but also on the control of women as symbols, consumers, workers, and emotional comforters" as well as "women-as-consumers." Thus Enloe found women, just not in the places international relations scholars normally look. She analyzed women in the tourism industry, in nationalism, in and around military bases, in diplomacy and as laborers in agriculture, textiles, and domestic service. She finds that, contrary to what realists would argue, "gender makes the world go round," implying that it is women that are the foundation of many elements of state power. In *The Morning After: Sexual Politics at the End of the Cold War* (1993), Enloe focuses again on identifying where women are, this time, however she also addresses "men as victims as well as perpetrators of militarism" (Sylvester, 2002, 39). She questions what a demilitarized post-Cold War world looks like, particularly if gender is ignored. An understanding of militarism, during and after the Cold War, must move beyond the traditional state-centric view and incorporate how gender and identity influence the military and politics.

All three works take an unorthodox approach in relation to traditional ontologies, epistemologies and methodologies in international relations. Like all feminist scholars, she challenges the ontological assumption of the primacy of the state and problematizes it alongside gender. Her analysis using narratives of the private lives of women (and men) aligns with the post-positive traditions and the feminist standpoint. Critics are quick to point out that much of this research is not located within the discipline of international relations, rather is it situated in geography (Peterson, 1998). Nonetheless, Enloe's work stands as a prominent contribution to the feminist international relations discipline.

J. Ann Tickner is generally considered a standpoint feminist but is clear that her goal is to transcend gender rather than privilege women over men. Much of her research examines the gender bias inherent in the discipline of international relations. She writes "As a scholar and teacher of international relations, I have frequently asked myself the following questions: Why are there so few women in my discipline? If I teach the field as conventionally defined, why are there so few readings by women to assign my students? Why is the subject matter of my discipline so distant from women's lived experiences? Why have women been conspicuous only by their absence in the worlds of diplomacy and military and foreign policy making" (Tickner, 1992, ix)? Thus, her interests lie in locating women within the discipline, within international relations theory, as well as within the practice of global politics. As a student of Robert Keohane, Tickner was schooled in the traditional approaches to the study of international relations and her 1992 publication is the first book to address international relations theory from a feminist perspective. Her traditional training and the topic of security provided Tickner a certain amount of gravitas as she proceeded to critique the prevailing paradigms in the field.

As an introductory international relations text, *Gender in International Relations: Feminist Perspectives on Achieving Global Security* (1992) challenges the realist, liberal, and Marxist paradigms. In particular, Tickner questions the primacy of the masculine voice and the marginalization of the feminine one inherent in all three. Her goal is to illustrate how gender permeates global politics and economics and how women are impacted by the gendered hierarchy characteristic of the international system. Tickner's solution, consistent with feminist theory, is to have more women in positions of economic, political, and even military power. She also calls for a re-evaluation of the importance of 'other' actors in international relations such as those involved in conflict resolution and relief work.

In "Hans Morgenthau's Principles of Political Realism: A Feminist Reformulation," Tickner seeks to understand why women are underrepresented at the highest levels of diplomacy, the highest ranks in the military, as well as in the international relations discipline. Ultimately, she focuses on the latter and uses Morgenthau's realist arguments to illustrate why a masculine worldview dominates the discipline. She proceeds to utilize feminist theory to first critique the principles as laid out by Morgenthau and then offers a feminist view arguing that "a truly realist picture of international politics must recognize elements of co-operation as well as conflict, morality as well as *realpolitik*, and the strivings for justice as well as order" (Tickner, 1998, 437). The themes found in Tickner's analysis are consistent throughout her work, particularly her interest in the underrepresentation of women in the field of international relations. She is also one of the strongest defenders of the feminist ontological, epistemological, and methodological perspectives as evidence by the Keohane debate (see Criticisms, below) as well as her 2005 article, "What is Your Research Program? Some Feminist Answers to International Relations Methodological Questions."

Collectively, Jean Elshtain, Cynthia Enlow, and J. Ann Tickner represent the big three when feminist international relations theory was in its infancy. That is not to say these are the only important scholars engaging in impactful contributions to the field. The work of Carol Cohn on the topic of nuclear weapons (see poststructural feminism) is but one example. Christine Sylvester (1949–) made a significant contribution to the furtherance of feminist international relations scholarship with *Feminist Theory and International Relations in a Postmodern Era* (1994) and the follow-up, *Feminist International Relations: An Unfinished Journey* (2002). In many ways, she serves as a bridge to the second generation of scholars. In her 1994 work, Sylvester provides an analysis of the epistemological divisions of feminist international relations posited by Harding (1986) as well as undertakes an analysis of the major debates in the field of international relations. She picks up these topics and others in the 2002 offering that explores her own journey through the discipline.

At the turn of the 21st century, the field witnessed the emergence of a second generation of feminist scholars. These scholars turned from challenging malestream international relations theory to applying feminist approaches to various issues facing the international system. These scholars accept that the practice and discipline of international relations is gendered and focus on addressing the marginalization of women. Moreover, these scholars point to the first generation of scholars as the influence and starting point for much of their own research. For example, in *The Global Construction of Gender* (1999), Elisabeth Prügl looks at the regulation of home-based work as an issue for global governance utilizing a rules-based constructivist approach (see Chapter 5). Prügl focuses on entitlement, identity and labor, which she argues is inherently biased toward men. She also studies the gender regimes of the agricultural sector of the European Union (2011). She concludes that masculine rules negatively impact women farmers and place them at a distinct disadvantage. Prügl also contributes to the development of feminist constructivism as a theory by offering guidance on how to reconcile feminism and constructivism into a coherent theory (Locher and Prügl, 2001). In a post-positive study in the poststructuralist feminist tradition, Charlotte Hooper analyzed the language utilized in *The Economist* to illustrate the continued masculine, in fact multiple mascunities, nature of states identified by Tickner (1992) as well as the masculine bias in the international system. In *Manly States: Masculinities, International Relations, and Gender Politics*, Hooper (2001, 219) argued, "that the discipline of IR is heavily implicated in the construction and promotion of Anglo-American models of hegemonic masculinity—and that this role continues in connection with globalization." These two examples are illustrative of the type of research that the current generation of scholars are conducting.

As a discipline, feminist international relations scholars recognize the difficulty in presenting their approach to rest of the international relations field. As such, several research agendas have been suggested: women and international relations, gender and international relations, and feminist international relations (Wibben, 2004; Youngs, 2004). The 'women and international relations' research agenda encapsulates the familiar question, "where are the women in international relations?" and seeks to locate and identify the role of women in the international arena. The work by Cynthia Enloe, for example, falls into this agenda.

Scholars examining how the discipline as well as politics is gendered fall into the 'gender and international relations' research agenda. We can locate the work of both Elshtain (gendered roles in the policy world) and Tickner (gender in the discipline) within this agenda. Last, the 'feminist international relations' agenda envisions scholarship that addresses how international relations would look if feminist scholarship were taken seriously. "Such an approach necessarily brings the political back into international politics, since feminism . . . entails a political project. While there are many feminisms . . . they agree on a common goal—to make the world a better place for women. So . . . they want to dismantle current hierarchies and reduce gender inequalities" (Wibben, 2004, 106). This is what we are currently seeing in the second generation of feminist international relations scholarship.

Criticisms of Feminism

Feminist international relations theory has faced criticisms from its inception, in part, due to its interdisciplinary nature, the perceived indiscernible differences between feminism as a movement and as an academic discipline, and the unconventional methodologies employed. One of the major concerns, however, is that feminist international relations theory is more likely to be ignored than directly criticized. When it is addressed, one of the main critiques is the perceived inability to separate itself from politics as "the political nature of feminist knowledge claims along with their adoption of what are seen as disruptive approaches constitute the main grounds on which feminists insights have been dismissed" (Wibbens, 2004, 102).

The "disruptive approaches" attracts a great deal of debate from those in the malestream of international relations. While the research that falls under the feminist empiricism umbrella often engages in the accepted epistemological and methodological norms of mainstream international relations, the rest of the feminist agenda is questioned for the perceived lack of rigorous and systematic scholarship (Jones, 1996). This criticism is at the heart of the debate sparked by Robert Keohane's article "International Relations Theory: Contributions of a Feminist Standpoint" in a 1989 issue of *Millennium*. Keohane provides an analysis of each epistemological perspective outlined by Harding (1986) and concludes that the feminist standpoint has the most promise, that empirical feminism must go beyond stating and studying the obvious "that women have been marginalized in the state, and in interstate politics" and finally that "this postmodernist project is a dead-end in the study of international relations—and that is would be disastrous for feminist international relations theory to pursue this path" (Keohane, 1989b, 249). Keohane applauds and welcomes the feminist standpoint approach to redefining key concepts in the discipline, particularly power, sovereignty, and reciprocity.

Cynthia Weber (1994, 337) represented the view of feminist international relations scholars, however, she makes it clear that she is responding to Koehane's text and his text only. She argues that his critique "is symptomatic of male paranoia, for wherever the feminist body of literature threatens to overflow the boundaries within which the discipline of International Relations has sought to confine it, Keohane's critique works to reimpose these boundaries or invent new ones around and within the feminist body of literature" (Weber, 1994, 338). She also points out that Harding (1986) and Sylvester (1989) approach international relations by looking through "*feminist* lenses" while "Keohane's text looks *at* them" (Weber, 1994, 339). In other words, "Keohane treats feminist IR as a subject to be studied, not a way of studying IR" (Wibbens, 2004, 103). This, and other critiques of feminist international relations, led Tickner (1997) to tell traditional scholars, "You just don't understand."

Similar to the critique of constructivism, critics also question whether international relations feminism is an actual theory or whether it co-opted elements of other theories by merely adding gender. For example, does feminism simply take from Marxism in the development of feminist or socialist Marxism? Does constructivism borrow from feminism or does feminism borrow from constructivism? J. Ann Tickner (1997, 614) argues that practically all international relations feminist scholars "use gender in a social constructivist sense." However, feminists are not credited with developing constructivism, rather that honor goes to Alexander Wendt, Nicholas Onuf, and John Ruggie (Sylvester, 2002) as discussed in Chapter Five. Feminist scholar Christine Sylvester (2002, 11) writes, "The possibility that some [feminists] . . . may have helped introduce aspects of constructivism to IR, as is arguably the case with Elshtain's *Women and War*—which is about the social constitution of gender through ideas carried in war stories—is not mentioned, let alone explored. All-embracing constructivism, therefore, comes out as fathered, like most IR."

Another debate in feminist international relations erupted with the publication in 1998 of "Women and the Evolution of World Politics" by noted scholar Francis Fukuyama.[16] He focuses on the differences between men and women from a biological perspective. Relying on evolutionary biology, Fukuyama (1998, 30) states "there are profound differences between the sexes that are genetically rather than culturally rooted, and that these differences extend beyond the body into the realm of the mind." Men are naturally violent and women are pacifists; men are prone to violence more than women. His concern, of course, is that states (particularly Western states) with female leaders will be ripe for the taking since they are less likely to lead their respective countries to war. Since differences are hard-wired into humans' DNA, Fukuyama basically argues that women are tilting at windmills in their attempt to change human nature (Wibbens, 2004). *Foreign Affairs* published a rejoinder in 1999 titled "Fukuyama's Follies: So What if Women Ruled the World." His critics point out that it should not "be assumed that the male monopoly on warfare has been as eternal and universal as Fukuyama imagines" when in fact historical evidence suggests that women are equally capable of collective violence (Ehrenreich, 1999, 119). Moreover, Fukuyama's reliance on evolutionary psychology for his conclusions are just wrong (Ferguson, 1999) and he ignores cultural and social influences on behavior (Pollitt, 1999). Ironically, Fukuyama's folly helped to highlight one of the major contributions of feminist scholarship: "that gender roles are influenced by a variety of factors and very cross-culturally and historically" (Wibbens, 2004, 99).

International relations feminism has brought to light several important facets of international relations. For example, this paradigm points out that the experiences of women in global politics afford them a unique perspective. "Out of oppression—physical, material, psychological, linguistic—comes epistemic advantage. Women's locations on the peripheries and margins of society place them in positions whereby their capacities for perceiving, seeing, and knowing the world are greater than those at the center . . . Feminism is necessary to begin to understand society from the perspective of the outsider, the immigrant, the stranger" (Zalewski, 1993, 21).

Case Study: Proliferation

The issue of nuclear weapons and the NPT serves as an excellent example of how feminism as a movement and feminism as a theory intersect. While this has been a critique of feminist international relations theory, many feminist scholars "do not believe that it is possible to separate thought from action, and knowledge from practice, they claim that feminist research cannot be separated from the historical movement for the improvements of women's lives of which it emerged" (Tickner, 2006, 28). Recall that feminists look to address questions that mainstream theories ignore such as roles assigned to women and men as well as the gendered nature of international relations. Thus, we focus here on two elements: first, who are the participants in the anti-war, disarmament, and nuclear nonproliferation movements and how do they participate, and second, how are nuclear weapons and the NPT gendered?

In 1961, approximately 50,000 women across 60 cities in the United States marched in protest against nuclear weapons. The sponsoring organization, Women Strike for Peace (WSP), attracted primarily white, educated, middle-class women, those indicative of the second feminist wave. In 1982, women, many born in war-time London, set up a camp near the Royal Air Force Station Greenham Common to protest the deployment of cruise missiles at the base. On December 12, 1983, over 30,000 women showed up, lined the wire fence around the base, and sang, "Give Peace a Chance" (The *Guardian*, 2015).[17] Protests against nuclear weapons continued in England throughout the summer of 1983 culminating in over 300,000 protesting in Hyde Park, London in October, which the *New York Times* called "the largest protest against nuclear weapons in British History" (Cortright, 2008, 148).

The WSP and the women at Greenham Common continued the long tradition of anti-war feminists, starting with the Women's International League for Peace and Freedom (WILPF) 1915. The WILPF claims several platforms including advancing women's rights by supporting the Convention on the Elimination of All Forms of Discrimination against Women (CEDAW) and programs that continue its activism in the area of nonproliferation and disarmament.[18] Reaching Critical Will (RCW), the disarmament program of the WILPT, "works for disarmament and arms control of many different weapon systems, the reduction of global military spending and militarism, and the investigation of gendered aspects of the impact of weapons and of disarmament processes."[19] The WILPF is also opposed to nuclear energy pointing to concerns about the nuclear fuel cycle citing problems at each stage (uranium mining, enrichment, reprocessing, and the disposal of radioactive waste), the controversies regarding the nuclear programs in Iran and North Korea, the relationship between nuclear energy and climate change, and the realities of nuclear disasters such as those at Three Mile Island in 1979, Chernobyl in 1986, and the Fukushima Diiachi Power Plant in 2011. As a women's organization, the WILPF also addresses gender and disarmament. They acknowledge the socially constructed nature of gender stating that "ideas about gender affect the way people and societies view weapons, war, and militarism. Considering gender can help in developing deeper understanding of 'gun cultures,' armament policies, or obstacles to disarmament."[20]

In 2015, they published, *Women Weapons, and War: A Gendered Critique of Multilateral Instruments* aimed at examining international treaties and agreements including the Arms Trade Treaty (ATT), the UN Programme of Action on trade in small arms and light weapons (UNPoA), resolutions from the UN Security Council, the UN Human Rights Council, and the UN General Assembly as well as other relevant instruments. Collectively, these instruments "fail to recognise the gendered power structures that prevent women's effective participation in peace and security issues, or that generate and sustain armed conflict and armed violence in the first place" (Acheson, 2015, 4). The report studies the language used in the ATT and UNPoA regarding women and gender and only finds three references to women. They are categorized as victims (in terms of gender-based violence) or members of vulnerable populations. Furthermore, the analysis revealed a lack of any references to their potential agency, for example as militants or fighters. The report concludes, "To group all women together, and to group all women with children and the elderly, as vulnerable or as victims, is to strip 50% of the populations of its agency and its diverse identities, experiences, and capacities. It also reinforces persistent constructions of women as the 'weaker sex' in need of protection, and of men as the more 'powerful'' sex with a given responsibility to 'protect' the women'" (Acheson, 2015, 8). Similar to the arguments made by academics, the report argues that the perpetuation of these constructed identities only prevents women from participating effectively in social, economic, and political roles.

A 2015 article by the Institute for Security Studies (ISS) asks what should by now be a familiar question, "In the debate towards nuclear disarmament, where are all the women?"[21] Contrary to the idea that participation in the non-proliferation regime is gender neutral (implying that it is open to participation by both women and men), the reality is that this world is still closed off to women (recall Carol Cohn's experience with nuclear defense intellectuals). For example, NPT review conferences are designed to assess the three major pillars of the treaty: disarmament, non-proliferation, and the peaceful use of nuclear energy. The ISS study found that in 2005, 17.8% of the overall participants were women. This number rose to 25.6% in 2010 and 27.2% in 2015. Examining participants by country, the study found that of the 181 countries that have participated, 25 countries have never sent a women representative. Women constituted at least half of the participants in only 24 or 13% of countries. The report concludes "this means that women are underrepresented in 87% of countries that have sent representatives to the review conferences." Like the report from the WILPF, the ISS calls for reform in order to empower women and open space for their participation.

The scope of women's participation in the area of security and conflict has historically been located at the margins. Due to labor shortages in World War II, women moved from the kitchen to the assembly line and the image of "Rosie the Riveter" became ubiquitous and her status as a feminist icon continues to be debated today.[22] At the end of the war, women were expected to quietly return to role of homemaker. And, many did drift back to the hearth, becoming the subject of Friedan's *feminist mystique*. Others became part of the second wave of feminism that were involved in the anti-war, civil, and women's movements of the 1960s, including the WSP. A 1984 WSP statement recounts their origins: "We came into existence on November 1, 1961, as a protest against atmospheric nuclear tests by the U.S. and the Soviet Union which were poisoning the air and our children's food. That year 100,000 women from 60 cities came out of kitchens and jobs to demand: END THE ARMS RACE—NOT THE HUMAN RACE, and WSP was born."[23] Beyond their opposition to nuclear weapons, many feminists are opposed to nuclear energy and engage in protesting the installation of nuclear power stations, particularly in light of the Fukushima nuclear disaster in Japan in 2011. So, what we see is women participating in NGOs, non-profits, and women's organizations at the

246 INTERNATIONAL RELATIONS THEORY

local, state, and international levels in anti-war and anti-nuclear organizations like the Campaign for Nuclear Disarmament (CND) headquartered in the United Kingdom and CODEPINK whose stated goals
are "to end U.S. wars and militarism, support peace and human rights
initiatives, and redirect our tax dollars into healthcare, education,
green jobs and other life-affirming programs."[24] A common thread is
that war and nuclear weapons are not only gendered, they are morally
wrong; however, feminists also take a pragmatic approach by addressing the costs involved in war-making (Cohn and Ruddick, 2004). These
costs cover not only the price of weapons, conventional and nuclear,
but also the opportunity cost to programs that would improve the lives
of women and other marginalized members of society.

Feminist international theory also addresses the issues of
nonproliferation and weapons of mass destruction important to
feminist anti-war activists, specifically within the context of national
security. The feminist security theory agenda focuses on the gendered
nature and economics of war as well as the leaders that are primarily men
(Blanchard, 2003). Feminists argue that nuclear weapons extend the
masculine/feminine dichotomy and point to the rhetoric of statesmen
as evidence. In 1998, India tested five nuclear devices prompting Hindu
leader Balasaheb Thackery to state, "we had to prove that we are not
eunuchs" (quoted in Cohn, Hill, and Ruddick, 2005, 3). As India was
pushed to sign the Comprehensive Test Ban Treaty, Brahma Chellaney,
a geostrategic analysis, argued "accession to these 'self-castration
measures' would leave India as a 'nuclear eunuch.'" In a subsequent
attack on India's self-restrained nuclear policy, Chellaney likened
India's "nuclear option" to "chronic impotence" and decried national
leaders for leaving the nation "naked" (Perkovich, 1999, 457–458).

Postmodern feminist Carol Cohn (see section on poststructuralism),
who also self-identifies as an anti-war feminist, argues that the nature
of nuclear weapons is gendered. Observing the language used among
defense intellectuals, she learned "pat the missile" has several meanings:
on the one hand it denotes affection and intimacy and even sexual possession, while on the other hand patting is something one does to children and pets. The image is either a sexual one or a maternal one, either
way not one that should be associated with a mechanism for destruction. Cohn also comments on the phallic worship she associated with the
nuclear industry citing the following sexual, as well as gendered, subtext
to weapons: "penetration aids," "more bang for the buck," "to disarm

is to get rid of all your stuff," "vertical erector launchers," and "thrust-to-waist ratios" (Cohn, 1987a, 1987b). Rejecting a reductionist argument that the arms race was in part a symptom of "missile envy," Cohn sought an alternative explanation for this particular form of discourse. What she found is that mastering the language of the discourse leads to power and agency, and in this case, a "militarization of the mind" (Cohn, 1987b, 715). Language also contributes to the development of culture, an argument shared by feminists and constructivists alike.

Feminist scholars and peace scholars invoke the concept of a positive peace as a goal, rather than peace in the negative sense, that is, the absence of war. They argue that even in times of peace states are constantly preparing for war, in other words, war is not bounded by time or space. Feminists do not adhere to the demands of the security dilemma like their realist counterparts, arguing that resources are better spent on improving the lives of all citizens within the state. As such, women were an integral part of the anti-nuclear movements during the second wave of feminism (1980s). However, they are not present in the decision-making processes and at the forums central to discussions regarding disarmament in general and the implementation of the NPT specifically. In addition, feminist international theory scholars argue that the starting point for examining war and weapons should be women's lives, specifically "the work women do and the distinctive bodily assaults war inflicts on women" (Cohn and Ruddick, 2004, 409). Ultimately, "State security may sometimes be served by war, but too often human security is not" (Cohn and Ruddick, 2004, 406).

Case Study: WTO

In the introduction to this chapter, we highlighted the general lack of women in positions of power in the political and economic sectors. Here we focus on female representation in the WTO and other international institutions as well as the impact of trade liberalization as "[g]lobalization and especially its neo-liberal market manifestation have had severe gender impacts, affecting and often devastating women's lives and family livelihood, and drastically reducing political space for making claims against the state" (Pettman, 2004, 86). Thus, we see that feminist international relations theory is at odds with liberalism when it comes to perceived benefits of the free trade regime.

TABLE 6.1 Feminism and Proliferation

Feminism	Theoretical Tenet	Proliferation Example
Liberal Feminism	A positivist approach to the study of gender and international relations that adheres to a liberal philosophy of equality and individualism. They argue that women and men are equals based on their shared humanity. They ask, "where are the women?' and focus on the underrepresentation of women in the political and business arena.	While feminists generally support the NPT, its development, ratification process, and now review process are examples of how women are underrepresented in areas that are generally considered "high" politics in the international system. Liberal feminists do not necessarily expect a different outcome from the inclusion of women in the nuclear industry.
Feminist Standpoint	Women have a unique view (i.e., standpoint) regarding how the world works due to the way their life experiences have been marginalized and the socially constructed nature of gender roles. The feminist standpoint looks at how race, class, and patriarchy help to explain the gendered nature of international relations.	The underrepresentation of women in the decision-making and review process of the NPT is a function of the gendered nature of the international system that views men as "warriors" and women as the "beautiful soul" in need of saving. These constructed roles are perpetuated and supported by the traditional patriarchal nature of the nuclear weapons industry.
Poststructural Feminism	The categories of masculinity and femininity are socially constructed and all claims of universal truths should be questioned. They focus on how language and discourse are utilized in the political, economic, and social arenas as tools to disseminate knowledge which is gendered in favor of men.	The language of the defense and military sector is gendered toward men creating an almost exclusive club that has a monopoly on the knowledge of the nuclear industry. This creates an additional barrier for women entering the field.

The Fourth United Nations World Conference on Women in Beijing (1995) developed a Platform for Action focusing on 12 areas of concern including "Institutional Mechanism for the Advancement of Women."[25] The platform calls for specific actions on the part of governments "to integrate gender perspectives in legislation, public policies, programmes, and projects" as well as to "generate and disseminate gender-disaggregated data and information for planning and evaluation." While this Platform for Action was directed at state governments, international institutions are also adhering to this initiative in what is referred to as "gender mainstreaming."[26] In addition, international institutions, as well as many governments are instituting gender quotas in an attempt to even the playing field (as well as comply with the Platform for Action). The goal was to achieve gender equality by the year 2000. Here we have an example of how feminist international theory led to a policy initiative, gender mainstreaming, demonstrating the connection between feminism as a discipline and feminism as a movement (True and Mintrom, 2001).

According to WomenWatch, there has been an increase in women employees at the United Nations to the extent that gender parity has occurred up to the P2 level. Unfortunately, this is the lowest level in the professional ranks (Haack, 2014). How does this compare to the number of women employed at the WTO? WomenWatch reports that female employment increased from 35% (14 out of 40) in 2001 to 42.2% (19 out of 45) in 2011 in the professional and higher categories ranks. However, the highest rank achieved by a female was that of a P-5 (the highest level of the professional ranks or what is called mid-level professional) and there were no women in the highest ranks of D1–2 (managerial or senior level professionals) or UG (decision-making ranks).[27] While women have been able to at least crack the glass ceiling in the United Nations by holding some leadership positions in certain programs, only four agencies have had a women leader. Fourteen agencies within the United Nations have never had a women hold the top position. Moreover, women tend to be leaders in the areas one might expect, that is in the traditional low politics issues of human rights, health care, education, and the environment, with men holding leadership positions in the high politics issues of military spending and trade, just to name a few (Haack, 2014). One bright spot is the appointment of Christine Lagarde as the Managing Director of the International Monetary Fund (IMF), becoming the first women to head the IMF in 2011. To date, women have not ascended to the highest ranks in the WTO leading feminist activists and scholars alike to pose the question again, "where are all the women?"

What does this lack of female leadership at the WTO mean in terms of trade policy? Historically, trade agreements between and among states focused exclusively on economic issues, ignoring social issues such as human rights, environmental impact, and of interest here, gender issues. Likewise, policymakers at the WTO as well as mainstream international relations theories treat the issues of trade, such as trade agreements, as gender neutral (Wagner, 2012). As was discussed in Chapter 3, the liberal paradigm suggests several benefits to trade liberalization including higher salary potential and increased employment opportunities including small businesses for women. Studies suggest that indeed, trade liberalization has increased opportunities for women as they constitute approximately 75% of the workers in the textile, apparel, and electronic sectors in the export processing zones (EPZs).[28] In addition, the Food and Agriculture Organization of the United Nations (FAO) reports that women produce over half of the world's food supply, this number is even higher in sub-Saharan Africa and the Caribbean where women are responsible for up to 80% of food production. In addition, women make up a significant percentage of agricultural consumers, an issue that is highly contested within the WTO.[29]

However, feminist scholarship has highlighted the gendered nature of trade pointing out women are rarely the beneficiary of liberal trade policies that fail to "take into account women's unpaid household work or unequal access to such assets as land, resources, and credit . . . While women's employment in the paid labour force often expands with trade liberalization, the jobs they gain entry into are usually poorly paid and highly vulnerable" (MacDonald, 2002, 153). Women's hidden labor, those in the informal and household sectors, remain unaccounted for as well (MacDonald, 2002; Riley and Mejia, 1996).

When it comes to addressing many of these issues the WTO has traditionally been silent, insisting that trade policy is generally considered gender-neutral. However, in 2010, under the auspices of the United Nations Conference on Trade and Development (UNCTAD), a study was prepared to assess the impact of trade liberalization on countries seeking to accede to the WTO, specifically addressing the "gender dimension."[30] The report acknowledges that the rules of the WTO impact men and women differently "even though the wording of the legal texts governing trade regulation is gender-neutral." The report concludes that much of the differing effects is dependent on the domestic conditions within the acceding state, for example whether the state is developed or less developed. Moreover, women within the same country might be affected differently depending upon their sector of employment. Ultimately, the findings indicate that "the likely effects are more similar among those countries with similar social views of women and girls— where females are considered equal to males and given opportunities to participate in the economic sphere, trade liberalization holds more potential than it does for women living in societies where the role of the female in public life is restricted." In other words, it is not the policies of the WTO, it is the conditions within the state that matter. The WTO, as well as other financial organizations, believe their role is to help facilitate the free market, which is considered the final arbiter of the production and distribution of goods. Feminist activists, feminist international relations theorists, as well as several UN organizations such as the UN Development Program (UNDP) reject the liberal philosophy that all boats rise in the sea of free trade. Moreover, free trade and economic liberalism does not guard against gender inequality much less address the issue of poverty (Riley and Mejfa, 1996).

TABLE 6.2 Feminism and the WTO

Feminism	Theoretical Tenet	WTO Example
Liberal Feminism	A positivist approach to the study of gender and international relations that adheres to a liberal philosophy of equality and individualism. They argue that women and men are equals based on their shared humanity. They focus on the underrepresentation of women in the political and business arena.	A call for gender mainstreaming and quotas to create gender equality at international institutions like the WTO have led to some improvements in women's representation. However, parity is only evident in the lower professional ranks with the highest ranks still out of reach for most women.
Marxist/ Socialist Feminism	Women have a unique view (i.e., standpoint) regarding how the world works due to the way their life experiences have been marginalized and the socially constructed nature of gender roles. Marxist feminists view women's inequality as a function of the capitalist system. Socialist feminists look to patriarchy as well as capitalism as explanations for the gendered nature of international relations.	The WTO and trade liberalization adhere to the liberal philosophy opposed by Marxist and socialist feminists. The WTO and other international institutions are tools of the capitalist state. The liberal trade policies of the WTO serve to perpetuate the capitalist and patriarchal oppression of women.
Postcolonial Feminism	The categories of masculinity and femininity are socially constructed and all claims of universal truths should be questioned. They look to race, ethnicity, culture and colonial history as tools of oppression that perpetuate gender inequality and discrimination.	They argue that women and other marginalized groups do not benefit from liberal trade policies as advertised, particularly due to the high level of hidden work performed by women in non-Western states.

Conclusion

In this chapter, we explored the genesis and evolution of the feminist movement and its connection to the evolution and development of feminist international relations theory. Feminist theorists across the epistemological spectrum are in agreement that the gendered nature of the international system has silenced the voices of women and a feminist framework is necessary to expose those who are oppressed and marginalized. We also examined how feminist international relations theory intersects with several of the other theories presented in this book. The final chapter explores the relationships between realism, liberalism, economic structuralism, constructivism, and feminism in more detail in order to illustrate how all five can be utilized to study and understand international relations phenomena.

Key Terms

Dimorphism

Gender

Difference feminism

Feminist empiricism

Feminist postmodernism

Feminist standpoint

Intersectionality

Liberal feminism

Marxist feminism

Patriarchy

Postcolonial feminism

Poststructural feminism

Radical feminism

Socialist feminism

For Further Reading

Elshtain, Jean Bethke. 1987. *Women and War*. New York: Basic Books.

Enloe, Cynthia. 1990. *Bananas, Beaches, and Bases: Making Feminist Sense of International Politics*. Berkeley: University of California Press.

Sylvester, Christine. 1994. *Feminist Theory and International Relations in a Postmodern Era*. Cambridge: Cambridge University Press.

———. 2002 *Feminist International Relations: An Unfinished Journey*. Cambridge: Cambridge University Press.

Tickner, J. Ann. 1992. *Gender in International Relations: Feminist Perspectives on Achieving Global Security*. New York: Columbia University Press.

———. 1997. "You Just Don't Understand: Troubled Engagements Between Feminists and IR Theorists." *International Studies Quarterly* 41:611–632.

Tickner, J. Ann and Laura Sjoberg, eds. 2011. *Feminism and International Relations: Conversations About the Past, Present, and Future*. New York: Routledge.

Endnotes

[1] Martha Lear is credited with coining the term "second feminist wave" in a 1968 article in the *New York Times Sunday Magazine*.

[2] Many feminists disagree with the idea of establishing waves of feminism as many do not fit nicely into the time periods that delineate the different waves (see Baumgardner, 2011).

[3] Alice Paul was a member of the National Women's Party (NWP) who advocated militant tactics, Carrie Chapman Carr was the president of the National American Women's Suffrage Association (NAWSA), and Anna Howard Shaw was considered a skilled orator. Maria Stewart was a gifted orator as well as a journalist and abolitionist. She was a member of the Massachusetts General Colored Association and published essays for abolitionist publisher William Lloyd Garrison. Born into slavery, self-named Sojourner Truth became an abolitionists and women's rights activist best known for her speech "Ain't I a Woman" at the Ohio Women's Rights Convention in 1851. Frances E. W. Harper was a poet, writer, and teacher as well as an abolitionist. She was active as a civil rights and women's rights activist during Reconstruction.

[4] Betty Friedan was also one of the feminists that formed the National Organization for Women (NOW) which sought legal means to achieve gender equality.

[5] "The Problem That Has No Name" is the title of the first chapter in Friedan's (1963) *The Feminist Mystique*.

[6] Angela Davis is the author of *Women, Race, and Class* (1983) and *Women, Culture and Politics* (1990). bell hooks is the pen name of Gloria Jean Watkins in honor of her great-grandmother. Lower case is her preferred punctuation. She is the author of *Ain't I a Woman? Black Women and Feminism* (1981) and *Feminist Theory: From Margin to Center* (1984).

[7] Feminists often utilized the term "malestream" in their critique of mainstream international relations.

[8] The published books are *Women and War* (1987) by Elshtain, *Bananas, Beaches and Bases* (1989) by Enloe, *Gender in International Relations: Feminist Perspectives on Achieving Global Security* (1992) by Tickner and *Feminist Theory and International Relations in a Postmodern Era* (1994) by Sylvester. The specific contribution of each of these theorists is discussed in more detail in the section, *Pioneers in the Field*.

[9] The categories of feminism included here are not meant to be the definitive nor exhaustive list. We focus on those representative of the field of international relations.

[10] Difference feminism is not generally considered part of the empiricist epistemology. It is discussed here in order to make a comparison to liberal feminism as both focus on the biological differences between men and women.

[11] The contribution of Cynthia Enloe is discussed in more detail in the section *Pioneers in the Field*.

[12] This is a reference to *Lean In: Women, Work, and the Will to Lead* (2013) by Sheryl Sandberg.

[13] Postcolonial feminism and Third World feminism are often used interchangeably. We utilize postcolonial as it is the preferred terminology in the discipline.

[14] Studies on SGD find support for the UN program to increase the number of women and girls participating in sporting activities as a means to "challenge and resist their domestic duties, improve their social networks and relations with communities, confront gender norms, boost self-confidence, advance communication skills and increase their ability to make decisions regarding their own well-being" (Hayhurts, 2011, 533).

[15] Tickner specifically points to the work done on military prostitution by Katharine Moon in *Sex Among Allies* (1997) and female domestic servants in Malaysia in Christine Chin's *In Service and Servitude* (1983). Moon addresses the literature on national security policy and Chin's work examines the intersection of development and the global political economy, however, they approach these male-dominated fields in very different ways.

[16] Francis Fukuyama (1989, 1992) is best known for his proclamation that we had witnessed "the end of history" in terms of political ideology. Western liberalism had triumphed over all other contenders, especially fascism and communism.

[17] See "That's Me in the Picture: Hazel Whiskerd, Protesting at Greenham Common, 1982" in *The Guardian* at http://www.theguardian .com/artanddesign/2015/aug/14/hazel-whiskerd-protesting -greenham-common.

[18] See the "Our Work" on the Women's International League for Peace and Freedom at http://wilpfus.org/our-work.

[19] Reaching Critical Will is available at http://www.reachingcriticalwill.org/.

[20] See the Gender and Disarmament page of Reaching Critical Will at http://reachingcriticalwill.org/resources/fact-sheets/critical-issues/ 4741-gender-and-disarmament.

[21] https://www.issafrica.org/iss-today/in-the-debate-towards-nuclear -disarmament-where-are-all-the-women

[22] In 2014 Beyonce posted an instagram photo imitating Rosie the Riveter sparking a social media debate as to the validity of Rosie as a feminist icon.

[23] Swarthmore College is the repository of the Women Strike for Peace, 1961–1996 records available at https://www.swarthmore.cdu/library/ peace/DG100-150/DG115/DG115WSP.html.

[24] See CODEPINK's website at http://www.codepink.org/about.

[25] The Fourth World Conference on Women Platform for Action can be accessed at http://www.un.org/womenwatch/daw/beijing/platform/.

[26] Examples include UN Security Council Resolution 1325 in 2000 (http://unscr.com/en/resolutions/1325) and UN Security Council Resolution 1820 in 2008 (http://unscr.com/en/resolutions/1820)

[27] Data accessed from the United Nations on November 30, 2015. http://www.un.org/womenwatch/uncoordination/documents/unentity/WTO/wto-factsheet.pdf

[28] Export processing zones (EPZs) are "areas within developing countries that offer incentives and a barrier-free environment to promote economic growth by attracting foreign investment for export-oriented production" (Papadopoulos 2007, 148).

[29] See "Women Feed the World" at http://www.fao.org/docrep/x0262e/x0262e16.htm.

[30] The countries under consideration were Azerbaijan, Bhutan, Cambodia, Cape Verde, Ethiopia, Iraq, Kazakhstan, Laos, Serbia, and Yemen. See the report at http://unctad.org/en/Docs/ditctncd20106_en.pdf.

CHAPTER 7
....

Conclusion

"The complexity of most large events in world politics precludes plausible unicausal explanations. The outbreak of World Wars I and II, the emergence of international human rights norms, and the evolution of the European Union, for example, are surely important enough events to merit comprehensive explanation even at the expense of theoretical parsimony."

—Andrew Moravcsik, "Theory Synthesis in International
Relations: Real Not Metaphysical"

After exposure to the five main theories of international relations in the preceding chapters, it would be expected that readers would wonder how all this adds up. As alluded to in the first chapter of this book, the five approaches presented have distinct features but also lines of connection and similarities. At times, they appear to be in direct challenge to one another, while at other times they complement and reinforce each other. This chapter ties them all together, highlighting their similarities and differences, filling in some gaps that exist in the coverage presented of the theoretical family of international relations, and discussing the future of international relations theory. Finally, we will leave you with the case studies discussed throughout this book: proliferation and the WTO. In each chapter, an explanation was provided to explain an aspect of each case study. It is important to note that there are additional explanations that could have been provided from each theoretical point of view, but for clarity sake, only a sampling of explanations was chosen. Here, they are tied together to demonstrate the benefits of a holistic or eclectic approach to theoretical application, and thus a broader understanding of the world around us.

Ontology and Epistemology Revisited

Before reading this book or entering the class for which it is assigned, you may never have heard the terms ontology and epistemology. After reading the preceding chapters, you should now have a better idea as to how the five approaches to studying international relations view the world and the acquisition of knowledge in that world. Recall that ontology refers to the nature of existence, and more specifically for the purpose here is whether or not there is a known, single reality in the world. In Chapter 2 we explained that realists believe that they know the world around them and that they analyze the world that actually is, not the world they wish existed. The central assumptions of realism highlight this belief, in that states are the principal actors in a self-help system of anarchy. As such, survival is their most important objective and they expect conflict rather than cooperation as the means to that end. This is the "reality" of world politics, according to realists. In Chapter 3, the points of ontological convergence and divergence between liberals and realists become clear. Liberals accept that the fixed reality of international relations is one of a system of anarchy. They disagree with realists in a number of other areas: individuals as well as domestic and non-state actors matter, individual and state behavior can be modified, and cooperation is possible in all important areas of concern. Although liberals "know" the reality, they believe the negatives of anarchy can be overcome through cooperation. Further, epistemologically, both realists and liberals are positivists, accepting a known reality and believing knowledge of this reality can be acquired empirically. As explained in Chapter 1, the decades following World War II witnessed the call for a more scientific approach to studying international relations. Recalling that this approach does not require quantitative methodology, international relations scholars attempted to create studies that could predict behavior and carry the weight assigned to methodologies pursued in the hard sciences and other social sciences such as economics. Hypothesis testing coupled with generalizing and predicting behavior was pursued in order to develop better explanations (realists) and, for some, to understand ways in which international relations could be changed for the better (liberals).

The other three worldviews look at the world quite differently. Chapter 4 presented the myriad approaches under the banner of economic structuralism. While some theorists (Marxist-based) who fall under economic structuralism argue there is a known reality, others disagree and question the existence of a fixed reality. The central assumptions of economic structuralism, however, demonstrate that there is a consensus that the system is not characterized by anarchy but it is capitalism and the hierarchy that flows from it that creates an inherently conflictual condition in international politics. As demonstrated in Chapter 5 and 6, constructivists and feminists are on the opposite end of the spectrum from realists and liberals in their ontological view. Constructivists accept the importance of the state, but not the fixed nature of anarchy or for that matter the fixed nature of any element of international relations. The "real world" is simply something we have constructed, thus we can deconstruct it and reconstruct it. Instead of being forced into behaviors by the structure of the system and its anarchical nature, behavior is guided by norms legitimized by the agents in world politics and followed freely and willingly by states. Similarly, some feminists, particularly liberal feminists, view the state as the central actor in world politics, but all question the gender bias of the state as an institution. International relations as a discipline also suffers a gender bias. The perceived reality is male-dominated and feminists of all types wish to alter this view to recognize how gender bias has contributed to its construction and to reorient that reality to include both men and women. Epistemologically, most economic structuralists, constructivists, and feminists are post-positivists. A major debate erupted in the 1960s concerning the applicability of the scientific method. Hedley Bull (1966) was a proponent of the classical approach of deriving theory from philosophy, history, and law and exercising judgment concerning the issues and behavior in international relations. He declared that "the scientific approach has contributed and is likely to contribute very little to the theory of international relations, and in so far as it is intended to encroach upon and ultimately displace the classical approach, it is positively harmful" (Bull, 1966, 366). The debate continues to this day.

Towards a Holistic Approach to Studying International Relations

For several decades there has been a lament amongst some scholars of international relations that the focus on theory has undermined the analysis of real-world issues and thus diminished the policy relevance of studies in international relations. If the work becomes too theoretical, or too scientific, policy-makers will not learn from it, either because they cannot see the relevance or because they simply cannot understand it. Many of the pioneers discussed in the preceding chapters have indeed intended for their work to be prescriptive to policy-makers. Although there are many more examples, the Spotlight on Policymakers feature in each chapter is intended to demonstrate how theorists work to apply their ideas (or have their ideas applied) to the "real world." But, if Joseph Nye (2009b) is correct, scholars have been pushed to the sidelines by the jargon, models, methodologies, and theories that policymakers cannot apply to the situations in which they find themselves. Part of the argument as to why this is so goes beyond the clear post-positivist critique of becoming too scientific and extends to the paradigmatic approaches presented in this book. If the theories of international relations take a silo approach, their explanatory value and their connection and relevance to non-academics is diminished. If theorists compartmentalize themselves, viewing the other approaches as contrary, they limit their own explanatory value. Paradigm-specific progress is often not "recognized or appreciated, either by the discipline writ large or by those outside the academe who look to social scientists for usable knowledge. Instead, scholarly discourse risks becoming dominated by self-referential academic debates at the expense of addressing the complexities and messiness of everyday problems" (Sil and Katzenstein, 2010, 2).

As such, the following two sections of this chapter address this concern from two different angles. First, there are established and influential theories of international relations that bridge the gap between the five theories presented in this book, and others that move beyond them by utilizing different lenses through which to view the world. Some of these theories incorporate aspects of two or more of the five approaches discussed in the preceding chapters, in addition to including factors not present in other theoretical approaches, in an effort to create a more applicable, less rigid, explanatory mechanism. Others touch on alterative perspectives and approaches. Some of the fundamental differences between these approaches and realism and liberalism are ontological and epistemological. All the worldviews presented below are post-positivist in nature and highlight the increasing movement of international relations theory in that direction. This discussion is not meant to diminish the value of the positivist, paradigm-specific approaches already discussed or the efforts of the scholars whose work manifests these approaches. The purpose here is to present a view of theoretical inquiry that crosses boundaries to highlight different ways of assessing the world around us. Thus, the tenets of the English School, critical theory, and postcolonialism will be discussed to demonstrate how crossing paradigms and/or viewing the world through an alternate lens than those presented by realism and liberalism, much like the approaches of constructivism, feminism, and economic structuralism, can result in rich methods of inquiry. It should be noted here that adherents to these approaches would accuse us of relegating these approaches to the status of second-class citizens by discussing them together at the end of this book, rather than providing each with a full explanation in its own chapter. While this book is intended to provide a primer of the five main theories of international relations, students are encouraged to further investigate the theories presented below as their study of international relations progresses.

Second, the case studies of proliferation and the WTO are addressed through an eclectic lens, meaning the explanations for elements of these real-world examples will be drawn from realism, liberalism, constructivism, economic structuralism, and feminism.[1] Sil and Katzenstein (2010, 10) define eclectic as "any approach that seeks to extricate, translate, and selectively integrate analytical elements—concepts, logics, mechanisms, and interpretations—of theories or narratives that have been developed within separate paradigms but that address related aspects of substantive problems that have both scholarly and practical significance." One's first thought might be that this is simply a "kitchen sink" approach: throw everything in that could have any explanatory value and all the bases will be covered. As explained in Chapter 1, theories are a way in which scholars and students of international relations seek to make sense of the complexities of world politics. For many, the **parsimony principle**, also known as the law of parsimony, is of value, meaning that the simplest explanation that fits the evidence is the best approach to take. This is an element of all scientific inquiry and postulates that variables should not be unnecessarily multiplied in seeking an explanation. Hence the best hypothesis is the one that requires the fewest number of explanatory variables. This is one of the benefits of realism, for example. Many proponents of realism argue it is the most parsimonious of the main theories of international relations—state behavior is explained through the need to pursue survival through the acquisition of power, both military and economic. Simple, straight-forward, and according to realists, explains international relations in a nutshell.

Throughout the chapters of this book, however, it has been shown that other approaches, with different variables and different epistemological views, possess significant explanatory weight, and in some cases, explain what realism cannot. If one's purpose is to apply theory to real-world events, having an impact on policy-makers and political outcomes, seeking explanations that are rich in content and accessible to policy-makers is key. To ignore variables that help to explain a situation also diminishes the possibility that a situation could be improved or avoided in the future. For example, if we ignore the impact of the inequality of trade on individuals, policy-makers and the WTO will be tempted to avoid finding solutions for the unequal effects of trade. Artificially forcing complex issues into a parsimonious package to satisfy a narrow paradigmatic approach undercuts the ability of international relations scholars to fully explain phenomenon in world politics and be policy-relevant. Combining paradigmatic explanations will result in a more robust inquiry and promote novel thinking about issues that dramatically impact states in the international system and the people who live within them.

English School

The English School is one of the more recent approaches to the study of international relations, with its genesis in the post–World War II era. The origins of the school are debated and unclear, but the name "English School" is widely accepted as a misnomer as adherents of this theory are not, and have not been, predominantly English. Intellectual precursors of this school are Hugo Grotius and Immanuel Kant (see Chapter 4), as well as E.H. Carr (1892–1982), who is thought of by many as a classical realist infused with liberal thought. The work of early English School scholars was virtually ignored in the United States, while others simply considered it a variant of realism. In the 1980s, the approach all but withered away in the face of its exclusion from the debate between realism and its critics as well as its apparent lack of applicability to critical new approaches, such as international political economy. In 1981, in his article "The English School of International Relations: A Case for Closure?" Roy E. Jones declared that the English School should be disbanded. The mid-1990s brought a resurgence of the English School, and today it is seen as a bridge between neorealism and neoliberalism on the one side, and radical alternatives such as critical theory and post-structuralism on the other side. Thus it occupies much the same space as constructivism, which you read about in

Chapter 5. There is no single view expressed by scholars of the English School, but instead it is made up of a series of scholars covering many theories and views of international relations.[2]

While often referred to as a branch of realism, this school of thought actually mixes components of realism, liberalism, and constructivism. Like realists, prominent English School scholars recognize the existence of a system of interstate relations. They differ from realists however in that their primary purpose for the system is to help elucidate the history of international society (Bull, 1977). Like liberals, rules and institutional arrangements, as well as non-state actors, are important components of international relations. English School scholars are not utopians, however, in that they do not believe that perpetual peace (as discussed in Chapter 3) will result from cooperation. The English School occupies the middle ground between realists and liberals, in that the world is not doomed to endless cycles of violence as rules, laws, and institutions are willingly established and followed by states, but there is no reason to believe that the international system will ever develop into the stability seen in domestic societies. Like constructivist scholars Ruggie and Wendt (see Chapter 5), English School scholars view interstate relations as occurring in a social sphere in which states are agents who are socialized to the rules of the system. Shared values and knowledge are the basis of the norms and institutions that operate in the social sphere. Despite similarities, the approaches differ in terms of the unit of analysis. While constructivists, like Wendt, view the state as the unit of analysis, English School scholars accept individuals and groups as important units of analysis (Dunne, 1998). Hence, the English School approaches the search for explanations in world politics from multiple levels of analysis (discussed in Chapter 1).

Following from the comparisons with realism, liberalism, and constructivism, the central traditions of the English School are elucidated. There are three traditions—realism, rationalism, and revolutionism (Wight, 1991). First, states and non-state actors operate in an anarchical environment. The role of power politics, inherent conflict between states, and war are all central features of this tradition. Second, despite this recognition of the anarchical nature of international relations, the focus is on the concept of "society." Rationalism in the English School refers to the rules, institutions, and laws that states establish, combined with power and balance of power, to create order in anarchy. The combination of realism and liberalism is evident in this regard. E.H. Carr is seen as laying the intellectual foundation for this approach. Carr (1939) argued for the middle ground between idealism and realism, rejecting the utopian view that moral consideration can be pursued at the expense of power and interests, while also rejecting the idea that values can be ignored all together. English School scholars do not deny the importance of power, but it is tempered by an institutional framework composed of norms, rules, laws and institutions.

Continuing from the rationalist tradition, perhaps the English School's most distinguishing feature is its argument that communities and cultures reside in states and these states in turn form an international society. Hedley Bull (1977, 13) provided the widely accepted definition of international society, classifying it as "a group of states, conscious of certain common interests and common values" who form "a society in the sense that they conceive of themselves to be bound by a common set of rules in their relations with one another, and share in the working of common institutions." English School scholars do not accept the argument postulated by realists that a lack of a world government to keep states in check prevents the existence of an international society. Like neoliberal institutionalists, rationalists argue that states are capable of creating and following a set of mutually advantageous rules. States are necessary, lest the world devolve into a Hobbesian state of nature, but they are capable and willing to accept a set of rules that protects their fundamental goal—the safety of their citizens. Following from this tradition, a major foci of English School theorists is how this international society is created and conversely how it can revert to a system of states. The creation of international society has a clear connection to constructivism, in that its formation is the outcome of centuries of human effort to influence the behavior of international actors. The rules, norms, laws, and institutions that bind international society together are all socially constructed. The constructs are not inevitable and they do not exist independently of the will and effort of people. There is also significant debate within the English School concerning what type of international society exists. Some accept the pluralist view of international law, in that states are only bound by rules to which they have given consent. Others, however, subscribe to the natural law view, in that states must obey laws even if they have declined to provide consent and there are basic rights to self-defense and punishment of those who violate the rules (Wight, 1979, 1991; Bull, 1977).

Third, although power and interests hold an important place in English School thought, the view espoused by Immanuel Kant concerning ethics and morality forms the basis for revolutionism. Revolutionists take the perspective that there are universal moral principles and the English School concept of world society (which is different than international society as explained above) flows from this perspective. The Kantian concept of world society adopted by the English School is that there is a world society of individuals and their rights and needs come prior to that of the society of states. States are responsible for protecting the well-being of their citizens and when they fail to do so, they lose their right to sovereignty. Individual protection trumps state protection (Bull, 1977).

All three traditions—realism, rationalism, and revolutionism—can exist simultaneously. All are the subjects of analysis for English School scholars and they represent their understandings of reality. The English School represents a diverse school of thought, intertwining these three traditions as well as elements of realism, liberalism, constructivism, and other critical views. The English School has assumed a prominent place in the study of international relations and it offers an approach rooted in history. But, it also faces significant criticism, much of which stems from its diversity. It is argued that the English School is conceptually underdeveloped, dismissive of gender roles and issues of the economy and human rights, and has unclear boundaries (Buzan, 2004). It is seen by many as a bit of a kitchen sink approach, as mentioned above. It has been viewed as an attempt to cope with a complex environment by failing to clarify an actual argument—hedge one's bet because if you consider so many variables, one is likely to be correct. Theory, history, power, morality, ideas and structure all matter. This heightens the uncertainty as to which theorists actually belong to this school and how it is truly different than any other.[3] Despite these criticisms, many argue this approach is to be lauded. A multifaceted approach is a way to avoid unwisely focusing on only one view or explanation of the world. As such, a fuller and richer understanding of international relations could be attained.

Critical Theory

As with the other theories discussed throughout this book, critical theories of international relations come in many forms. The genesis of critical theory can be found in the works of several intellectuals working simultaneously in different parts of Europe during the 1920s. While Antonio Gramsci (see Chapter 4) was in Italy writing and opposing the rise of fascism, a group of German-Jewish scholars and thinkers formed an intellectual circle during the interwar years that came to be known as the **Frankfurt School** (*Franfurter Schule*). Originally associated with Goethe University in Frankfurt Germany, many of these individuals lived and worked in exile in the United States as the war in Europe approached. These intellectuals critiqued both the left and right wing governments of the day, both socialist and capitalist economies. They were also critical of the positivist approach arguing that it limited the types of questions one could pursue. Gramsci and members of the Frankfurt School expounded and expanded Marxist philosophy while questioning the social, political, and economic consequences of the capitalist economy. As pioneers of critical theory, they established a paradigm that wanted to not only understand the world in which they lived, but wanted to affect change. In particular, the focus was and is on analyzing bourgeois society and how it misrepresents most of society.

According to Robert Cox (1981, 129) whose contributions to critical theory are discussed below, critical theory "stands apart from the prevailing order of the world and asks how that order came about. Critical theory . . . does not take institutions and social and power relations for granted but calls them into question by concerning itself with their origins and how and whether they might be in the process of changing." In addition, critical theorists criticize "the image of social actors as atomistic egoists, whose interests are formed prior to social interaction, and who enter social relations solely for strategic purposes. They argued, in contrast, that actors are inherently social, that their identities and interests are socially constructed, the products of intersubjective social structures" (Reus-Smit, 2013, 221). Beyond these ontological differences, critical theorists also question the positivist epistemological perspective of neorealism and neoliberalism, arguing that an interpretive understanding of international relations is more appropriate. We saw these ideas developed within the constructivist paradigm in Chapter 5.

Despite differences between critical theorists, they operate based on two main premises. First, the goal of emancipation was and is always at the forefront. Emancipation requires the removal of restraints on human equality and the end of human exploitation (Linklater, 1990). This requires a critical assessment of the role of power in international relations and its impact on people. Critical theory is designed to encourage transformation of the social and political order through emancipatory politics. To accomplish this goal, international politics must be understood and scrutinized. This requires historical analysis and a willingness to engage in a critical assessment of past and current practices in international relations. As the goal here is transformation, this approach runs counter to the aspirations of realists and liberals. If we look at realism and liberalism as policy prescriptions, both are concerned with stability, politically and/or economically. For example, realists, like Waltz, are concerned with maintaining a balance of power to ensure a stable political order. The outcome is to maintain the status quo, rather than the transformation of the international system. Along similar lines, neoliberals are concerned with maintaining stability to promote economic gain. As seen in Chapter 4, however, that economic gain benefits those with power, further intensifying economic inequality.

Providing direction on how to pursue social and political transformation is a cornerstone of critical theories. Andrew Linklater (1949–) focuses on issues of identity and community in creating an approach to transformation.[4] The rethinking of political community is carried out on three dimensions. First, the normative dimension critiques the idea that the state is accepted as the form of political organization and looks toward the ethical and moral understanding of societies' role in promoting justice. Critical theorists view the sovereign state as a central barrier to emancipation because it promotes an "us" versus "them" mentality through exclusion, injustice, and violence between self-interested states. Second, the sociological dimension accounts for the evolution of the modern international system and the harm it has brought to many. Critical theorists reject the realist claim of the inherent condition of anarchy and self-interested states. Like constructivists, critical theorists believe that such international structures are constructed through social interaction. Understanding the development of these structures accounts for the ways in which states view their moral and legal responsibilities. Flowing from this knowledge, critical theorists seek to promote transformation through the understanding of existing social inequality and the harm it causes. Linklater (2011, 5), in particular, has sought to "understand whether, or how far, the modern world has made progress in making harm a key moral and political question for humanity as a whole." Third, human action and behavior are viewed through the lens of how to reconstruct the international system towards the emancipatory goals of justice, freedom, and equality. In this regard, Linklater (1998) identifies a "triple transformation" consisting of the universalization of certain moral, political, and legal principles, the reduction of material inequality, and the need for deeper respect for ethnic, cultural, and gender differences. In order to reconfigure the existing political system, the state must be reconstituted towards more inclusion and democratic participation. This system would be post-Westphalian, abandoning the idea that power resides in the hands of a centralized entity (the state government) and instead adopting broader communities of dialogue (Linklater, 1990, 1998).

The second main premise of critical theories is that there is a link between knowledge and politics/interests. Theorists are not objective or detached from the subjects they discuss. On the contrary, the theorist is entangled with the political process and social life in which she or he resides. Robert Cox (1926–) is best known for his statement, "Theory is always *for* someone, and *for* some purpose" (Cox, 1981, 128). He contends that theorists are incapable of separating their own values from this analysis. Thus, the source of theory needs to be analyzed along with the theory itself. Who does the theory benefit? What is the purpose of the theory? According to Cox, realist theories benefit those in charge, that is, great power states and more specifically, the hegemon. He studies hegemony and how the powerful states shaped the system to their own interests. Much like Lenin internationalized Marxist theory, Cox internationalized Gramsci's argument regarding hegemony (see Chapter 4). Cox is interested in explaining how the current global structure came into being and the likelihood that change is possible through what he calls "counter-hegemonic movements." It is through the emancipatory actions of such movements we will see an end to the exploitative nature of capitalism and the inequalities it produces (Cox, 1981, 1983). The critical approach allows the social scientist to understand and question not only the actions of the dominant actors in the international system, but also their motives. Only in understanding the underlying motives can affective change occur that will emancipate those most marginalized in society.

Critical theory has added significantly to the understandings of states and other system structures as mutable entities. In addition, it focuses attention on human values, equality, and freedom through the struggle against the exclusionary nature of state power. As space was created for this type of theoretical discussion during the Third Debate (see Chapter 1), for many it was apparent that post-positivist approaches were gaining traction and the future of international relations theory would be along these lines. Despite this, mainstream theories of international relations (realism and liberalism) have all but ignored critical theory. When they do engage the arguments, it is to levy criticism based on ontological and epistemological grounds. Critical theory is charged with being an exercise in wishful thinking, unsubstantiated concepts, and with no evidence or connection to reality (Schweller, 1999). If one is to believe that international relations theory is to become more focused on the post-positivist approach, critical theory will have to address being challenged by the need to be more policy relevant. This criticism of course is situated in the notion that there is a known reality and policy relevance is based on understanding and operating within that reality. A notion critical theorists reject.

Postcolonialism

While postpositivist approaches were gaining traction during the Third Debate, one approach continued to be left at the margins, that of the developing world or the Global South. Western voices continue to dominate the discourse in international relations, and while these approaches may talk about the developing world, they do so through a Western lens, grounded in Western experiences and discourse. Postcolonial[5] scholars look both historically (colonial) and currently (postcolonial) at the power dynamics between the developed and developing worlds, focusing on marginalized peoples. As with other approaches, it cannot be classified by a single, cohesive, generalizable thought. It is multidisciplinary and inclusive, partially born from the dissatisfaction with the traditional international relations focus on war, states, and power. Identities, culture, people, race, and gender are of particular importance to postcolonial scholars, and they seek to understand both the former colonizer (the Western countries of Europe and North America) and the former colonized (primarily in Latin America, Africa, and Asia). While former colonies are now independent sovereign countries participating in international society, hierarchy continues as the ideas that define the relationship between the former colonizers and the former colonized reflect the Western concept of the world. Postcolonialism seeks to undermine **Eurocentrism**, promoting alterative analysis that respects the formerly colonized areas and their marginalized people.

Postcolonialists are postpositivists and share some kinship with both Marxism and feminism. The postcolonial focus on the marginalized, and their use of the term **subaltern** (a term coined by Gramsci), ties them to Marxism. The connection to feminism comes with the focus on gender and gender-based oppression. Like critical theories, postcolonialism seeks to transform international order and the conceptions of society and morality while undoing the legacy of European colonialism and imperialism. The writings of Mahatma Gandhi, Franz Fanon, and R. Siva Kumar, to name a few, are part of the inspiration as well as the enunciation of postcolonialism. These authors exposed the impacts of colonialism on societies, identities, and cultures and their writings helped create an alternate history from that presented by Western scholars, one that presents the experiences of the marginalized. This counter-narrative is an important component of the postcolonial approach.

An important inspiration for postcolonialism is **poststructuralism**. Poststructuralism is not a theory or paradigm of international relations, but instead it represents a critical approach that questions the ways in which mainstream approaches present issues in global politics, including identity, power and knowledge, and representation. The dominant approaches in international relations are based on historical practices, but they are not the only possible explanations for the way in which the world works. The traditional international relations' focus on states, interests, security, and economic processes are driven by Western thinkers, thus taking a particular vantage point and framing the discussion from a certain perspective. Critical perspectives, including poststructuralism which came into the international relations debate in the 1980s, take issue with these interpretations and promote the evaluation of international relations from differing perspectives. The poststructural approach in the 1980s began with the critique of realism and how realism shaped the view of international relations. Realism was, and is, seen as excluding important actors, issues, and, most relevant here, marginalized peoples and perspectives. Poststructuralism does not identify different actors and interests like theories, but instead creates a new set of questions to be answered and analyzed. Theory is seen as a player in-and-of itself, establishing parameters about knowledge and power, and hence is a unit of analysis in poststructural analysis. In other words, how theories are constructed, how we know what we claim to know, and who can know it are central to understanding world politics.⁶ Thus, poststructuralism is related to critical theory, discussed above, feminism, discussed in Chapter 6, and postcolonialism.

While one cannot identify central assumptions of postcolonialism, there are common concerns that permeate many of the writings in this area. First, postcolonialism revolves around issues of power and legitimacy, and recognizes that Western powers seek to maintain hegemony in politics as well as in the defining of concepts such as morality, ethics, law, and order. Unlike realists and liberals who see power as residing with the state through military and economic means, postcolonial scholars view power as knowledge produced through discourses that creates understanding of social reality. Discourses do not simply describe the world, they actually create the objects contained therein as well as how those objects are understood.⁷ For postcolonialists, they seek explanations as to how ways of understanding in world politics became dominant thus opening the door to altering those understandings.

One of the foundational works of postcolonialism that highlights the impact of discourses on the objects themselves and the corresponding policy response is *Orientalism* (1978, 2003) by Edward Said (1935–2003). The focus of this work is on the ways the Orient is compared to the West in Western art, literary works, and biographies, with the former characterized as backward and despotic, while the latter is seen as advanced and democratic. The Western works depicted the Orient as a place of cultural rituals that were seen as indulgent by European standards; a place that could be easily conquered and enjoyed. The men of the Orient were seen as weak or unjustifiably cruel and cunning, and the women were simultaneously modest and sexualized. The Middle East and Asia are seen as the antithesis of the West, and thus cannot be a part of mainstream international relations. There is little respect for the achievements of the Orient, cultural differences are constantly reaffirmed, and the area and people are seen as marginal and subordinate to the West in international relations. These stereotypes of a culture and people produced Western beliefs, and those beliefs directly impact policy-making. While *Orientalism* is a seminal work in postcolonialism, it is often criticized for its use of fiction to explain aspects of international relations and for ignoring the voices of women, both Western women who wrote about the Middle East and Asia as well as the women in these areas who defied the images written about by Western men.

The power of these discourses is seen today. Areas of the Middle East and Africa, in particular, are viewed as backwards, uncivilized, underdeveloped, despotic, and in need of Western intervention. These views are in turn used to legitimize political actions by Western powers, most recently in Afghanistan, Iraq, Iran, Syria, Libya, Congo, and elsewhere in the two regions. These political actions range from armed intervention to sanctions to diplomatic pressure. States in these regions fall within the discourse of "fragile states," formerly referred to as "failed states"—an interesting act of discourse in and of itself. The Fund for Peace produces an annual "Fragile States Index" to raise warning flags for countries that appear headed toward conflict or collapse.[8] All states are ranked along sets of social, economic, and political and military indictors including human flight and brain drain, state legitimacy, and human rights and the rule of law. The definition and the level of relevance assigned to each indicator are assessed through the Western lens and Western definitions. States that do not meet the Western standards are infantilized in international relations discourse by both scholars and policy makers. Much akin to colonial discourse, these states are viewed as helpless entities destined for chaos and violence if the Western world does not come to their rescue. In 1993 (and republished in 2010), for example, Gerald B. Helman and Steven R. Ratner[9] argued for UN conservatorship for failed states. They used the analogy of domestic systems that seek to help those in need by arguing that in these systems "the polity confronts persons who are utterly incapable of functioning on their own, [and] the law often provides some regime whereby the community itself manages the affairs of the victim." Further, "guardianship or trusteeship" are often the remedy for "broken families, serious mental or physical illness, or economic destitution. The hapless individual is placed under the responsibility of a trustee or guardian, who is charged to look out for the best interests of that person." This type of discourse undermines the legitimacy of non-Western states and reinforces the notion that Western states are superior and lack any responsibility for the conditions in developing countries. This is in spite of the fact that many of the conflicts in those areas are a direct result of colonialism and the proceeding economic and political liberalization policies imposed as the remedy for the failures of colonial policy.

Two additional themes common in postcolonial writings are identity and resistance and their relation to each other. The identities of the colonized were significantly and unavoidably transformed by the colonial experience. The cultures in former colonies are thus a mix of traditional and colonial elements and as a consequence, cultural identity and practice, as well as psychological impact, are at the center of postcolonial studies. There is an identified postcolonial self, and it is widely accepted that there can be no return to the precolonial authentic self (Fanon, 1986). The mix or hybridity that exists is seen by many postcolonial writers as evidence of the resistance of the colonized. The colonizers were unable to completely dominate the colonized and unable to destroy the essence of who they are; they never succeeded in recreating them in their image. These hybrid identities serve to disrupt the colonial authority, rendering their domination incomplete (Bhabha, 1994).

Despite the notion that there can be no return to a pure, precolonial identity, an important element of resistance is ensuring the survival of the cultures of the marginalized or subaltern. Without the continued existence of the traditional ways, colonial domination will be complete. This is a struggle within postcolonial writings. Postcolonial scholar Gayatri Spivak (1942–) argues for "strategic essentialism," which recognizes certain attributes of the subaltern's identity for the purpose of resistance, but recognizes that there is no return to precolonial identity purity (Spivak, 1985). Strategic essentialism aims to create a unity within a group to heighten their societal presence. Homi Bhabha (1949–) takes resistance to another level is describing "dissemi-Nations." These nations occur when people with hybrid identities move from the developing world to the developed world, undermining the fixed notion of identity and power within a territorial state (Bhabhi, 1994). Postcolonial writers further pursue resistance through giving voice to the marginalized by retelling history from their perspectives thus creating a space for the previously unseen and unheard. This is also seen as a way to break the hegemonic dominance of discourse in international relations. Postcolonial forms of resistance are less likely to embrace traditional international relations behavior such as uprisings and armed conflict. Instead they focus on everyday forms of resistance, such as mockery, cartoons, and slogans (Scott, 1999; Mbembe, 2001).

The focus on resistance is one of the main areas of criticism leveled against postcolonialism. Critics argue that the focus on discourse and rewriting history does nothing to actually assist the marginalized

(Dirlik, 1994). If one's goal is to improve the condition of the subaltern, mockery and cartoons does little towards this goal. The structural inequalities must be addressed if there is to be an actual improvement in the distribution of resources that works to maintain the system of exploitation experienced by the marginalized. Postcolonialists argue, however, that altering the discourse is the starting point for changing the structure. Disrupting the hegemonic discourse exposes the bias inherent within it, and critiques of it can transform the social and political environment. In addition, more recent postcolonial writings have paid attention to contemporary issues, dealing more with political actions and outcomes rather than culture. Postcolonial works in the last two decades have focused on issues of security, war, and political economy. Despite this, postcolonial theory remains at the margins of international relations and is likely to maintain that position for the foreseeable future. It is, however, insightful and highly valuable in posing challenges to the tradition theories of international relations.

Case Studies: A Holistic Approach to Proliferation and Trade Liberalization

In the preceding chapters there has been significant discussion of the issues of proliferation and trade (specifically the WTO). In Chapter 1 important foundational principles and understandings of the issues were presented to frame the theoretical discussion in the later chapters. Chapter 2 presented an application of elements of realism to explain the behavior of North Korea in developing its nuclear weapons program as well as the response of those states attempting to stop and now reverse it. The discussion also highlighted the differences within the realist school—they all want stability, but the means by which it is pursued differ. Realist principles were also applied to states' decisions to join the WTO and comply with its rulings. This discussion demonstrated the fact that both strong and weak states join the WTO for their own national interests, but also that the strong states can compel the weaker to take actions they would not otherwise choose. In Chapter 3, the neoliberal perspective is applied to show why international regimes designed to control the proliferation of WMDs were created, specifically the NPT, CWC, and BWC. These regimes demonstrate the neoliberal principle that states join and adhere to cooperative regimes in order to reap mutual benefits. Similarly, the case of state membership and compliance in the WTO illustrates the adherence to liberal principles of free trade, interdependence, and cooperation.

In Chapter 4, the view of economic structuralists as it relates to the "have nots" of nuclear weapons is presented. The inequality inherent in the status afforded nuclear powers and the struggle of "have nots" in developing peaceful nuclear power are used to highlight the disparities that exist between the developed and developing states and the continuing impacts of the inequality of power that exists between them. Similarly, the discussion of the WTO illustrates the disparity of economic power between the core on the one hand and the semi-periphery and the periphery on the other. Developing states remain in a weakened position due to the legacy of imperialism, and the WTO, as controlled by the developed states, fails to adequately address their concerns. In Chapter 5, the constructivist lens is applied to explain the development of the nuclear taboo through the United States' role as a norm entrepreneur, while simultaneously providing a view as to why North Korea and Iran pursue nuclear weapons despite the existence of the de facto norm against their use. The pursuit of nuclear weapons by these two states is explained through the role of identity creation and maintenance. Further, constructivism is applied to explain the establishment and acceptance of the norm of tree trade and the role of the WTO. China's acceptance of that norm and its admittance into the WTO is used to demonstrate the important role played by identity, in that China entered the WTO as a developing state, but in its relations with others, China is viewed as a powerful economic and military state. Lastly, Chapter 6 applies one of many feminist approaches to explaining proliferation by focusing on the gendered language and discourse surrounding weapons, war, and security. This approach highlights one feminist contention concerning the role of men in decision-making posts versus that of women. The feminist approach presented concerning the WTO focuses on the limited number of women in positions of power in the WTO and the fact that trade liberalization has both positive and negative impacts on women. Attempts to address the negative ramifications on women would receive additional attention if more women were in decision-making roles in the WTO.

The explanations provided from the various paradigmatic perspectives are only a sampling of the ways in which these approaches could explain these central international relations issues. As highlighted in each chapter, there are a multitude of variables present in each paradigm and varying strands of adherents to each approach. Recall, for example, that there are different kinds of realists, including classical, structural, offensive, defensive, and neoclassical. Similarly, there are many types of feminists, including liberal, radical, postmodern, standpoint, and postcolonial. To assist in demonstrating their explanatory value, the approach in this book has been to explain each phenomenon (proliferation and trade liberalization) from a limited set of standpoints within each paradigm to provide the starting point for students of international relations to begin applying the theories to real-world cases. From here, students should now be able to combine elements of the theories presented to create a more robust explanation of events. It is important to remember that this is not an attempt to create a synthesized approach or to create a new paradigm, but instead the purpose is to highlight connections between the approaches studied in this book and demonstrate the relevance of inclusive thinking about problems in world politics. This discussion also does not ignore the problems of incommensurability. Thomas Kuhn (1962), for example, argued that different paradigms cannot overlap because they use different vocabulary, training, and ideas on how to solve problems or even if certain phenomenon are problems at all. While this is a relevant concern and one that should be kept in mind, as demonstrated in the paradigm-specific chapters, theorists within a single paradigm or worldview experience this same challenge. Intra-paradigmatic views of how to solve problems vary, as do the definitions of certain terms. If this were an attempt to synthesize the approaches presented in this book, this might be an insurmountable problem. As long as one is cautious not to use concepts carelessly and since the purpose here is to demonstrate how the consideration of various variables can work together to provide a greater elucidation of phenomenon is world politics, this challenge is not insuperable.

Below is an exercise to demonstrate how all five main theories presented in this book can link together to explain phenomena seen in world politics. Figure 7.1 illustrates the impact of realism, liberalism, economic structuralism, constructivism, and feminism on the two case studies presented throughout this book. The same explanatory value can be seen through other issues in global politics as well; in other words any number of issues can go in the circle where proliferation and trade liberalization are situated. Although there are many elements of both major issues that can be explained, each of the

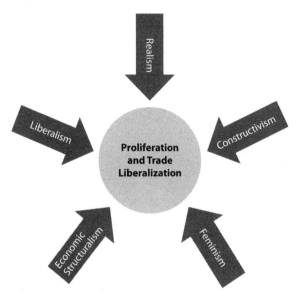

FIGURE 7.1 **Proliferation and Trade Liberalization.**

following sections focuses on one element of each issue to demonstrate the connecting of the approaches explained in this book. The proliferation discussion will focus on the development of nuclear weapons, while the trade section will focus on why states pursue trade liberalization. As one reads this discussion, you might find some elements more powerful in their explanatory value than others, or the inclusion of all five approaches may seem overwhelming or unnecessary. It may be that at the end of this exercise, one decides they prefer a more parsimonious approach offered by one the myriad of theories of international relations or a combination of fewer approaches. One might be drawn to a particular ontological or epistemological view of the world, or one of the approaches described earlier in this chapter may seem more relevant or important. This is all a part of the process of being a student of international relations.

Proliferation

It should be clear from the discussion in the previous chapters that there are multiple explanations for the decision to acquire nuclear weapons or not. Neorealist explanations have long been the cornerstone for explaining why states acquire such weapons—they feel insecure and to enhance their own security, they seek the world's most effective deterrent, nuclear weapons. Let's assume for a moment that this explanation satisfies our curiosity as to why the Soviet Union (Russia), France, Great Britain, China, India, Pakistan, Israel, and North Korea have developed nuclear weapons since the US development and use of the technology against Japan in World War II. How does one then explain why all the other states with legitimate security concerns of their own have refrained from developing or acquiring such weapons? Many nations, including South Korea, Japan, Egypt, Saudi Arabia, and Taiwan, to name a few, have faced significant threats to their sovereignty and territorial integrity, and yet none have developed nuclear weapons. One could also wonder the same for a few of the former republics of the Soviet Union, most notably Ukraine. In fact, in the 1990s, Ukraine negotiated removing former Soviet nuclear weapons from its territory and moving them to the physical control of Russia. The events of 2014/2015, during which Russia annexed Crimea and continues to threaten the sovereignty of Ukraine, have made that negotiated agreement seem unwise. Neorealists would tell us that states that exist under the nuclear umbrella of another state need not waste their resources developing their own arsenal. That has long been the argument about Japan, South Korea, and the states in NATO who do not possess their own nuclear weapons. They are protected by the nuclear deterrent of the United States. If this is enough, why did France develop its own weapons? A main part of the argument for France possessing its own nuclear deterrent was based on the notion of **extended deterrence** lacking credibility. The French did not believe that the United States would start a nuclear war to protect Paris if the consequence was losing a major US city in retaliation. If we look at Ukraine, and assume for the moment it felt it was protected by the US nuclear umbrella even though it is not a part of NATO, the umbrella failed to protect its territorial integrity from its aggressive neighbor, Russia. Thus, the notion that existing under another state's nuclear umbrella eliminates the need to develop one's own weapons is an unsatisfactory explanation. Neorealism may provide a compelling explanation for one element of the proliferation argument, but fails to satisfactorily explain it in its entirety.

Neoliberal institutionalism takes an additional step in explaining proliferation. If we continue along the argument above, the states who choose not to develop their own nuclear arsenal, despite legitimate security concerns, do so as an element of the cooperative regime created through the NPT. From the neoliberal perspective, adherents to the NPT believe their interests are met through cooperation in that behavior is coordinated and modified. Confidence-building measures promote good relations across issues thus improving the security of states who join the NPT. Of the 191 members of the NPT, it would be safe to say that a vast majority of them have never been threatened with the use of nuclear weapons and thus annihilation by a nuclear state. Neoliberals would argue that the NPT promotes alternative dispute resolution (in other words not threatening an adversary with nuclear weapons) and promotes a cooperative relationship across issue areas. A further argument against the acquisition of nuclear weapons comes from the feminist school. Although there are many strands of feminism, most would promote the non-acquisition and non-use of nuclear weapons, as weapons are inherently a tool of domination related to the overall view of war and militarism as male-dominated and oppressive. That oppression is felt most acutely by women and children, but the decisions about weapons and war are predominately made by men. The goal of feminists to end oppression can be broadly conceived, in that the goal is to end oppression of all people and nations. As such, the NPT is viewed as a vehicle to end the oppression of the many by the few through disarmament of all nations as called for in the NPT. The use of nuclear weapons would cause immeasurable damage and suffering, and thus the goal is for all states to disarm, not just prevent the further proliferation of these weapons (Peach, 2004).

If it is true that being non-nuclear states and members of the NPT promotes good relations, then why do Israel, India, Pakistan, South Sudan, and North Korea remain outside the treaty? Four of those states, Israel, India, Pakistan and North Korea developed nuclear weapons, while South Sudan has been preoccupied with internal problems since its independence in 2011 and thus joining the NPT would not be high on its list of priorities. While a neorealist argument focusing on security possesses explanatory power in these cases (perhaps as the only explanation in Israel's case), it ignores other variables that undoubtedly influenced the development of nuclear weapons in these states. With nuclear weapons comes international prestige. Constructivists argue that although there is a norm against nuclear weapons' acquisition, some states pursue these weapons because there is a socially constructed idea that such weapons enhance status, image, and prestige in the system. India and Pakistan, for example, while possessing legitimate security concerns, particularly with one another, both sought nuclear weapons to improve their image in the international community. For Pakistan, its status as the first Muslim country to develop nuclear weapons is a source of pride and prestige. In India, immediately after their successful nuclear tests in 1998, headlines such as "Explosion of Self-Esteem" and "Megatons of Prestige" were seen on editorials (Bidwai and Vanaik, 2000, 44). In addition, North Korea is attempting to flout the rule of nonproliferation set by the hegemonic power of the United States. Constructivists argue that this is the creation of a new norm of noncompliance, while economic structuralists add to that the element of resistance from a state that has been disadvantaged by an unequal international environment as epitomized by the divide between the wealthy and the poor. In fact, India, Pakistan, and North Korea all fit the economic structuralist argument of states adversely impacted by imperialism and the related privileged status of the core over the periphery and semi-periphery. The development of nuclear weapons is seen as a deterrent from this perspective, but it is economic exploitation that is being deterred. For countries that are, or in the case of these three countries were, outside the nuclear club, the original nuclear weapons states (the United States, Russia, Great Britain, France, and China) have broken their agreement to work towards eliminating nuclear weapons. Their refusal to do so marks the continued unequal distribution of power intended to be used to further exploit the periphery and semi-periphery. The development of nuclear weapons in this scenario is seen as an equalizing force, at least to some extent. Nuclear weapons will prevent direct attack, thus protecting sovereignty, and affording these states legitimacy and power.

Taken together, the different elements of realism, liberalism, feminism, constructivism, and economic structuralism paint a robust picture as to the proliferation of nuclear weapons. As a whole they can explain why some states have chosen to develop nuclear weapons, while most have not. The same motives and goals do not apply to each state and thus pulling the most applicable variable from each theory provides a more satisfactory explanation. As previously mentioned, there are many other elements of the theories that could be applied but the purpose of this discussion is to demonstrate how variables taken from the various approaches can tie together to more fully explain phenomenon in world politics.

Trade Liberalization and the WTO

The previous chapters covered numerous aspects of trade liberalization policies and the role of the WTO in promoting those policies. In this section the focus is on why states pursue trade liberalization while also adopting elements of protectionism, or another way of looking at it is why states join the WTO and yet pursue policies (protectionism) counter to its goal (free trade). (Neo)liberalism is the cornerstone of this explanation and its dominance in this area has marginalized the other theories presented in this book, including realism. The correlation between free trade and economic growth drives states to engage in trade liberalization policies in their own self-interest. For (neo)liberals, the benefits of free trade, open markets, and capitalism are obvious. Economic growth equals economic power, and if all states engage in liberal economic policies, all states will benefit. Constructivists add another dimension to this argument in explaining the creation of the norm of free trade. The belief that free trade produces economic benefits is a fundamentally held belief in international relations, adopted in the developed as well as developing worlds. The establishment of GATT followed by the WTO promoted the idea that free trade was in a state's best interest and the acceptance of this norm is evidenced by the fact that the organization has 162 members and states have clamored to gain entrance even in the face of prolonged accession processes (for example, China, Russia, Saudi Arabia). In addition, in May 2016, there were 21 applicants in the accession process, indicating a near universal desire among states to gain membership.

If it is true that all states benefit from free trade and open markets, and there is a clear desire for membership in the WTO, then why do states pursue protectionist policies? It is here that we begin to see how economic theories collide in the real world. Neomercantilists (realism) support the idea of free trade and open markets, but only when they do not impede national interests. From this, protectionist policies emerge. Let's take Brazil as an example. Brazil is a member of the WTO and to avoid running afoul of WTO policies, carefully designs buy-local policies to boost its domestic industries. For example, in 2012, Brazil was seeking ways to increase domestic car sales. The government introduced Inovar-Auto, a program that required car manufacturers (which are all foreign owned) to invest in local innovation (in particular fuel saving measures) and engineering. If the companies failed to comply, they would face higher taxes on domestic sales. Brazil's protectionist policies do not end with cars. They have forced their state-owned oil company to buy domestic products and their state-controlled development bank to dramatically increase local investment. While one can understand the logic behind protecting and promoting a domestic industry, often these plans are counterproductive. In Brazil, the state-owned oil company has suffered from a limited capacity to produce oilfield equipment and the new engines produced through Inovar-Auto have restricted the potential for exports (*The Economist*, 2013). Despite the widespread belief that free trade leads to economic growth, and the knowledge that protectionism often leads to negative consequences, states engage in protectionist policies nonetheless. As such, protectionist policies run counter to national interests, making the (neo)liberal and neomercantilist arguments unsatisfying on their own.

Economic structuralism provides an added avenue of explanation. Although developing states engage in free trade and join the WTO, the legacy of imperialism and the world capitalist system that perpetuates the disparity between the rich and the poor compels states of the periphery and semi-periphery to seek alternative ways of protecting their domestic industries and people from the continued exploitation by the core. Brazil is a newly industrialized country and a member of the BRICS association, which contains five of the major emerging national economies: Brazil, Russia, India, China, and South Africa. While this status affords Brazil some power in the economic arena, it continues to run the risk of exploitation by the developed states. Since the WTO is a creation of the Western states and the advanced capitalist states maintain their influence over the organization, states like Brazil must protect themselves from the organized attempts to exploit their resources and people. Hence, subtle protectionist policies that do not technically violate WTO rules provide them some means to exercise control over their own destiny, while still allowing them to reap the benefits of WTO membership (in particular access to the markets of other WTO members).

Feminism adds one additional element to our explanation. When economic structuralists talk of protecting their resources and people, very often it is women who face a disproportionate amount of the exploitation. As free trade has expanded, production facilities and the assembly lines that accompany them have moved to the developing world. This has been a blessing and a curse for women. On the positive side, this movement of production has provided jobs for many women who would have remained unemployed and has thus afforded them a level of power not previously attained. One the negative side, working conditions in these factories are poor, women are abused, exploited, and paid unfair wages. Foreign companies from the developed world engage in this exploitation, often in collusion with the host governments. Many feminists argue that if there were more women in decision-making positions in the host countries, in the WTO, and in the multinational corporations that operate in the developing world, conditions for women worldwide would improve. For example, if more women were in positions of power in the WTO perhaps the WTO would be more nuanced in its application of rules against agricultural subsidies and quotas in developing countries. The forced removal of these protectionist measures allowed for a flood of cheaper agricultural goods (often from developed countries that are subsidizing their farmers) and this reduced the share of the market for small farmers. This reduction has a significant impact on women who were forced from their farms onto the assembly lines. Women in power would be more likely to take into account the deleterious impact on women in the developing nations and seek alternate solutions.

As with proliferation, this discussion provides a multifaceted explanation encompassing elements from all five main theories of international relations. One approach alone cannot adequately explain every aspect of this issue, but taking a holistic approach to the analysis creates a more robust explanation. This type of analysis may bridge the gap between theory and practice, thus making international relations scholarship increasingly relevant in the policy world. It may be, however, that social science researchers are satisfied with containing their debates within academia. If so, paradigmatic approaches offer compelling and more parsimonious explanations. As students of international relations, you can now consider the approach you wish to pursue. You may choose a strict paradigmatic approach, like the positivist theories of realism and liberalism. You may lean towards the postpositivist approaches that have been gaining traction for the last several decades and that take a critical view of the mainstream theories of international relations. Or you may choose a more holistic path that seeks to incorporate elements of a number of approaches as demonstrated in this section.

Where Do We Go from Here?

As we endeavor to make sense of the world around us through the use of international relations theories, the discussion in this book highlights the wide-ranging nature of the approaches to studying international relations. Emphasized in this chapter has been their interconnectivity to one another, but these approaches do not exist in a vacuum, as they borrow and intertwine with approaches in other fields and disciplines. Neoliberal institutionalism borrows heavily from economics, economic structuralism ties to IPE (international political economy), poststructuralism has foundations in philosophy, and postcolonialism in cultural studies. Feminism ties to a multitude of sources, including sociology, political science, and philosophy. The cross-pollination of disciplines, and thus the interdisciplinary nature of international relations scholarship, creates broader perspectives on global phenomena and thus can bring creative thought processes to the intellectual, social, and political problems that plague global society.

Chapters 1 presented the "great debates" in international relations. So as we assess where the field is going, we should know where we are. Ole Wæver[10] (2013, 322) explains that we are still in the period "after the fourth debate"[11] in that the categories from the fourth debate "are still around as the main signposts in the landscape. We are neither in a total interregnum, nor in a fifth debate." Neorealists and neoliberals spend little time mired in the fourth debate nor debating each other. There are, however, healthy internal debates harkening back to the days of the first "debate axis" in that defensive realism (discussed in Chapter 2) is closer to liberalism than it is to offensive realism, and the neoliberal debate is closer to a debate with realism over power versus institutions (Wæver, 2013, 322). While one could argue that positivist approaches remain central, we do see the continued growth and expansion of the postpositivist approaches in international relations. The focus on how to study world politics rivals that of using theory to explain global phenomenon. The foreseeable future certainly holds a continuation of the ontological, epistemological, and methodological debates in international relations. As highlighted in Chapter 1, there has been an ebb and flow of these debates, and there is little doubt that will continue.

It is important to keep in mind that we should not expect one theory or approach to answer every question, explain all key structures, and fully assess the dynamics of international relations. Hopefully through reading this book you have discovered that there are many ways to view international relations, and many ways to ask and answer questions about the phenomena that occur in world politics. It is also important to remember that those phenomena are not static, and the changing nature of world politics will serve to expand, alter, and challenge existing theories and approaches. The ever-increasing importance of the environment, the activities of international terrorists and the corresponding responses, the advent of new military and communications technology, the growth of intrastate conflict, global and regional financial crises, and the growing number and influence of non-state actors will force existing theories and approaches to confront their applicability to real world events. International relations theorists will continue to ask and seek answers to a multitude of questions for which there are no universally accepted answers. What should be the focus of international relations scholars? What is the role of gender, identity, globalization, and imperialism? How do we study international relations? Is the scientific method a legitimate enterprise in international relations, or is the world too complex for anything other than the classical approach? Is there objective knowledge in the field, or is all inquiry biased by political, social, and cultural perspectives and discourses? There is no correct answer to be found concerning which approach is best, and we hope that students of international relations will continue to view the world through the varied lenses presented here and investigate further theoretical approaches not presented.

Key Terms

Eurocentrism
Extended deterrence
Frankfurt School
Parsimony principle
Poststructuralism
Subaltern

For Further Reading

Bhabha, H. 1994. *The Location of Culture*. New York: Routledge.
Bull, Hedley. 1977. *The Anarchical Society: A Study of Order in World Politics*. London: Macmillan.

Buzan, B. 2004. *From International to World Society.* Cambridge: Cambridge University Press.

Moravcsik, Andrew. 2003. "Theory Synthesis in International Relations: Real Not Metaphysical." *International Studies Review,* 5 (1), pp. 131–136.

Sil, Rudra. and Peter J. Katzenstein. 2010. *Beyond Paradigms: Analytical Eclecticism in the Study of World Politics.* New York: Palgrave Macmillan.

Endnotes

[1] Analytical eclectism as applied by Sil and Katzenstein explores connections between realism, liberalism, and constructivism. The approach taken in this chapter is to find points of explanatory value in all five approaches discussed in this book. This is not a synthesis of the five theories or the creation of one all-encompassing theory, but instead an attempt to demonstrate the explanatory value in looking at events from a multitude of perspectives.

[2] For a history of the English School, see Tim Dunne. 1998. *Inventing International Society: A History of the English School.* New York: Palgrave.

[3] For criticisms of the English School, see Martha Finnemore. 2001. "Exporting the English School?" *Review of International Studies,* 27, (3) and Barry Buzan. 2004. *From International to World Society? English School Theory and the Social Structure of Globlisation.* Cambridge: Cambridge University Press.

[4] In *The Transformation of Political Community: Ethical Foundations of the Post-Westphalian Era* (Polity Press, 1998), Linklater drew on the work of Jurgen Habermas on communicative action, Immanuel Kant on cosmopolitanism, and Charles Taylor and Michael Walzer on communitarianism. For more on these approaches see, Diez, M. and Steans, J. (eds). 2005. "A Useful Dialogue? Habermas and International Relations," *Review of International Studies,* 31/1 and Edkins, J. and Vaughan-Williams, N. (eds). 2009. *Critical Theorists and International Relations* (London: Routledge).

[5] The term postcolonial is not meant to indicate an end to the impacts of colonialism. While the process of colonization has ended (thus the direct control of land and resources), the lasting effects of its structures continue.

[6] To gain a better understanding of post-structuralism, see Der Derain, J. and Shapiro, M.J. 1989. (eds). *International/Intertextual Relations: Postmodern Readings of World Politics*. Lexington, KY: Lexington Books and Der Derain, J. 2009. *Critical Practices on International Theory: Selected Essays*. New York: Routledge.

[7] Much of this view of power is drawn from poststructuralists. For seminal work in this area, see Michel Foucault. 1972. *The Archeology of Knowledge*, translated by A.M. Sheridan Smith. London: Tavistock Publishers.

[8] To view the latest "Fragile States Index", visit http://library.fund forpeace.org/fsi.

[9] Helman served in the Foreign Service, was US Ambassador to the United Nations in Geneva, and deputy to the under-secretary of state for political affairs. Ratner served in the State Department's Office of the Legal Advisor and an international affairs fellow at the Council on Foreign Relations.

[10] Ole Wæver is Professor of International Relations at the University of Copenhagen and director of the Centre for Advanced Security Theory.

[11] Recall from Chapter 1, most scholars refer to this as the Third Debate, as we have throughout this book.

GLOSSARY

....

Anarchic (anarchy) – absence of a central government in the international system.

Atomist egoist – an actor whose interests are formed prior to any social interaction with other states or non-state actors in the system.

Balance-of-power – one of the early realist theories that describes an arrangement of states in the international system to maintain parity in terms of power; the power of each state in the arrangement is checked by the power of the other states.

Bandwagoning – when states ally themselves with other states to take advantage of their strength; states attempt to increase their gains and lessen their losses by joining with the stronger side.

Bipolar – one configuration of the distribution of power in the international system where two states have a preponderance of power; used to describe the international system during the Cold War ideological battle between the USSR and US.

Bismarckian alliance system – a succession of alliances constructed by Otto von Bismarck after the unification of Germany in 1871.

Bourgeoisie – the capitalist class in Marxism.

Buckpassing – states sitting on the sidelines while other states do the fighting.

Capitalism – economic system in which the means of production are privately owned for profit. Capitalism includes free markets, wage labor, and private property.

Classical mercantilism – a period of history in the fifteenth through eighteenth centuries, a time when the modern nation-state emerged in Europe. During this period, economies were used to create wealth and power in the name of national security.

Cognitive consistency – the desire to make information fit into pre-existing beliefs through the use of heuristic devises such as schemas and analogies.

Collective security – a liberal approach whereby each state in the system agrees that an attack on one is an attack on all and pledge to respond to the aggressor state. It was the framework of the League of Nations.

Comparative advantage – people and states should produce the goods they are most efficient at producing, based on their available resources, and trade for all others.

Complex interdependence – mutual dependence characterized by multiple channels of contact between states, limited use of force to resolve disputes between states in the interdependent relationship, and a nonhierarchical view of state goals and issues.

Concert of Europe – describes the period of relative peace among the great nations of Europe in the years between the end of the Napoleonic Wars in 1815 and World War I.

Core – wealthy, industrialized area in Immanuel Wallerstein's world systems theory; used to describe the richest states in the international system.

Corn Laws – tariffs and other agricultural restrictions designed to protect British landowners in the late 18th century and early 19th century. The laws were repealed in 1846.

Defensive realists – theorists including Kenneth Waltz, Barry Posen, Jack Snyder, and Stephen Van Evera, who believe that states seek power as a means of security to balance and defend themselves against other states. They argue that there is an offense–defense balance that is weighted in the defender's favor and that aggressive states seeking additional power and territorial gains will end up fighting a string of losing wars or expending significant resources holding conquered territories that in the end will be detrimental to their own power.

Dependency (*dependencia*) – theoretical approach originating in Latin America in the 1950s that describes the economic division of labor between the wealthy core states and the poor periphery states.

Democratic Peace Theory – following from the writings of Immanuel Kant, democratic institutions are conducive to peace between democracies.

Deterrence – while applicable to conventional weapons, it generally refers to the threat of force (the use of nuclear weapons) to prevent an attack from a rival before it occurs.

Difference feminism – feminist approach that concludes that the biological differences between women and men are significant and meaningful in that women are naturally more nurturing and caring. If women assume positions of power, their unique abilities will transform the international system.

Dimorphism – the division of humans into two distinct categories based on their physical form.

Economic base – term used by Marx to describe the economic structure of a society.

Economic nationalism – to prevent dependency on other nations, economic nationalism promotes strong and independent domestic economies. The interests of the nation supersede the interests of the individual, and state action is needed to promote wealth and power.

Economic structuralism – a theory of international relations with Marxist roots that focuses on the hierarchy of states based on economic class and on the historical and continued division between rich and poor states in the international system.

End of history – an argument made by Francis Fukuyama that mankind has reached the endpoint of its ideological evolution with Western liberal democracy as the final form of human government. The liberal, democratic, capitalist society under construction by the European powers is the closest to achieving this endpoint.

Epistemic communities – groups of people with knowledge in a particular issue area.

Epistemological (Epistemology) – the study of knowledge and how humans acquire knowledge

Epochs – term used by Marx to describe five specific historical stages of economic development including primitive, slave, feudal, capitalism, and finally, socialism.

Eurocentrism – viewing the world through European values and experiences, highlighting the preeminence of European culture, politics, and society.

Extended deterrence – dissuading an attack on an ally.

Feminist empiricism – a perspective on feminist research that accepts that a known reality exists and that we gain knowledge based on experience. The scientific method is used as the means to make sense of all knowledge. The study of international relations has a male bias that would be removed by including more women researchers in international relations scholarship. Represents the philosophical underpinning of liberal feminism.

Feminist postmodernism – feminist approach that postulates that the categories of masculine and feminine are socially constructed. This approach questions the existence of any universal truths, focusing on relative truths instead, and rejects the idea that scholarship must be objective, arguing that it is impossible to separate the researcher from the subject. Contends that power exists in the state, the dominant class, and in symbols, language, and knowledge. Poststructural and postcolonial feminism are strands of feminist postmodernism.

Feminist standpoint – feminist approach that argues that due to their historical and now structural subordination in terms of patriarchy, women have a unique view or standpoint on how the world works and knowledge in general. As such, women are in a better position to understand certain aspects of the world. Radical, Socialist, and Marxist feminism are strands of the feminist standpoint.

Frankfurt School – an intellectual circle of German–Jewish scholars and thinkers formed during the years between World I and World II who were pioneers of critical theory; critiqued both the left- and right-wing governments of the day, both socialist and capitalist economies, as well as the positivist approach, arguing that it limited the types of questions one could pursue.

Functionalism – a theory pioneered by David Mitrany that postulates that multilateral arrangements and institutions will be created to deal with the plethora of problems that one state cannot solve alone. This cooperation will necessarily spill over into other areas.

Game theory – an approach that utilizes mathematical and logical analysis to explain interactions among actors to demonstrate the difficulties of cooperating and the means to overcome them. Outcomes are produced based on the utilities of the actors and they often result in unintended consequences, leaving the actors worse off than they planned.

Gender – the social construction of the meaning of masculine and feminine.

Globalization – process by which the world and its people are increasingly interconnected and interdependent. The spread of cultural, economic, and social relations.

Great powers – the states in the international system with high levels of economic and military power that set them apart from other states in the system.

Group of 20 – a group of 19 large and emerging economies and the European Union; the countries include: Argentina, Australia, Brazil, Canada, France, Germany, India, Indonesia, Italy, Japan, Republic of Korea, Mexico, Russia, Saudi Arabia, South Africa, the United Kingdom, and the United States.

Hegemonic stability theory – the argument of offensive realists who postulate that having a preponderant power or a hegemon leads to stability.

Hobbesian anarchy – a form of anarchy that is hostile in nature.

Imperialism – the control, economically and politically, of another country in order to increase a state's empire.

Idealist (idealism) – an approach or belief that individuals and their ideas can affect international relations in a positive manner; an approach deemed utopian by realists.

Intergovernmental organizations (IGOs) – international institutions which have states as members.

Intersectionality – institutions and systems of oppression, domination, and discrimination, such as racism, sexism, and homophobia, overlap and cannot be studied separately from one another.

Intersubjectivity – the process of shared ideas and social interaction over time.

Just War Theory – a central feature of idealism that establishes a set of criteria about when it is acceptable to use force (jus ad bellum) and a set of criteria establishing acceptable conduct of combatants in a war (jus in bello).

Kantian anarchy – a form of anarchy that is based on peaceful relationship and friendship.

Keynesianism – a strain of liberal economics developed by John Maynard Keynes in the 1930s in response to the Great Depression. Keynes focused on total spending in the economy and how to avoid inflation through increased government spending and lower taxes to stimulate demand and create jobs.

Laissez faire – a market free from political restrictions and regulations except those that are absolutely necessary for the proper functioning of the market.

Law of the Concentration of Capital – one of Marx's three laws of capitalism; capital accrues in the hands of fewer and fewer capitalists resulting in an increase in the impoverished masses.

Law of Decreasing Profits – one of Marx's three laws of capitalism; a decrease in the rate of return that results when the concentration of capital and surplus occurs.

Law of Disproportionality – one of Marx's three laws of capitalism that focuses on the how lower wages lead to underconsumption that results in a surplus.

Law of Uneven Development – contribution of Lenin to Marxism; the overabundance of capital due to the three laws of Marx leads to uneven economic development among the capitalist states. This uneven development increases the conflict in the international system.

Liberal feminism – feminist approach with a focus on the underrepresentation of women in positions of power, particularly in terms of political office, international organizations, and business. Holds that women and men are equal based on their shared humanity and as such, women should have the same rights as men. Analyzes how conflict and economic issues impact the lives of women as well as how women act during times of war and peace.

Lockean anarchy – a form of anarchy that is characterized by rivalry.

Logic of appropriateness – engaging in behavior based on accepted norms deemed legitimate by other agents in the structure.

Logic of consequences – engaging in behavior that produces the maximum utility and satisfies the actor's interests.

Long cycle theory – a theory posited by George Modelski, identifying regular cycles of world leadership and global war, each of which lasts about 100 years; each cycle contains a global war, a global power (hegemon), delegitimation (the hegemon faces a decline in relative power) and deconcentration (the hegemon is challenged by emerging rivals).

Means of Production – term used by Karl Marx to describe the raw materials as well as the tools necessary for production, such as facilities, machines, land, and infrastructure.

Methodological (Methodology) – the manner in which data is acquired and analyzed.

Marxism – ideology developed by Karl Marx as a critique of capitalism focusing on the unequal economic relationship and the struggle between the worker and the owner.

Marxist feminism – feminist approach that advocates changing the economic structure of the international system because women's inequality is seen as a function of the capitalist system.

Modernist constructivism – a constructivist approach that is more likely to adhere to the scientific method in the study of intersubjective meaning between agents and structure.

Monetarism – theory developed by Milton Friedman that postulates that inflation will be controlled by a regulated money supply (keeping the supply and demand at equilibrium), so the maintenance of price stability should be the main focus of monetary authorities.

Most Favored Nation (MFN) – a policy in international trade whereby an importing country will not discriminate against another country in favor of a third.

Mode of Production – term used by Karl Marx to describe how the state organizes the means of production of goods and services, for example, feudalism or capitalism.

Multinational corporations (MNCs) – companies that have operations in more than one country with the headquarters usually located in the advanced, developed world.

Mutually constituted – the relationship of two forces that co-determine each other and can only be understood in reference to each other.

Mutually Assured Destruction (MAD) – a condition that describes the relationship between two nuclear states such that if one side launched a nuclear attack, the other side could retaliate, inflicting unacceptable losses. The end result is that neither side will launch an attack.

Natural law – universal laws that are common to all human beings, derived from nature and not from political and social rules.

Naturalist constructivism – primarily the view of Alexander Wendt focusing on factors beyond the material world to include the immaterial and social nature of the international system.

Neofunctionalism – created by Ernest Haas, a theory of integration that is the basis for European integration.

Neomercantilists – economic theorists who believe economic power is used to ensure the survival of a state; they support free trade and open markets as long as they do not impede national interests. If free trade counters national interests, subtle trade protectionist policies, or non-tariff barriers, are pursued.

Nongovernmental organizations (NGOs) – international organizations made up of individuals and not states, usually focusing on a particular issue area such as the environment, human rights, or nuclear non-proliferation.

Non-tariff barriers – a protectionist economic policy, other than taxation, designed to protect domestic markets; examples include quotas and product labeling.

Norm cascade – the general acceptance of a new norm in the international system due to the work of norm entrepreneurs and adoption of the norm by a significant number of states.

Norm entrepreneur – an agent possessing a strong notion about appropriate behavior and who works to call attention to issues and promote a change in behavior.

Offensive realists – theorists, including John Mearsheimer, who work from the assumption that more power is always better in securing the survival of the state, thus they seek maximum or dominant power. They argue that the historical record shows that the side that takes the offensive wins more often than not, thus great powers will constantly be seeking dominance over one another with the ultimate prize being hegemony.

Ontological (Ontology) – the theory or study of being; refers to the nature of existence; addresses what kinds of things actually exist and operate in the universe.

Paradox of thrift – A term coined by John Maynard Keynes to describe when a society is faced with recession or depression and individuals are faced with unemployment. If a person fears unemployment, one rational response is to save money and spend less. Spending less slows the economy, and as purchasing falls, so does production and employment. A spiral ensues of decreasing employment, purchasing, and production, and an economic catastrophe ensues.

Parsimony principle – the simplest explanation that fits the evidence is the best approach to take; variables should not be unnecessarily multiplied in seeking an explanation.

Patriarchy – a societal structure or government in which men hold the primary power and women are largely excluded from positions of power.

Peace of Westphalia – Treaty that ended the Thirty Years' War in 1648 and established the modern international state system through the principle of sovereignty.

Periphery – term used to describe the poorest areas and states in dependency and world-systems theory.

Positivists – theorists who argue that there is a known reality apart from our own existence and this knowledge is acquired in an empirical fashion.

Positive-sum – the outcome of absolute gains when describing the relations between states; describes a situation where all states benefit, albeit not necessarily equally.

Postcolonial feminism – feminist approach, also referred to as Third World feminism, that criticizes mainstream feminism for overlooking issues of race, ethnicity, culture, and colonial history in how women encounter discrimination and inequality within societies. Focusing on women as a whole fails to address the unique experiences of women from colonized areas.

Postmodernist constructivism – focuses on the development of norms, ideas, values, and beliefs through language and discourse utilizing a post-positive approach.

Postpositivists – theorists who contend that there is no single reality and that the acquisition of knowledge is multifaceted.

Poststructural feminism – A feminist approach focusing on how the use of language in the political, economic, and social arenas impacts women, specifically when it comes to the dissemination of knowledge.

Poststructuralism – not a theory or paradigm of international relations, but instead it represents a critical approach that questions the ways in which mainstream approaches present issues in global politics, including identity, power and knowledge, and representation; focused on language and discourse.

Power transition theory – theory by A.F.K. Organski that postulates that conflict is most likely when the top nation and its allies are challenged by a great power in a secondary position.

Principal-agent theory – An element of neoliberal thought that questions how much authority states are willing to entrust to international institutions. States are the principals and they delegate authority and tasks to institutions as their agents.

Proletariat – the working class in Marxism.

Proliferation – an increase in the number of actors possessing certain weapons.

Protectionism – economic policies designed to protect domestic markets and industries from international competition.

Quotas – a protectionist economic policy that limits the quantity of goods that can be imported.

Radical feminism – feminist approach that postulates that the oppression and discrimination of women is fundamental and occurs before race and class discrimination.

Realpolitik – power politics in which foreign policy is guided by national interests.

Regimes – arrangements that bind states to rules, norms, and principles related to their conduct in given areas such as trade, proliferation, the movement of hazardous waste, and the protection of wildlife and fauna. Regimes are voluntary constructs and states create them to provide a sense of order in international relations. Although voluntary, they do provide a regulatory function and states disobey them at a cost.

Relations of Production – describes the relationship between the capitalist, or the owners of the means of production, and the workers.

Republic – a state in which the citizens vote for elected officials who represent them in a government operated by the rule of law.

Revolutions of 1848 – A series of upheavals throughout Europe in response to dissatisfaction with political leadership and the conditions of the working class. The demands centered around political participation and democratic reforms.

Security dilemma – As one state arms itself for self-defense, other states become fearful of this build-up of weaponry and view it as aggressive rather than defensive, leading them to build their own defenses, resulting in an arms race.

Semi-periphery – the states that occupy a political and economic space between the core and the periphery in world-systems theory.

Social contract – individuals consent to the creation and power of a government to protect their rights and promote the public good.

Social facts – the collective institutional practices of a state.

Socialist feminism – feminist approach examining women's oppression stemming from patriarchy and capitalism, focusing on how women are generally omitted from economic decision-making and ultimately are the most vulnerable economically.

Soft power – a term coined by Joseph Nye, Jr. that describes the exercise of power through a state's own values, ideas, wealth, and culture. States can attract and influence others because they respond positively to its values and beliefs.

Sovereignty – a key characteristic of the modern international system denoting political authority and self-determination over a defined territory and the people within it.

Subaltern – the marginalized and oppressed.

Subsidies – a type of protectionist policy whereby a government provides an additional payment to producers enabling them to sell their product at lower prices in the international market, increasing their competitiveness.

Superstructure – term used by Marx to define and describe the laws, institutions, and culture of a society.

Tariffs – a protectionist policy whereby importers pay a tax on products entering a country.

Theory – a set of statements that explains particular events and acts as a conceptual framework to understand phenomena in world politics.

Theory of Surplus Value – the added value applied to the raw materials by labor.

Transnational – operating across or transcending national boundaries.

Transnational advocacy network – a type of norm entrepreneur or group of activists who are motivated by a central principled idea or value.

Underconsumption – a condition in society resulting in a decline in the purchase of goods due to low wages.

Weapons of Mass Destruction (WMDs) – a class of weapons defined by the United Nations in 1948 that includes biological, chemical, and nuclear weapons.

World Health Organization (WHO) – specialized agency of the United Nations founded in 1948 to direct and coordinate international health within the United Nations' system.

World Systems Theory – a theory developed by Immanuel Wallerstein to describe how states are arranged economically in the international system, based on the capitalist system.

World Trade Organization (WTO) – the international institution created in 1995 to replace the General Agreement on Tariffs and Trade (GATT); it regulates trade between states.

Worldviews – how an individual looks at the world and a belief about how the world works.

Zero-sum – the outcome of relations where one state's loss is another's gain.

WORKS CITED

"X" [George F. Kennan]. 1947. "The Sources of Soviet Conduct." *Foreign Affairs* 20: 556–582.

Acheson, Ray. 2015. *Women, Weapons, and War: A Gendered Critique of Multilateral* New York.: Reaching Critical Will of the Women's International League for Peace and Freedom.

Adler, Emanuel. 1997. "Seizing the Middle Ground: Constructivism in World Politics." *European Journal of International Relations.* 3(3): 319–363.

Akiyama, Nobumasa and Kenta Horio. 2013. "Can Japan Remain Committed to Nonproliferation?" *The Washington Quarterly* 36(2): 151–165.

Arms Control Association. "Nuclear Weapons: Who has what at a Glance." Accessed June 26, 2014, https://www.armscontrol.org/factsheets/Nuclear weaponswhohaswhat.

Ashley, Richard. 1984. "The Poverty of Realism." *International Organization* 38: 225–286.

Axelrod, Robert. 1984. *The Evolution of Cooperation.* New York: Basic Books.

Babst, Dean V. 1964. "Elective Governments—A Force for Peace." *The Wisconsin Sociologist* 3(1): 9–14.

Bairoch, Paul and Gary Goertz. 1986. "Factors of Urbanization in the Nineteenth Century Developed Countries: A Descriptive and Econometric Analysis." *Urban Studies* 23: 285–305.

Balaam, David N. and Bradford Dillman. 2014. *Introduction to International Political Economy,* 6th ed. Boston: Pearson.

Balaam, David N. and Michael Veseth. 2005. *Introduction to International Political Economy,* 3rd ed. New Jersey: Pearson.

Baran, Paul A. 1957. *The Political Economy of Economic Growth.* New York: Monthly Review Press.

Barkin, Samuel J. 2003. "Realist Constructivism." *International Studies Review* 5: 325–342.

Barton, John H., Judith L. Goldstein, Timothy E. Josling, and Richard H. Steinberg. 2010. *The Evolution of the Trade Regime*. Princeton: Princeton University Press.

Baumgardner, Jennifer. 2011. *F'em: Goo Goo, Gaga and Some Thoughts on Balls*. Berkeley: Seal Press.

Beaud, Michel. 2001. *A History of Capitalism*. New York: Monthly Review Press.

Bellany, Ian. 1977. "Nuclear Non-Proliferation and the Inequality of States." *Political Studies* 25(4): 594–598.

Benenson, Peter. 1961. "The Forgotten Prisoners." *The Observer*, 28 May 1961.

Berger, Peter L. and Thomas Luckmann. 2011. *The Social Construction of Reality: A Treatise in the Sociology of Knowledge*. New York: Open Road Integrated Media.

Bhabha, H. 1994. *The Location of Culture*. New York: Routledge.

Bidwai, Praful and Achan Vanaik. 2000. *New Nukes: India, Pakistan and Global Nuclear Disarmament*. Oxford: Signal Books.

Blanchard, Eric M. 2003. "Gender, International Relations, and the Development Feminist Security Theory." *Signs: Journal of Women in Culture and Society*. 28(4): 1289–1312.

Bryson, Valerie. 2004. "Marxism and Feminism: Can the 'Unhappy Marriage' be Saved?" *Journal of Political Ideologies*. 9(1): 13–30.

Bull, Hedley. 1966. "International Theory: The Case for a Classical Approach." *World Politics* 18(3): 361–377.

———. 1977. *The Anarchical Society: A Study of Order in World Politics*. London: Macmillan.

Burch, Kurt. 2002. "Toward a Constructivist Comparative Politics." In Daniel M. Green, ed. *Constructivism and Comparative Politics*. Armonk, NY: M.E. Sharpe, 60– 87.

Buzan, Barry. 2004. *From International to World Society? English School Theory and the Social Structure of Globlisation*. Cambridge: Cambridge University Press.

Cardosa, Fernando Enrique and Enzo Faletto. 1979. *Dependency and Development in Latin America*. Berkeley: University of California Press.

Carr, E.H. 1939. *The Twenty Years' Crisis*. London: Macmillan.

Chin, Christine. 1983. *In Service and Servitude: Foreign Female Domestic Works and the Malaysian "Modernity" Project*. New York: Columbia University Press.

Chowdhry, Geeta. 1994. "Women and the International Political Economy." In Beckman, Peter R. and Francine D'Amico, eds. *Women, Gender, and World Politics*. Westport, CT: Bergin and Garvey, 155–171.

Christian, David. 2011. *Maps of Time: An Introduction to Big History*. Berkeley: University of California Press.

Christensen, Thomas J. 1996. *Useful Adversaries: Grand Strategy, Domestic Mobilization and Sino-American Conflict, 1947–1958*. Princeton: Princeton University Press.

Clatanoff, William C., C. Christopher Parlin, Robert Jordan, and Jean-Francois Seznec. 2006. "Saudi Arabia's Accession to the WTO: Is a 'Revolution' Brewing?" *Middle East Policy.* Vol. XIII, No. 1.

Clausewitz, Carl Von. On War. 1976. Translated and edited by Michael Howard and Peter Paret. Princeton, N.J.: Princeton University Press.

Clay, Jason. 2013. "Are agricultural subsidies causing more harm than good?" *The Guardian.* Accessed June 24, 2015, http://www.theguardian.com/sustainable-business/agricultural-subsidies-reform-government-support.

Cohn, Carol. 1987a. "Slick 'Ems, Glick 'Ems, Christmas Trees, and Cookie Cutters: Nuclear Language and We Learned to Pat the Bomb." *Bulletin of the Atomic Scientists.* 43(5): 17–24.

————. 1987b. "Sex and Death in the Rational World of Defense Intellectuals." *Signs: Journal of Women in Culture and Society* 12(4): 687–718.

Cohn, Carol and Sara Ruddick. 2004. "A Feminist Ethical Perspective on Weapons of Mass Destruction." In Sohail H. Hasmi and Steven P. Lee, eds. *Ethics and Weapons of Mass Destruction: Religious and Secular Perspectives.* Cambridge: Cambridge University Press, 405–435.

Cohn, Carol, Felicity Hill, and Sara Ruddick. 2005. "The Relevance of Gender for Eliminating Weapons of Mass Destruction, No 38." *Stockholm: The Weapons of Mass Destruction Commission.*

Copeland, Dale C 2000. "The Constructivist Challenge to Structural Realism." *International Security.* 25(2): 187–212.

Cortright, David. 2008. *Peace: A History of Movements and Ideas.* Cambridge: Cambridge University Press.

Cox, Robert. 1981. "Social Forces, States and World Orders: Beyond International Relations Theory." *Millennium: Journal of International Studies* 10(2): 126–155.

————. 2010. "Gramsci, Hegemony, and International Relations." In Paul R. Viotti and Mark V. Kauppi, eds. *International Relations Theory,* 4th ed. New York: Longman.

Crenshaw, Kimberlé. 1989. "Demarginalizing the Intersection of Race and Sex: A Black Feminist Critique of Antidiscrimination Doctrine, Feminist Theory and Antiracist Policies." *University of Chicago Legal Forum* 140: 139–167.

Davey, William. 2009. "Compliance Problems in WTO dispute settlement." *Cornell International Law Journal* 42.

Davis, Angela. 1983. *Women, Race, and Class.* New York: First Vintage Books.

————. 1990. *Women, Culture and Politics.* New York: First Vintage Books.

De Beauvoir, Simone. 1953. *The Second Sex.* New York: Knopf.

Deutsch, Karl and J. David Singer. 1964. "Multipolar Systems and International Stability." *World Politics* 16(3): 390–406.

Dirlik, Arif. 1994. "The Postcolonial Aura: Third World Criticism in the Age of Global Capitalism" *Critical Inquiry* 20(1): 328–356.

Donald, Moira. 1993. *Marxism and Revolution: Karl Kautsky and the Russian Marxists, 1900–1924*. New Haven and London: Yale University Press.

Dos Santos, Theotonio. 1970. "The Structure of Dependence." *American Economic Review* 60: 235–46.

Dunne, Tim. 1998. *Inventing International Society: A History of the English School*. New York: Palgrave.

Ehrenreich, Barbara. 1999. "Men Hate War Too." *Foreign Affairs*. 78(1): 118–122.

Eichengreen, Barry. 2006. *The European Economy since 1945*. Princeton: Princeton University Press.

Elshtain, Jean Bethke. 1981. *Public Man, Private Woman: Women in Social and Political Thought*. Princeton: Princeton University Press.

————. 1987. *Women and War*. New York: Basic Books.

Engels, Frederick. 1902. *The Origin of the Family, Private Property, and the State*. Chicago: Charles H. Kerr & Company.

Enloe, Cynthia. 1983. *Does Khaki Become You? The Militarization of Women's Lives*. New York: South End Press.

————. 1989. *Bananas, Beaches, and Bases: Making Feminist Sense of International Politics*. Berkeley: University of California Press.

————. 1993. *The Morning After: Sexual Politics at the End of the Cold War*. Berkeley: University of California Press.

————. 2000. *Maneuvers: The International Politics of Militarizing Women*. Berkeley: University of California Press.

Fanon, F. 1986. *Wretched of the Earth*, translated by C. Farrington. New York: Grove Press.

Ettinger, Elzbieta. 1979. *Comrade and Lover: Rosa Luxemburg's Letters to Leo Jojiches*. Cambridge: MIT Press.

Evans, Peter. 1979. *Dependent Development: The Alliance of Multinational, State, and Local Capital in Brazil*. Princeton: Princeton University Press.

Ferguson, R. Brian. 1999. "Perilous Positions." *Foreign Affairs* 78(1): 125–127.

Finnemore, Martha. 1996. *National Interests in International Society*. Ithaca, NY: Cornell University Press.

Finnemore, Martha and Katherine Sikkink. 1998. "International Norm Dynamic and Political Change." *International Organization* 52(4): 887–917.

————. 2001. "Taking Stock: The Constructivist Research Program in International Relations and Comparative Politics." *Annual Review of Political Science* 4: 391–416.

Ford, Jane. 2002. "A Social Theory of Trade Regime Change: GATT to WTO." *International Studies Review* 4(3): 115–138.

Frank, Andre Gunder. 1969. *Capitalism and Underdevelopment in Latin America*, rev. ed. New York and London: Modern Reader Paperbacks.

Freedom House. 2015. *Freedom in the World – Electoral Democracies.* Accessed July 20, 2015, https://freedomhouse.org/sites/default/files/Number%20and%20 Percentage%20of%20 Electoral%20Democracy%2C%20FIW%201989–2015.pdf.

———. 1979. *Dependent Accumulation and Underdevelopment.* New York: Monthly Review Press.

Freidan, Betty. 1963. *The Feminine Mystique.* New York: W. W. Norton and Co.

Friedman, Milton. 1962. *Capitalism and Freedom.* Chicago: University of Chicago Press.

Fukuyama, Francis. 1989. "The End of History?" *National Interest*, no. 16.

———. 1992. *The End of History and the Last Man.* New York: Free Press.

———. 1998. "Women and the Evolution of World Politics." *Foreign Affairs* 23(2): 24–40.

Gimenez, Martha and Lise Vogel. 2005. "Marxist-Feminist Thought Today." *Science & Society.* 69(1): 5–10.

Goldstein, Joshua S. 2011. "Think Again: War; World Peace Could Be Closer than You Think." *Foreign Policy.* Accessed July 17, 2015, http://foreignpolicy .com/2011/08/15/think-again-war/?wp_login_redirect=0.

Gordon, Linda. 2013. "Socialist Feminism: The Legacy of the 'Second Wave.'" *New Labor Forum* 22(3): 20–28.

Grosfoguel, Ramón. 2000. "Developmentalism, Modernity, and Dependency Theory in Latin America." *Nepantla: Views from South* 1(2): 347–372

Grotius, Hugo. 2005. *The Rights of War and Peace*, Books I–III, edited and with an introduction by Richard Tuck. Indianapolis: Liberty Fund.

———. 2006. *Commentary on the Laws of Prize and Booty*, edited with an introduction by Martine van Ittersum. Indianapolis: Liberty Fund.

Haack, Kirsten. 2014. "Breaking Barriers? Women's Representation and Leadership at the United Nations." *Global Governance* 20: 37–54.

Hamilton, Alexander. 2007. *Report on the Subject of Manufactures.* New York: Cosimo, Inc.

Haas, Ernest. 1958. *The Uniting of Europe: Political, Social and Economic Forces 1950–1957.* Stanford: Stanford University Press.

Hansen, Lene. 2009. "Ontologies, Epistemologies, Methodologies." In Laura Shepherd, ed. *Gender Matters in Global Politics: A Feminist Introduction to International Relations.* New York: Routledge, 17–27.

Harding, Sandra. 1986. *The Science Question in Feminism.* Ithaca: Cornell University Press.

Hartman, Heidi. 1979. "The Unhappy Marriage of Marxism and Feminism: Towards a More Progressive Union." *Capital and Class* 3(2): 1–33.

Hayek, Friedrich. 1944. *The Road to Serfdom.* Chicago: University of Chicago Press.

Hayhurst, Lyndsay MC. 2011. "Corporatising Sport, Gender and Development: Postcolonial IR Feminisms, Transnational Private Governance and Global Corporate Social Engagement." *Third World Quarterly* 32(3): 531–549.

Helman, Gerald B. and Steven R. Ratner. 2010 [1993]. "Saving Failed States." *Foreign Policy*, last modified June 15, 2010, accessed November 15, 2015, http://foreignpolicy.com/2010/06/15/saving-failed-states/.

Hixson, Walter L. 1989. *George Kennan: Cold War Iconoclast*. New York: Columbia University Press.

Hobson, John. 1900. *The War in South Africa*. London: James Nisbet & Co., Limited.

————. 1938, *Imperialism: A Study*. 3rd ed. London: Unwin Hyman.

Hollande, Francois. 2012. "67th United Nations General Assembly." September 15, 2012, accessed November 20, 2015, http://www.ambafrance-uk.org/President-Hollande-issues-global.

Hooks, Bell. 1981. *Ain't I a Woman? Black Women and Feminism*. South End Press.

————. 1984. *Feminist Theory: From Margin to Center*. South End Press.

Hooper, Charlotte. 2001. *Manly States: Masculinities, International Relations, and Gender Politics*. New York: Columbia University Press.

Hopf, Ted. 1998. "The Promise of Constructivism in International Relations Theory." *International Security* 32(1): 171–200.

Hudson, Valeria. 2012. "What Sex Means for World Peace." *Foreign Policy*. April 24.

Hunt, Swanee. 2007. "Let Women Rule." *Foreign Affairs* 83(3): 109–120.

Jackson, Ian. 2009. "Nuclear Energy and Proliferation Risks: Myths and Realities in the Persian Gulf." *International Affairs* 85(6): 1157–1172.

Jones, Adam. 1996. "Does 'Gender' Make the World Go Round? Feminist Critiques of International Relations." *Review of International Studies* 22(4): 405–429.

Jones, Roy E. 1981. "The English School of International Relations: A Case for Closure." *Review of International Studies* (7)1: 1–13.

Kant, Immanuel. 1996. "Perpetual Peace: A Philosophical Sketch." In John A. Vasquez. *Classics in International Relations*, 3rd ed. New Jersey: Prentice Hall. Originally published in 1795.

Kaplan, Morton A. 1966. Some Problems of International Systems Research. *International Political Communities: An Anthology*. Garden City, N.Y.: Anchor, pp. 469–486. Quoted from John A. Vasquez. 1996. *Classics of International Relations*, 3rd ed. New Jersey: Prentice Hall.

Kautsky, Karl. 1970. "Ultra-Imperialism." *New Left Review*. 59: 41–46.

Keck, Margaret, and Kathryn Sikkink. 1998. *Activists Beyond Borders: Advocacy Networks in International Politics*. Ithaca, NY: Cornell University Press.

Kennan, George F. 1951. *American Diplomacy, 1900–1950*. Chicago: University of Chicago Press.

Keohane, Robert O. 1984. *After Hegemony: Cooperation and Discord in the World Political Economy*. Princeton: Princeton University Press.

————. 1989a. "Neoliberal Institutionalism: A Perspective on World Politics." In *International Institutions and State Power: Essays in International Relations Theory*. Robert O. Keohane ed. Boulder: Westview Press.

_____. 1989b. "International Relations Theory: Contributions of a Feminist Standpoint." *Millennium: Journal of International Studies* 18(2): 245–253.

Keohane, Robert O. and Joseph Nye Jr. 1971. *Transnational Relations and World Politics*. Cambridge, MA: Harvard University Press.

_____.1977. *Power and Interdependence: World Politics in Transition*. Boston: Little Brown.

Keynes, John Maynard. 1963. *The End of Laissez-Faire: Essays in Persuasion*. New York: W.W. Norton. Originally published in 1926.

Khan, Mohammad Tanzimuddin. 2004. "China, WTO and the developing countries: a constructivist analysis." Working Paper, Center for Strategic Research, Ministry of Foreign Affairs of the Republic of Turkey. http://www.sam.gov.tr/volume9a.php.

Kissinger, Henry A. 2011. The Age of Kennan. *The New York Times*. Accessed July 18, 2014, http://www.nytimes.com/2011/11/13/books/review/george-f-kennan-an-american-life-by-john-lewis-gaddis-book-review.html?pagewanted=all&_r=0.

Klabbers, Jan. 2015. "Book Reviews." *The European Journal of International Law* 25(4): 1195–1208.

Krasner, Stephen D. 1991. "Global Communications and National Power: Life on the Pareto Frontier." *World Politics* 43(3).

_____. ed. 1983. *International Regimes*. Ithaca: Cornell University Press.

Kratochwil, Friedrich and John Gerard Ruggie. 1986. "International Organization: A State of the Art on an Art of the State." *International Organization* 40(4): 753–775.

Kratochwil, Friedrich. 1991. *Rules, Norms, and Decisions: On the Conditions of Practical and Legal Reasoning in International Relations and Domestic Affairs*. Cambridge: Cambridge University Press.

_____. 1993. "The Embarrassment of Changes: Neo-realism as the Science of Realpolitik Without Politics." *Review of International Studies* 19(1): 63–80.

Kristensen, Hans M. and Robert S. Norris. 2015. "Pakistani Nuclear forces, 2015." *The Bulletin of the Atomic Scientists*. Accessed November 30, 2015, http://thebulletin.org/2015/november/pakistani-nuclear-forces-20158845.

Krolokke, Charlotte and Anne Scott Sorensen. 2006. *Gender Communication: Theories and Analyses*. London: Sage Publications.

Kuhn, Thomas. 1962. *The Structure of Scientific Revolutions*. Chicago: University of Chicago Press.

Kwon, K.J. and Jethro Mullen. 2013. "North Korea Says New Nuclear Test Will Be Part of Fight Against the U.S." *CNN.com*. Accessed June 26, 2014, http://www.cnn.com/2013/01/23/world/asia/north-korea-nuclear-test/.

Lear, Martha W. 1968. "The Second Feminist Wave." *New York Times Magazine* 3/18/68.

Lebow, Richard Ned. 2001. "Thucydides the Constructivist." *American Political Science Review* 95(39): 547–560.

Leier, Mark. 1995. "Book Review" *Marxism and Revolution: Karl Kautsky and the Russian Marxists, 1900–1924.* New Haven and London: Yale University Press. In *The International History Review.* XVII, 2: May.

Lemkin, Raphael. 2013. *The Autobiography of Raphael Lemkin.* Edited by Donna-Lee Frieze. New Haven: Yale University Press.

———. 1944. *Axis Rule in Occupied Europe: Laws of Occupation: Analysis of Government; Proposals for Redress.* Washington, DC: Carnegie Endowment for International Peace.

Lenin, V. I. 1965. *Imperialism, the Highest Stage of Capitalism: A Popular Outline.* New York: International Publishers.

Linklater, Andrew. 1990. *Men and Citizens in the Theory of International Relations.* London: Palgrave Macmillan.

———. 1998. *The Transformation of Political Community: Ethical Foundations of the Post-Westphalian Era.* Cambridge: Polity Press.

———. 2011. *The Problem of Harm in World Politics: Theoretical Investigations.* Cambridge: Cambridge University Press.

Lobell, Steven E., Norrin M Ripsman, and Jeffrey W. Taliaferro. 2009. *Neoclassical Realism, the State, and Foreign Policy.* Cambridge: Cambridge University Press.

Locher, Birgit and Elisabeth Prügl. 2001. "Feminism and Constructivism: Worlds Apart or Sharing the Middle Ground?" *International Studies Quarterly* 45: 111–129.

Locke, John. 1689. *Two Treatises of Government.* P. Laslett (ed.), Cambridge: Cambridge University Press, 1988.

Lodgaard, Sverrre. 2001. *Nuclear Disarmament and Non-Proliferation: Towards a Nuclear-Weapon-Free World.* London and New York: Routledge.

Lomnitz, Claudio. 2012. "Time and Dependency in Latin America Today." *The South Atlantic Quarterly* 111: 347–357.

Love, Patrick and Ralph Lattimore. 2009. "International Trade: Free, Fair and Open?" *OECD Insights.* Paris: OECD Publishing. DOI: http://dx.doi.org/10.1787/9789264060265-en.

Luxemburg, Rosa. 1900. Reform or Revolution. Available online at https://www.marxists.org/archive/luxemburg/1900/reform-revolution/.

MacDonald, Laura. 2002. "Comparing Women's Movements' Responses to NAFTA in Mexico, the USA, and Canada." *International Feminist Journal of Politics* 4(2): 151–172.

Machiavelli, Niccolo. 1981. *The Prince.* England: Penguin Classics.

Maliniak, Daniel, Susan Peterson, and Michael J. Tierney. 2012. *TRIP Around the World: Teaching, Research, and Policy Views of International Relations Faculty in 20 Countries.* Williamsburg: The College of William and Mary.

Maoz, Zeev and Bruce Russett. 1993. "Normative and Structural Causes of Democratic Peace, 1946–1986." *American Political Science Review* 87(3) (September): 624–638.

Marchand, Marianne H. 2009. "The Future of Gender and Development after 9/11: Insights from Postcolonial Feminism and Transnationalism." *Third World Quarterly* 30(5): 921–935.

Marsh, D. and Furlong, P. 2002. "A Skin Not A Sweater: Ontology and Epistemology in Political Science." In D. Marsh and G. Stoker, eds. *Theory and Methods in Political Science*, 2nd ed., 17–41.

Marx, Karl. 1970. *Wage Labour and Capital*. 7th printing. Moscow: Progress Publishers.

———. 1977. "Preface to *A Critique of Political Economy*". In McClellan, David, ed. *Karl Marx: Selected Writings*. Oxford: Oxford University Press, 388–392.

———. 1990. *Capital, Vol. 1*. London: Penguin Classics.

———. 2007. *Economic and Philosophic Manuscripts*. Mineola, NY: Dover Publications, Inc.

Maschler, Michael, et al. 2013. *Game Theory*. Cambridge: Cambridge University Press.

Mbembe, A. 2001. *Postcolony*. Berkley: University of California Press.

McLaughlin, Janice. 2003. *Feminist Social and Political Theory*. New York: Palgrave Macmillan.

Mearsheimer, John J. 1983. *Conventional Deterrence*. Ithaca, NY: Cornell University Press.

———. 1994. "The False Promise of International Institutions." *International Security* 19(3): 5–49.

———. 2001. *The Tragedy of Great Power Politics*. New York: W.W. Norton.

———. 2011. *Why Leaders Lie: The Truth about Lying in International Politics*.

———. 2013. "Structural Realism." In Dunne, Tim, Milja Kurki, and Steve Smith, *International Relations Theories: Discipline and Diversity*, 3rd ed. Oxford, UK: Oxford University Press, 71–88.

Mearsheimer, John J. and Stephen Walt. 2007. *The Israel Lobby and U.S. Foreign Policy*. New York: Farrar, Straus and Giroux.

Mearsheimer, John J., Russell Hardin, Robert E. Goodin, and Gerald Dworkin (eds.). 1985. *Nuclear Deterrence: Ethics and Strategy*. Chicago: University of Chicago Press.

Mill, John Stuart. 1848. *Principles of Political Economy with Some of the Applications to Social Philosophy*. New York: Charles C. Little and James Brown.

Minty, Abdul Samad. 2012. Quoted in Fredrick Dahl, "Non-Nuclear States Lobby Big Powers to Disarm Faster." Reuters, May 4, 2012. Accessed November 20, 2015, http://www.reuters.com/article/2012/05/04/us-nuclear-disarmament-divisions-idU SBRE8431CV20120504#7kjFArPugCzsWFIB.97.

Mitchell, B. Ronald. 1994. "Regime Design Matters: International Oil Pollution and Treaty Compliance." *International Organization* 48(3): 425–458.

Mitrany, David. 1966. *A Working Peace System*, reproduced with introduction by Hans. J. Morgenthau. Chicago: Quadrangle.

Modelski, George. 1987. *Long Cycles in World Politics*. London: Macmillan.

Moon, Katharine. 1997. *Sex Among Allies*. New York: Columbia University Press.

Moravcsik, Andrew. 2003. "Theory Synthesis in International Relations: Real Not Metaphysical." *International Studies Review* 5(1): 131–136.

Morgenthau, Hans. 1948. *Politics Among Nations*. New York: Knopf.

Nagdy, Mohamed and Max Roser. 2015. "International Trade." *OurWorldInData.org*. Accessed July 23, 2015, http://ourworldindata.org/data/global-interconnections/international-trade/

Nye, Joseph Jr. 2005. *Soft Power: The Means to Success in World Politics*. New York: Public Affairs.

———. 2009a. "Get Smart: Combining Hard and Soft Power." *Foreign Affairs*. Accessed August 6, 2015, https://www.foreignaffairs.com/articles/2009-07-01/get-smart.

———. 2009b. "Scholars on the Sidelines." *Washington Post*, April 13, 2009. Accessed October 16, 2015, http://www.washingtonpost.com/wp-dyn/content/article/2009/04/12/AR2009041202260.html.

Onuf, Nicholas G. 1989. *World of Our Making: Rules and Rule in Social Theory and International Relations*. Columbia, SC: University of South Carolina Press.

Organski, A.F.K. 1958. *World Politics*. New York: Knopf.

Papadopoulos, Nicolas. 2007. "Export Processing Zones in Development and International Marketing: An Integrative Review and Research Agenda." *Journal of Macromarketing* 27(2): 148–161.

Patel, Khadija. 2015. "Q&A: Exploring Sweden's 'Feminist' Foreign Policy." Al Jazeera, June 15, 2015. Accessed August 6, 2015, http://www.aljazeera.com/indepth/features/2015/06/southafrica-au-sweden-feminism-foreign-policy-150615140028265.html.

Peach, Lucinda Joy. 2004. *Ethics and Weapons of Mass Destruction: Religious and Secular Perspectives*. Edited by Sohail H. Hashmi and Steven P. Lee. Cambridge: Cambridge University Press.

Pease, Kelly-Kate S. 2012. *International Organizations* 5th ed. Boston: Longman.

Perkovich, George. 1999. *India's Nuclear Bomb: The Impact on Global Proliferation*. London: University of California Press.

Peterson, V. Spike. 1992. "Transgressing Boundaries: Theories of Knowledge, Gender and International Relations." *Millennium: Journal of International Studies* 21(2): 183–206.

———. 1998. "Feminisms and International Relations." *Gender & History* 10(3): 581–589.

———. 2004. "Feminist Theories Within, Invisible To, and Beyond IR." *Brown Journal of World Affairs* 10(2): 35–46.

Pettman, Jan Jindy. 2004. "Feminist International Relations After 9/11." *Brown Journal of World Affairs* 10(2): 85–96.

Phillips, Andrew Bradley. 2007. "Constructivism." In Martin Griffiths, ed. *International Relations Theory for the Twenty-First Century: An Introduction.* London & New York: Routledge, 60–74.

Pollitt, Katha. 1999. "Father Knows Best." *Foreign Affairs* 78(1): 122–125.

Price, Richard. 1995. "A Genealogy of the Chemical Weapons Taboo." *International Organization* 49(1): 73–103.

————. 1998. "Reversing the Gun Sights: Transnational Civil Society Targets Land Mines." *International Organization* 52(3): 613–644.

Price, Richard and Christian Reus-Smit. 1998. "Dangerous Liaisons? Critical International Theory and Constructivism." *European Journal of International Relations* 4(3): 359–294.

Prügl, Elisabeth. 1999. *The Global Construction of Gender.* New York: Columbia University Press.

————. 2009. "Does Gendering Mainstreaming Work? Feminist Engagements with the German Agricultural State." *International Feminist Journal of Politics* 11(2): 174–195.

————. 2011. *Transforming Masculine Rule: Agriculture and Rural Development in the European Union.* Ann Arbor: University of Michigan Press.

Putnam, Robert D. 1988. "Diplomacy and Domestic Politics: The Logic of Two-Level Games." *International Organization* 42(3): 427–460.

Racine, Louise, and Amelie Perron. 2012. "Unmasking the Predicament of Cultural Voyeurism: A Postcolonial Analysis of International Nursing Placements." *Nursing Inquiry* 19(3): 190–201.

Rampton, Martha. 2015. "Four Waves of Feminism." Accessed on November 22, 2015, http://www.pacificu.edu/about-us/news-events/four-waves-feminism.

————. 1997. "The Constitutional Structure of International Society and the Nature of Fundamental Institutions." *International Organization* 51(4): 555–589.

————. 1999. *The Moral Purpose of the State: Culture, Social Identity, and Institutional Rationality in International Relations.* Princeton: Princeton University Press.

————. 2013. "Constructivism." In Scott Burchill, Andrew Linklater, Richard Devetak, Jack Donnelly, Terry Nardin, Matthew Paterson, Christian Reus-Smit, and Jacqui True, eds. *Theories of International Relations,* 5th ed. New York: Palgrave Macmillan.

Riley, Maria and Rocio Mejia. 1996. "Gender in the Global Trading System: Analysis and Strategies from a Gender Focus." Unpublished document submitted to the 1996 WTO Ministerial Conference. Washington DC: Center of Concern.

Ricardo, David. 1973. *The Principles of Political Economy and Taxation.* London: Dent.

Rose, Gideon. 1998. Neoclassical Realism and Theories of Foreign Policy. *World Politics* 51(1): 144–177.

Rothschild, Nathalie. 2014. "Swedish Women vs. Vladimir Putin." *Foreign Policy*. December 5, 2014. Accessed on August 6, 2015, http://foreignpolicy.com/2014/12/05/can-vladimir-putin-be-intimidated-by-feminism-sweden/.

Rouhani, Hassan. 2013. "Statement by H.E. Dr. Hassan Rouhani, President of the Islamic Republic of Iran, on Behalf of the Non-Aligned Movement at the High Level Meeting of the General Assembly on Nuclear Disarmament." September 26, 2013. Accessed November 20, 2015, http://www.un.org/en/ga/68/meetings/nucleardisarmament/pdf/IR_en.pdf.

Ruggie, John Gerard. 1975. "International Responses to Technology: Concepts and Trends." *International Organization* 29(3): 557–583.

————. 1983. "Continuity and Transformation in the World Polity: A Neorealist Synthesis." *World Politics* 35(2): 261–285.

————. 1998a. "What Makes the World Hang Together? Neo-utilitarianism and the Social Constructivist Challenge." *International Organization* 52(4): 855–885.

————. 1998b. *Constructing the World Polity: Essays on International Institutionalization*. London and New York: Routledge.

Rupert, James. 2015. "Sweden's Foreign Minister Explains Feminist Foreign Policy." Accessed on August 6, 2015, http://www.usip.org/olivebranch/2015/02/09/sweden-s-foreign-minister-explains-feminist-foreign-policy.

Sachs, Jeffery D. and Andrew Warner. 1995. "Economic Reform and the Process of Global Integration." *Brookings Papers on Economic Activity* 26(1): 1–118.

Sagan, Scott. 1994. "The Perils of Proliferation: Organization Theory, Deterrence Theory, and the Spread of Nuclear Weapons." *International Security* 18(4) (Spring, 1994): 66–107.

Said, Edward. 1978. *Orientalism*. New York: Vintage Books.

Sandberg, Sheryl. 2013. *Lean In: Women, Work, and the Will to Lead*. New York: Alfred A. Knopf.

Schweller, Randall L. 1998. *Deadly Imbalances: Tripolarity and Hitler's Strategy of World Conquest*. New York: Columbia University Press.

————. 1999. "Fantasy Theory." *Review of International Studies* 25 (01): 147–150.

Schouten, P. 2008. "Theory Talk #13: Immanuel Wallerstein on World-Systems, the Imminent End of Capitalism and Unifying Social Science". *Theory Talks*, last modified April 8, 2008, http://www.theory-talks.org/2008/08/theory-talk-13.html.

Scott, David. 1999. *Refashioning Futures: Criticism after Postcoloniality*. Princeton, NJ: Princeton University Press.

Searle, John R. 1995. *The Construction of Social Reality*. New York: Free Press Shanker, 2012.

Shepherd. Laura J. 2009. "Sex or Gender? Bodies in World Politics and Why Gender Matters." In Laura J. Shepherd, ed. *Gender Matters in Global Politics: A Feminist Introduction to International Relations*. New York: Routledge, 3–16.

Sherrill, Clifton W. 2102. "Why Iran Wants the Bomb and What it Means for US Policy." *Nonproliferation Review* 19(1): 31–49.

Sil, Rudra Peter J. Katzenstein. 2010. *Beyond Paradigms: Analytical Eclecticism in the Study of World Politics*. New York: Palgrave Macmillan.

Sjoberg, Laura. 2009. "Introduction to Security Studies: Feminist Contributions." *Security Studies* 18: 183–213.

Skidelsky, Robert. 2003. *John Maynard Keynes 1883–1946: Economist, Philosopher, Statesman*. New York: Penguin Books.

Smith, Adam. 1964. *The Wealth of Nations*. New York: Dutton.

———. 1759. *The Theory of Moral Sentiments*, reproduced in 2011. New York: Gutenberg Publishers.

Smith, Tony. 1979. "The Underdevelopment of Development Literature: The Case of Dependency Theory." *World Politics* 31(2): 247–288.

Spivak, G.C. 1985. "Subaltern Studies: Deconstructing Historiography." In Ranajit Guha, ed., *Subaltern Studies IV*. New Delhi: Oxford University Press, 330–363.

Stanglin, Doug. 2014. "Jonathan Pollard: Israel's Prolific American Spy." *USA Today*.

Stanley, Liam. 2012. "Rethinking the Definition and Role of Ontology in Political Science." *Politics* 32(2): 93–99.

Stiglitz, Joseph E. 2007. *Making Globalization Work*. New York: W.W. Norton & Company.

Stockholm International Peace Research Institute (SIPRI), "Report on Military Expenditures." http://www.sipri.org/.

Sylvester, Christine. 1989. "The Emperor's Theories and Transformations: Looking at the Field Through Feminist Lenses." In Dennis Pirages and Christine Sylvester (eds.), *Transformations in the Global Political Economy*. London: Macmillan, 230–253.

———. 1994. *Feminist Theory and International Relations in a Postmodern Era*. Cambridge: Cambridge University Press.

———. 2002. *Feminist International Relations: An Unfinished Journey*. Cambridge: Cambridge University Press.

Tannenwald, Nina. 2005. "Stigmatizing the Bomb: Origins of the Nuclear Taboo." *International Security* 29(4): 5–49.

———. 2007. *The Nuclear Taboo: The United States and the Non-Use of Nuclear Weapons since 1945*. New York: Cambridge University Press.

Tertrais, Bruno. 2010. "The Illogic of Zero." *The Washington Quarterly* 33(2): 125–138.

The Economist. 2011. "China's Economy and the WTO: All Change." Accessed June 24, 2015, http://www.economist.com/node/21541448.

———. 2013. "The Hidden Persuaders." Accessed November 20, 2015, http://www.economist.com/news/special-report/21587381-protectionism-can-take-many-forms-not-all-them-obvious-hidden-persuaders.

Thorburn, Diana. 2000. "Feminism Meets International Relations." *SAIS Review* 20(2): 1–10.

Thucydides. 1954. "The Melian Dialogue." *History of the Peloponnesian War*, translated by Rex Warner. New York: Penguin Books.

Tickner, J. Ann. 1992. *Gender in International Relations: Feminist Perspectives on Achieving Global Security*. New York: Columbia University Press.

———. 1997. "You Just Don't Understand: Troubled Engagements Between Feminists and IR Theorists." *International Studies Quarterly* 41: 611–632.

———. 1998. "Hans Morgenthau's Principles of Political Realism: A Feminist Reformulation." *Millennium* 17(3): 429–440.

———. 1999. "Why Women Can't Rule the World: International Politics According to Francis Fukuyama." *International Studies Review* 1(3): 3–11.

———. 2005. "What is your Research Program? Some Feminist Answers to International Relations Methodological Questions." *International Studies Quarterly* 49: 1–21.

———. 2006. "Feminism Meets International Relations: Some Methodological Issues." In Brook A. Ackerly, Maria Stern., and Jacqui True. Eds. *Feminist Methodologies for International Relations*. Cambridge: Cambridge University Press, 19–41.

Toloraya, Georgy. 2008. "The Six Party Talks: A Russian Perspective." *Asian Perspective* 32(4): 45–69.

True, Jacqui. 2003. "Mainstreaming Gender in Global Public Policy." *International Feminist Journal of Politics* 5(3): 368–396.

True, Jacqui and Michael Mintrom. 2001. "Transnational Networks and Policy Diffusion: The Case of Gender Mainstreaming." *International Studies Quarterly* 45: 27–57.

Tzu, Sun. 1963. *The Art of War*, translated by Samuel B. Griffith. Oxford: Oxford University Press.

United National Conference on Trade and Development (UNCTAD). 2010. "Assessment of the Impact of Trade Policy Reform in Countries Acceding to the World Trade Organization: The Gender Dimension." New York and Geneva: United Nations. Accessed November 20, 2015, http://unctad.org/en/Docs/ditctncd20106_en.pdf.

U.S. Department of Agriculture, Economic Research Service. "Sugar and Sweeteners." Accessed June 24, 2015, http://www.ers.usda.gov/topics/crops/sugar-sweeteners/policy.aspx.

U.S. Department of State. "Remarks to the Press on the Six Party Talks. 2010. Stephen W. Bosworth. 2010. Tokyo, Japan." Accessed March 29, 2015, http://www.state.gov/p/eap/rls/rm/2010/02/137384.htm.

U.S. Trade Representative. 2014. "2014 Report to Congress on China's WTO Compliance." Accessed June 25, 2015, https://ustr.gov/sites/default/files/2014-Report-to-Congress-Final.pdf.

van Wyk, Jo-Ansie and Linda Kinghorn, Hollie Hepburn, Clarence Payne, and Chris Sham. 2007. "The International Politics of Nuclear Weapons: A Constructivist Analysis." *Scientia Militaria, South African Journal of Military Studies* 35(1): 23–34.

Vidal, John. 1999. "Real Battle for Seattle." *The Guardian*. Saturday, December 4. Accessed October 30, 2015, http://www.theguardian.com/world/1999/dec/05/wto.globalisation.

Wacziarg, Romain, and Karen Horn Welch. 2008. "Trade Liberalization and Growth: New Evidence." *World Bank Economic Review* 22(2): 187–231.

Wagner, Constance Z. 2012. "Looking at Regional Trade Agreements Through the Lens of Gender." *Saint Louise University School of Law* 31: 497–537.

Walker, Rebecca. 1992. "Becoming the Third Wave." *Ms. Magazine* 11(2): 39–41.

Wallerstein, Immanuel. 2004. *The Modern World-System I: Capitalist Agriculture and the Origins of the European World-Economy in the Sixteenth Century.* New York: Academic Press.

————. 2004. *World-Systems Analysis: An Introduction.* Durham and London: Duke University Press.

Walt, Stephan M. 1998. "International Relations: One World, Many Theories." *Foreign Policy, No. 110, Special Edition: Frontiers of Knowledge.* (Spring, 1998), 29–32; 34–46.

Waltz, Kenneth N. 1988. "The Origins of War in Neorealist Theory." *Journal of Interdisciplinary History* 18(4): 615–628.

————. 1979. *Theory of International Politics.* New York: McGraw-Hill.

Wæver, Ole. 2013. "Still a Discipline After All These Debates?" In Tim Dunne, Milja, and Steve Smith, *International Relations Theories: Discipline and Diversity*, 3rd Edition. Oxford: Oxford University Press 288–308.

Weber, Cynthia 1994. "Good Girls, Little Girls and Bad Girls: Male Paranoia in Robert Keohan's Critique of Feminist International Relations." *Millennium: Journal of International Relations* 23(2): 337–349.

Weber, Max. 1949. *Max Weber on the Methodology of the Social Sciences.* Free Press.

Weiner, Tim and Barbara Crossette. 2005. "George F. Kennan Dies at 101: Leading Strategist of Cold War." *New York Times*, March 18, 2005. Accessed July 17, 2014, http://www.nytimes.com/2005/03/18/politics/18kennan.html?pagewanted=all&_r=0.

Wendt, Alexander. 1992. "Anarchy is Want States Make of It: The Social Construction of Power Politics." *International Organization* 46(2): 391–425.

————. 1994. "Collective Identity Formation and the International State." *American Political Science Review* 88(2): 384–396.

————. 1999. *Social Theory of International Politics.* Cambridge and New York: Cambridge University Press.

Weymouth, Stephen and J. Muir MacPherson. 2012. "The Social Construction of Policy Reform: Economists and Trade Liberalization Around the World." *International Interactions* 38: 670–702.

Whitworth, Sandra. 1994. "Feminist Theories: From Women to Gender and World Politics." In Beckman, Peter R. and Francine D'Amico, eds. *Women, Gender, and World Politics.* Westport, CT: Bergin and Garvey, 75–88.

Whyte, Christopher. 2011. "Why Israel Fears a Nuclear Iran: Realism, Constructivism and Iran's Dual-National Identity." *CEJISS* 3: 141–162.

Wiarda, Howard J. 1985. "Toward a Nonethnocentric Theory of Development: Alternative Conceptions from the Third World." In Wiarda, Howard J. ed. *New Directions in Comparative Politics*. Boulder: Westview.

Wibben, Annick T.R. 2004. "Feminist International Relations: Old Debates and New Directions." *Brown Journal of World Affairs* 10(2): 97–114.

Wight, Martin. 1979. *Systems of States*. Leicester: Leicester University Press.

———. 1991. *International Theory: The Three Traditions*. Leicester: Leicester University Press.

Wilson, Bruce. 2007. "Compliance by WTO Members with Adverse WTO Dispute Settlement Rulings: The Record to Date." *Journal of International Economic Law* 10(2): 397–403.

Wohlforth, William Curti. 1993. *The Elusive Balance: Power and Perceptions during the Cold War*. Ithaca, NY: Cornell University Press.

Wollstonecraft, Mary. 1792. A Vindication of the Rights of Woman. Available at https://www.marxists.org/reference/archive/wollstonecraft-mary/1792/vindication-rights-woman/.

Wood, Julia 1994. *Gendered Lives: Communication, Gender, and Culture*. 10th edition. New York: Wadsworth.

World Bank. 2015. "Trade Data." Accessed July 17, 2015, http://data.worldbank.org/topic/trade.

World Health Organization. 2015. "Ebola Virus Disease Fact Sheet." Accessed July 21, 2015, http://www.who.int/mediacentre/factsheets/fs103/en/.

World Trade Organization. 2014. "International Trade Statistics." Accessed July 23. 2015, https://www.wto.org/english/res_e/statis_e/its_e.htm.

———. 2015. "Dispute Settlement: The Disputes, Chronological List of Disputed Cases." Accessed June 24, 2015, https://www.wto.org/english/tratop_e/dispu_e/dispu_status_e.htm.

———. 2015. "The Case for Open Trade." Accessed July 30, 2015, https://www.wto.org/english/thewto_e/whatis_e/tif_e/fact3_e.htm.

Youngs, Gillian. 2004. "Feminist International Relations: A Contradiction in Terms? Or: Why Women and Gender Are Essential to Understanding the World 'We' Live In." *International Affairs* 80(1): 75–87.

Zakaria, Fareed. 1998. *From Wealth to Power: The Unusual Origins of America's World Role*. Princeton: Princeton University Press.

Zaleswksi, Marysia. 1993. "Feminist Standpoint Theory Meets International Relations Theory: A Feminist Version of David and Goliath?" *Fletcher Forum of World Affairs* 17(2): 13–32.

Zhang, Xiaowen and Xiaoling Li. 2014. "The Politics of Compliance with Adverse WTO Dispute Settlement Rulings in China." *Journal of Contemporary China* 23(85): 143–160.

INDEX

....